CORPORATE
IMAGINATION *Plus*

CORPORATE *Plus*
IMAGINATION

*Five Steps to Translating
Innovative Strategies
into Action*

JAMES F. BANDROWSKI

THE FREE PRESS
A Division of Macmillan, Inc.
NEW YORK

Collier Macmillan Publishers
LONDON

FREE PRESS
Rockefeller Center
1230 Avenue of the Americas
New York, New York 10020

Manufactured in the United States of America

10 9 8 7 6 5 4 3 2 1

Library of Congress Catalog-in-Publication Data

Bandrowski, James F.
Corporate imagination plus: five steps to translating innovative strategies into action / James F. Bandrowski.
     p.   cm.

ISBN 0-7432-0549-9

1.   Corporate planning. 2. Strategic planning. 3. Organizational change. I. Title.
HD30.28.B349 1990
658.4'012—dc20

*To Stella and Stanley Bandrowski,
my parents*

Contents

Preface:
The Essence
of Business

HIGHLY successful organizations are innovators. This goes for corporations, nonprofit institutions, civic groups, religious organizations, sports franchises, public service agencies, governments, or entire countries.

What do winners like Compaq Computer, American Airlines, 3M, Honda, Digital Equipment Corporation, McDonald's, Federal Express, Citicorp, Hewlett-Packard, Procter & Gamble, and Merck & Co. all have in common? They all won command of their marketplace by creatively restructuring the success formula for their industries. They changed the way the game is played, and they outplayed their competitors under the new rules. This is business in its highest form.

Perhaps the most persuasive case for strategic innovation was made by John F. Welch, who at the age of forty-five became chairman of the board at General Electric. In his April 26, 1984, speech at Cornell University entitled "Competitiveness from Within—Beyond Incrementalism," Welch called for a new spirit of strategic change.

> I'm convinced that if the rate of change inside the institution is less than the rate of change outside, the end is in sight. The only question is the timing of the end.
>
> But in truth, the wisdom may lie in changing the institution while it's still winning—re-invigorating a business, in fact, while it's making more money than anyone ever dreamt it could make.

For those companies that have recently restructured, Walter Kiechel of *Fortune* presented a challenge in the February 29, 1988 issue: "Okay, Mr. Chief Executive," he gently needled, "so you restructured, cut costs, and even managed to lift your stock price out of takeover range for the time being. What do you do now?"

Outthinking and out-implementing the competition is required to get on top. And to stay there as well. "Buck" Rodgers, past vice president of marketing for IBM, stated in a provocative 1984 speech, "The trophies on one's shelf do not win tomorrow's games."

Notice that I do not emphasize just creativity, or just innovation for that matter. Implementation is at least as important as imagination. If strategy is king, execution is queen.

Think about it. Business at its essence is two things: ideas plus action. Thinking and doing. Having a dream and making it happen. Not only do you need to formulate a competitive edge, you need to have a capable, committed organization to put it into action. Successful companies are great at both. On the other hand, falling down in either can lead to financial disaster. Imagination is not enough. But it is essential.

PLANNING AND EXECUTION

What is the principal vehicle that organizations use to set future courses and monitor implementation? Strategic planning. Ironically, much business planning, and strategic planning in particular, does little to stimulate imagination or assure effective execution. Incrementalism (5 to 10% annual increases in profits, for example) dominates most thinking. Many times the quantum leaps and the creative sparks to fuel them—as well as the details of turning ideas into realities—are not even considered part of planning. Here are some top management comments I've heard:

- "Our planning is half cosmetic and half procedural nuisance."
- "It's the bland leading the bland."
- "Our strategic plan and other tall tales."
- "Our planning could win the duel of the dull."

Pick up any book on business strategy or planning and you probably won't even find the words "imagination" or "creativity" in the index. Yet the purpose of planning is to *create* and *implement* ways to beat the competition. This book was written to fill this void in the marketplace.

Through hundreds of examples, this book will give you a total approach to creating profit—for your company, your division, your department, and even yourself. There is something for both seasoned executives and management trainees in organizations of any size.

Chapter 1 outlines the five-step Creative Planning process. This universal approach can help a CEO create a vision for the company, help a manager set direction for his department, or help a professional organize and motivate a project team.

Part One, "Imaginative Strategic Thinking," contains a chapter on each of three ways to generate ideas—insights, leaps and connections—for use at all levels of organizations. It concludes with a chapter on how to refine new ideas to increase their positive impact and feasibility.

Part Two, "Make It Happen," explains how to put your plan into action. It begins with decision-making tools for selecting the best options. Then it shows how to crystallize one's mission, objective, strategy, and action plans. How successful companies implement their plans is covered. A chapter on leading creative teams details ways to facilitate the planning effort and to stimulate vigorous teamwork in general.

Part Three, "Insightful Strategic Analysis," devotes a chapter to each of the six key aspects of any organization: profitability, positioning, competitors, technology, operations, and organization. This provides the complete picture needed for strategic thinking. Many creative approaches, illustrated by examples, are included in each chapter.

Part Four, "Corporate Restructuring," describes how companies revitalize themselves by making major changes in the business they are in, how they operate, and how they are financed. The first chapter explains corporate planning for multibusiness companies: how to identify future winners and losers, and how to allocate resources accordingly. Next comes how to achieve major shifts in business direction by making acquisition bargains and divestiture coups. The subject after that is turnarounds. The "lean, mean profit machine" techniques used in saving sick companies apply to healthy ones as well.

The book concludes with a chapter on how and when to start creating profit in your organization, and what the United States could do to increase its competitiveness. A peek into the minds of creative geniuses is provided in the Appendix.

Acknowledgments

MANY people encouraged me to write this book and helped me to do it. Don Bohl, group editor of management briefings and surveys at the American Management Association, was the first person to recognize the significance of my ideas on creativity in strategy development. He guided me through my first two publications, monographs entitled "Creative Planning Starts at the Top" for the Presidents Association, and "Creative Planning Throughout the Organization" for all 75,000 AMA members.

I would like to thank all those executives who attended my speech in 1985 at the Tenth International Conference of the Planning Forum. They rated my presentation the "most useful" of the twenty-five speeches given, 79 percent of the participants assigning it the highest possible score. I must have hit a responsive chord. This confirmed that I was on to something powerful and spurred me on to develop my concepts further.

Another who motivated me to put my thoughts into book form was Michael Ray, professor of marketing and communications at Stanford Graduate School. Author of *Creativity in Business*, he also teaches a course by that name. I must also thank my fiancée, Linda Atwood, who endured my long hours in front of my computer, and my parents, Stanley and Stella Bandrowski, who encouraged me to earn an undergraduate degree in chemical engineering and two postgraduate degrees.

This book would not have been possible without the cooperation of numerous executives who allowed me to interview them at length. Many are mentioned in the pages following, while others will remain anonymous, as I promised them, in exchange for their candor. I also owe a great deal to my clients, from which I continuously learn.

Finally, I must thank Sally Bracket for her word processing; Tom Carter, a professional writer in San Francisco who polished the final draft; Robert Wallace, senior editor and vice president at The Free Press, for his support and guidance; and Laura Rosenfeld and Edith Lewis, who edited and coordinated the production of this book.

1

The Creative Planning Process

THE September 26, 1988, issue of *Fortune* put the challenge this way: "The 1990s will be tougher than the 1980s, which have seemed pretty . tough."

Fine, you say. All very interesting. But how do I go about developing a strategy that will beat out the competition? How do I effectively interweave imagination and planning so as to increase both short- and long-term profitability? And won't using a structured planning process inhibit the creative thinking that I am trying to achieve in the first place? The solution I've seen in numerous high-performing companies starts with three premises:

1. *Strategy development is a creative exercise.* This may seem obvious. Aren't we trying to determine what new to do? But in my fifteen years of experience as a corporate planning director and a management consultant, I have rarely seen the two concepts—creativity and planning—effectively coupled.

2. *Planning must result in action.* It must be provocative yet practical. Broad generalizations on what a company's strategy is are of little or no value to middle and lower management—the implementers.

Concrete ways to put the corporate competitive advantage into action are compulsory.

3. *Imagination starts at the top.* Top management must set the example. If a CEO lacks the inclination or the flair to become a highly creative executive, he or she must at least develop sufficient understanding of the innovation process to keep other minds from closing and keep them active. It is vital that the CEO not inhibit fresh strategic thinking within the organization.

When I use the phrase "Creative Planning," I don't mean the traditional mechanical analyses that have been used—and in most cases abused—over the last two decades: the experience curve, the growth/market share matrix (cash cows, stars, question marks, and dogs), and the like. I am referring to the overall thought process of strategy development and execution, the intellectual and emotional sides of it.

STRUCTURED CREATIVITY

One misconception I run into often is that great ideas are conceived and implemented in unstructured ways, as if ideas just pop into an executive's mind from nowhere, then are implemented on the spot. Sure, this happens occasionally, but not very often, particularly in the case of a corporate strategy. Strategic thinking and planning are being done at all successful companies, whether or not they go by that name.

Strategy development requires directed creativity, not blue-sky thinking. Creativity without direction is like a runaway horse—wasted energy. Saddling it up ensures productive, innovative thinking. This requires some structure and focus for the thought process and, ultimately, wise decisions.

But wait, you might say, didn't Peters and Waterman find in researching their book *In Search of Excellence* that successful companies like 3M did *not* do strategic planning? That may have been true when the book was written, but things are different now, especially in the St. Paul corporate headquarters of 3M.

"This company was very late in adopting any kind of formalized, explicit style of strategic planning," says Livio D. DeSimone, executive vice president of 3M's industrial and consumer product sector. Actually, it started when Lewis Lehr took over as chairman and CEO in 1980. "We had pushed decisions down to the product level of the company, and cross-functional teams were doing a pretty good job, but they weren't steering the company," explains Michael Tita, director of planning services and development. A more structured system of thinking about the future of the company has been adopted. But DeSimone adds, "One of the things we tried to do early on was to break away the accountability segment from the free-thought segment."[1] Keeping imagination separate from judgmental thinking will be a recurring theme.

QUALITIES OF SUCCESSFUL CEOs

Of great concern to me in developing my Creative Planning process was that it had to appeal to senior executives, to be user-seductive. If it wasn't, they wouldn't bother. So it had to be a nice, trim package of thought processes and actions that successful CEOs execute naturally in leading their organizations.

What are the platinum characteristics executives have that enable them to take their companies to the top? Here's what I believe they are.

1. *Industry Savants.* They realize there is no substitute for knowing their business, both the broad picture of their industries and the fine details of their companies. But they go beyond just awareness of what is. They constantly develop new insights into what is going on, what may happen, and how their companies can capitalize on the change.
2. *Imaginative Thinkers.* They add to their understanding an active imagination about how their business can compete to win. They are constantly looking for new ideas and providing the climate within their organizations that fosters creative thinking throughout.
3. *Astute Decision Makers.* They know how to move ideas forward to the point where they can identify the diamonds from cut glass. They are masters at the art of making decisions and do not let their emotions and egos get in the way. Most of all, they bring many managers into the process to achieve consensus and solidify commitment.
4. *Superior Strategists.* They are visionaries, but practical ones. They can clearly see why and how their company will beat the competition. They translate this vision into achievable objectives, then formulate flexible action plans that have been tested for contingencies.
5. *Masterful Motivators.* Their own love for accomplishment, combined with their ability to communicate the company's plans to their entire organization, inspires everyone to deliver at maximum performance. Once plans are in action, they continually tune in to new developments to take advantage of unplanned opportunities.

These five qualities build on one another. It would be difficult to generate options without a thorough understanding of the business and its environment. Decision making without options is irrelevant—no choices are possible except to not do anything. Detailed strategy follows decision making. And communicating is certainly easier when you know what you want to accomplish. It is the way all five of these qualities are integrated together that is important. Excelling in one, two or even three isn't good enough.

The unique value of Creative Planning is that it blends these seemingly disparate leadership qualities into a cohesive process. The essentials you have just read, in fact, correspond to the five steps of Creative Planning:

1. Analysis
2. Creativity
3. Judgment
4. Planning
5. Action

These represent the executive thought process—an intellectually driven approach to strategy development and execution which is prolific yet pragmatic. And as you will find, these steps are a strict departure from textbook planning.

OVERVIEW OF THE PROCESS

Exhibit 1–1 presents a summary of the Creative Planning process. As shown, you gain momentum as you progress toward implementation. But don't be fooled by its apparent simplicity. It is not quite as easy to follow as it looks. There are no exact recipes for strategic innovation. In going through the process, particularly if you are the facilitator, you have to be a sensitive chef, one who imagines the finished product—how it looks, feels, and tastes. Combining the ingredients, the master chef constantly tastes and improves, realizing that a rote, mechanical mixing of ingredients yields mediocrity at best. The same is true of Creative Planning.

Step One: Analysis

You begin by defining the situation and what will happen to it over time, both outside and inside your organization. The important thing at this point is to focus on the external world more than the internal aspects of your

EXHIBIT 1–1

The Creative Planning Process

Copyright © 1986 Strategic Action Associates

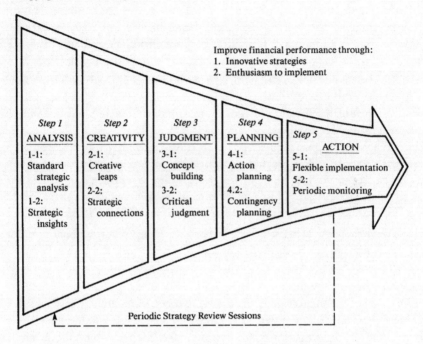

Improve financial performance through:
1. Innovative strategies
2. Enthusiasm to implement

Step 1 ANALYSIS	*Step 2* CREATIVITY	*Step 3* JUDGMENT	*Step 4* PLANNING	*Step 5* ACTION
1-1: Standard strategic analysis	2-1: Creative leaps	3-1: Concept building	4-1: Action planning	5-1: Flexible implementation
1-2: Strategic insights	2-2: Strategic connections	3-2: Critical judgment	4-2: Contingency planning	5-2: Periodic monitoring

Periodic Strategy Review Sessions

company. (You will get to them later.) Kent Dorwin, senior vice president of planning for Charles Schwab, says that in the company's first formal strategic planning process in 1987, management focused 80 percent of its attention on the strategic environment and only 20 percent inside the organization. I'll discuss Charles Schwab's "strategic revisioning," as he calls it, that resulted from the process, in Chapter 7.[2]

Evaluate your company and its environment from six different angles: profitability, markets, competitors, technologies, operations, and organization. (Part Three of this book contains a chapter on each of these areas.) But this is only the first half of your analysis step.

The equally if not more important aspect is to develop creative insights into your business and industry. A variety of techniques are used to get at the heart of the situation by breaking it down and ranking the parts. Chapter 2 covers eight of them in considerable depth. Included are identifying all of the issues facing your company, the blocks to increasing profitability, the traditions in your industry or company that no longer make sense, and many others.

Step Two: Creativity

The analysis you did and the insights you gained in the first step provide the platform from which to launch into imaginative strategic thinking. You and your management team generate ideas for all aspects of your company—ways to increase the value of your products and services to customers, improve productivity, beat out the competition, increase financial performance, et cetera. All issues and challenges are addressed, and all opportunities explored.

Brainstorming is only one of many tools for looking beyond conventional solutions. The real payoff comes from employing creativity techniques to leave the past and leap to the future. Twenty are covered in Chapters 3 and 4, and these make your planning sessions electric. Ideas combine with one another. New paths of thinking are opened. Fresh possibilities for increasing your competitive advantage are identified.

Step Three: Judgment

Your team goes through two stages of decision making. First is concept building, where you give shape to imagination. You make wild ideas feasible by toning them down, stripping out costs, and reducing risk. Second- and third-generation ideas emerge. You then combine them into strategic concepts.

You refine your concepts further until they become feasible options. Then you evaluate them against a common set of strategic criteria, which you develop specifically for your company. This produces a list of options prioritized from the most attractive to the least.

You blend your most attractive options together to see if they make sense as a whole and have a common theme. They cannot go off in all directions. The strategy you will pursue is beginning to come into focus.

Step Four: Planning

You stand back from the details and crystallize your company's mission. More important, you develop a vision of where your organization is going in the long term. Next is positioning. This describes how unique your company is (or will be), as perceived by your target customers. Then you set your objectives. They state in a measurable way what your organization will achieve over, say, the next three years.

You now formulate your strategy, which plots how you are going to achieve your objectives. In one or two sentences, you describe the essence of what your organization will do over the next two to three years. This is reinforced by a summary of your strategic values or guiding principles—what your company stands for and how it will operate. It is then back to the details, where you work out your company's strategic action programs, resource allocations, financial forecast, and contingency plans.

Step Five: Action

This is where you make things happen. You know that the proof of your ideas is in their implementation.

You present your company's plan to all management personnel, and eventually everyone in the company. Their roles are explained, and you solicit their contributions. Your plan becomes a framework for decision making throughout the company. Then each business unit and department develops a brief strategic plan of its own, showing how it integrates with the whole. Your organization becomes strategically aligned and motivated to put the plan into action.

Periodically, perhaps quarterly, strategic action programs are monitored for adjustments and refinements. Flexibility in implementation is paramount so that your organization can continually take advantage of opportunities as they arise. And you start the whole planning approach over again when needed—within one to three years is most common.

MODERATION LEADS
TO MEDIOCRITY

In the Preface I said that creating profit boils down to doing two things well: strategy development and execution, ideas plus action. Now I have given you five steps. Actually, the two concepts interrelate.

Take a look at Exhibit 1–2. I call it "the physics of planning." It shows two cycles of a sine wave—one for strategy and one for action. The five steps (and the substeps) of Creative Planning fall on different places on the curve. The vertical scale indicates the balance of creativity and reality. Wild, blue-sky thinking is at the top, and harsh, "this-is-not-going-to-work" thinking is at the bottom. How you are thinking at any given moment

EXHIBIT 1–2

Extreme Thinking Desirable

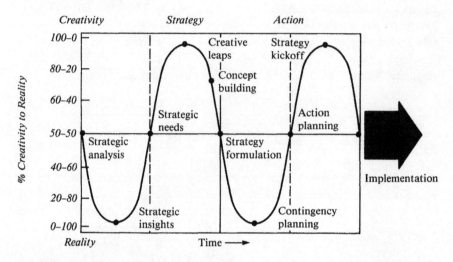

can be signified by a creativity/reality ratio: 100% creative–0% reality, 50%–50%, 20%–80%, et cetera.

We start the planning effort with strategic analysis, which is at a balance of 50%–50%. The task is to collect facts on the organization, its markets, the competition, and other areas. Not much creativity or judgment at this point. With facts in hand, we go into a relatively negative step, strategic insights (10%–90%). We identify all of the issues facing the company, pet peeves of customers, what doesn't make sense in the industry—we get it all out on the table. In fact, the more challenges we identify, the greater the possibility we will solve them and move forward.

We then jump to idealistic thinking (90%–10%) by taking creative leaps. We develop ideal solutions to the problems and challenges we've identified. This is where radically new strategic moves are hatched. We then come down the curve and undertake concept building. Our thinking at this point is 70% creative and 30% reality. It is the friendly reception area for our wild ideas. It's too soon to judge them, otherwise few if any of our ideas would make the grade. We spend time trying to make them more feasible.

Then we come further down to a 50%–50% point and evaluate the ideas in a balanced frame of mind. We don't want to be too negative yet, or optimistic either for that matter. The outcome is a prioritized list of strategic options that are to be formulated into a master plan. This completes the first cycle in the Creative Planning process.

It is now time for meticulous management—to test our strategy in the real world. Negative thinking (10%–90%) is encouraged by asking and answering: "What could go wrong with this plan?" This is commonly called contingency planning. Once we have assessed and dealt with risks, we move back up to balanced thinking and complete our action planning (50%–50%). We don't want to be overly optimistic or pessimistic when settling on strategies and setting objectives, particularly financial ones. Last, we move up to the top of the curve (90%–10%) to optimistically kick off the strategy and communicate it to our organization. Implementation then occurs.

The point of this model is that extreme thinking is essential if strategic planning is to be productive. For this to happen, there has to be both a process and a forum for it. Too often, there is neither. Visualize the curve in Exhibit 1–2 with no peaks or valleys. On one hand, highly creative ideas are suppressed in the name of practicality. On the other, negative thinking is not allowed because certain issues are not to be brought up, or the boss doesn't want to hear why his idea won't work. What results is "bureaucracy in chains," and little or no strategic innovation. The net result will be a predictable strategy and no excitement about implementing it.

People follow actions, not words, so one of the most important things a leader can do is to encourage new ideas, and not be closed-minded when they are forthcoming. The latter is the most difficult, but it is imperative in order to not stop the flow. Donald E. Noble, CEO of the highly successful Rubbermaid Inc., put it this way in a speech to the Cleveland chapter of the Association for Corporate Growth:

> To be successful, the CEO must encourage the expression of innovative ideas, recognizing that the majority of those ideas will not stand the tests to which they must be put to finally be successful. He must recognize that, unless all innovative ideas are encouraged, the ones that might ultimately be successful will never even be born."[3]

Beating your competition requires both dreamers and doers in your organization. The most successful executives are both. The beauty of Creative Planning is that it maximizes the contributions of both of these types of people.

SUCCEEDING AT IT

Throughout this book you will see suggestions on how to formulate and implement a strategy successfully. But there are a few that are so crucial to your success that they need to be presented up front. Here they are:

1. *Sequential Approach.* Creative Planning opens up your management team's thinking by means of analysis, expands its thinking to new creative levels, gradually selects the best strategic options, translates them into an action plan, and helps you execute the plan with enthusiasm. The five steps must be executed in the proper sequence. If your team gets ahead of itself, the most likely result will be a plan based on an incorrect diagnosis of the situation, an unimaginative, straight-line extrapolation of last year's strategy, or, worst of all, a combination of both.

2. *Maximize Participation.* Involving a variety of executives in the process increases the number of ideas, improves their quality, leads to better decisions, and enhances commitment to the strategy. At the very least, the chief executive officer, the chief operating officer, and the heads of finance, marketing, sales, research, engineering, operations, quality, and human resources should attend each strategy session. Employees from middle management should also attend when they can be expected to make a contribution. Lower-level people can also participate as members of task forces to address issues and champion selected ideas. The more participation the better, because creativity leads to commitment, which generates action.

3. *Delay Setting Objectives.* Objectives for the company and its business units should not be set until Step 4 (planning), after you have had a chance to look at all ideas for building the business. Preselecting a narrow range of objectives constrains creative thinking, because it tells the participants that certain issues and opportunities are closed or "out of bounds." It may even taint the assessments of the future. There is no reason to constrain anyone from thinking big early in the process. Objectives should be one of the outcomes of planning, not the starting point.

4. *Downplay Numbers.* There is no question that numbers are used to measure the performance of the company and to evaluate the planning done. However, at many companies planning means "pushing the nums." The result is a sterile, uncreative atmosphere and a plan made up of financial forecasts based on historical trends. So delay the consideration of financials (with the sole exception of finding out where your company really makes profit and return on investment, as explained in Chapter 10) until they are needed: to evaluate the attractiveness of options, in resource allocation, and finally in making a projection. Even in these cases, rounding to two figures is sufficient.

5. *Don't Rush It.* Rome wasn't built in a day, New York wasn't built in a week, and General Electric's strategy wasn't developed in a month. It takes time to conceive and refine a winning plan. So don't try to do it in a single three-day strategy retreat. At best, you will only be able to identify

the major issues and agree on some straightforward action programs. Outthinking the competition takes longer. Generally, a minimum of five meetings (one for each step) is required to create an innovative strategy for an organization. If the company contains a number of separate divisions, more meetings or entirely separate strategic planning programs for each may be necessary.

6. *Keep It Flexible.* Too often, strategic planning and operational planning are undertaken strictly by the book. As a result, they become exercises in filling out the forms—a lot of work, but not much thought. I have a standard set of forms for strategic planning, but I use them only occasionally. The reason is that every company's situation is different: the nature of its markets, competitors, issues, and opportunities. Sometimes the forms fit. Otherwise, all of the planning is kept flexible. The basic steps in the process remain the same, but almost everything else changes.

7. *Customize the Process.* In the same vein, Creative Planning must be customized to fit the financial position of the company, the style and personalities of the management team, the time they have available for meetings, the size and complexity of the company, and many other factors. No two companies are alike, even in the same industry. How many meetings, how they are facilitated, who participates, who does the strategic analyses, and many other questions cannot be answered until the organization is understood. This book will help you do this.

Creating a superior strategy is not easy. Then again, it need not be impossible, either. You can get ahead of your competitors if you infuse imaginative thinking and build implementation into your strategic planning. The Creative Planning process is designed for this. And since creativity is the most misunderstood aspect of strategy development, I will cover it first. It is also the most fun.

PART
ONE

*Imaginative
Strategic
Thinking*

2

Developing Strategic Insights

IN 1963 a man in his late twenties named Ray Dolby had a Ph.D. and was a research fellow at Cambridge. One of his hobbies was tape recording university musicians. Even though he had excellent equipment, there was a hiss on his tapes. It irritated him to no end.

Two cures for hiss already existed. Both had flaws. One filtered out the high-pitched hiss, but all the high-frequency music sounds went with it. The second amplified all of the high-frequency sounds before they were recorded, then reduced them to their original level when the tape was played back. But boosting already loud sounds created distortion, which is what you hear when a stereo is turned up too loud.

While Dolby was working for UNESCO as an adviser to the government of India, a thought occurred to him: "It was absurd to manipulate the whole signal to get rid of a very small amount of hiss."[1] It should be eliminated only in quiet moments, when the hiss would be noticeable. So he used a version of the second solution, above, to eliminate the annoying sound selectively (see Exhibit 2–1).

Ray Dolby patented his circuit and started his company in 1965 with $25,000 in savings and loans from friends. Today, more than 200 million

EXHIBIT 2–1

How the Dolby Circuit Removes Hiss

As drawn for author by William Jasper, president of Dolby Laboratories, February 25, 1987

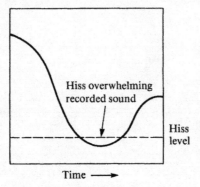

Tape recording without Dolby.

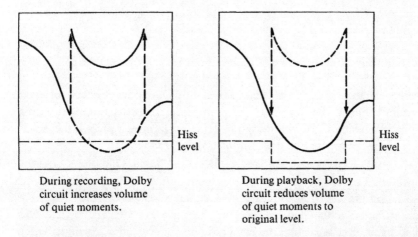

During recording, Dolby circuit increases volume of quiet moments.

During playback, Dolby circuit reduces volume of quiet moments to original level.

audio cassette decks, car stereos, videotape recorders, and personal tape players are equipped with Dolby technology. Some technical innovations from Dolby Laboratories are used in every country where sound recordings are made. Beginning with *Star Wars* in 1978, every movie to win an Academy Award for best sound has used Dolby technology.[2]

What happened to Ray? He had an insight. He recognized a problem, redefined it, and isolated the cause. Then he developed an ideal solution, reduced it to practice, and introduced it to the world. One other thing: He made a pile of money.

EVERYONE HAS INSIGHTS

Have you ever stood in line at the bank or supermarket, looked at the flow of people, said to yourself, "There has got to be a better way," and tried to think of one? If so, you started down the path to a strategic insight. You acknowledged dissatisfaction and began looking for solutions.

Unfortunately, most of us are far better at finding fault with organizations other than our own. Challenging our own thinking and ways of doing things upsets our homeostasis. It can downright hurt. But executives at winning companies do it constantly. Whenever possible, they create shared perceptions about the need for change. Then they make the change, and ahead of the competition, too.

This chapter will give you a variety of new ways to look at your business. As GE Credit Corporation's advertisement used to say, "You can't *do* things differently until you *see* things differently."

Problem Definition and, More Important, Redefinition

Reality is what we perceive it to be. There are no absolutes. So sticking with our first definition of a strategic situation is dangerous. We could end up spending a lot of time, and considerable corporate resources, adeptly solving the wrong problem. Therefore the best way to approach an open-ended challenge such as strategy development is to try to define it from a variety of perspectives. This prevents us from trying to solve all problems with the same approach. Without a variety of them it can be like trying to eat soup with a fork. By the way, when I say the word "problem," I'm using the term in both the positive and the negative sense. In the words of Henry Kaiser, "Problems are actually opportunities disguised in work clothes."

Here are four guidelines to help in your quest for understanding your strategic situation:

1. Redefine it in as many ways as possible. The more ways you look at your industry, the greater the chance you will develop a new insight into it. Think of strategy development as exfoliation. It's like peeling an onion. The outer layers have to be removed before you get to the good stuff.

2. Get as much participation in the problem definition stage as in the problem solving one to come later. People want to work on their own problems as much as they want to work on their own ideas.
3. Do not evaluate the correctness of the problem definitions as they are being generated, at least not at first. Numerous new perspectives is the initial objective.
4. Later, sort the trivial from the important. This is the only way to home in on the heart of the matter.

The object of developing insights, then, is not to search for solutions *per se*, but to seek new ways of viewing your business. Each is a mechanism to trigger fresh strategic thinking. There are many ways to do this. Here are eight.

1. *Issues and Challenges.* My survey of twenty-five planning officers indicated that most major corporations started using an issue-driven planning approach in the mid-1980s. Instead of aimlessly analyzing their environments, management teams are brainstorming lists of issues and opportunities at the start of their planning cycle. This puts the problems and challenges first, where they belong. The strategic thinking to follow is not blue-sky, but highly focused on what needs to be addressed. The organizing effect is highly beneficial.

What is a strategic issue? It is anything that may substantially impact your organization. Other ways to think of strategic issues are: all major questions needing answers; decisions needing to be made; things about the organization that need to be changed, corrected, or improved; or the primary challenges the organization faces. I'm purposely defining strategic issues broadly. Why? It is paramount to suspend judgment on whether an issue is strategic or not when the list is being developed. Debate will kill spontaneity. And what initially appears to be tactical can, upon inspection, be a widespread issue.

Once generated, group issues into a manageable number of categories, placing subissues under broad headings. Then have issue management teams (or individuals, if your group is small) creatively attack each with vigor. My work with the Mott Children's Health Center in Flint, Michigan, serves as an example of how this works. Dr. Roy Peterson, the organization's dynamic president, wanted to maximize creativity and participation in their planning. A task force of twenty-two managers and twelve board members, over the course of three months, was exposed to a wealth of outside stimuli: market trends, luncheon speeches by outside experts, customer surveys, et cetera. The thirty-four participants were then asked to list all issues and challenges facing the organization. Sixty-five were compiled. Those in turn were prioritized and grouped into six overall issues: (1) enhance responsive care, (2) develop services for special populations, (3) expand marketing and outreach efforts, (4) control costs and enhance revenue, (5) develop human resources, and (6) increase accountability throughout the organization.

Volunteer issue managers, with a task force of six to eight team members, were assigned to each issue. Over the course of three months, many ideas were conceived to resolve them. Volunteer idea champions emerged and presented their solutions. Eventually more than a hundred people were involved. Two major off-site meetings were held to select the best ideas, formulate an overall strategy, allocate resources, and launch the plan.

This process demonstrated the power of participation. One of the most controversial issues at Mott was productivity improvement. The vice president of health affairs along with other doctors initially were adamantly (I'm not sure that word is strong enough) against increasing the number of patients. They justifiably feared decreasing service quality. Dr. Peterson sagely asked the vice president of health affairs to be the issue manager for productivity. His team came up with numerous ways to increase it, including reorganizing various medical and dental departments, altering facility layouts, changing medical procedures, and reducing such inefficiencies as patient no-shows. In the final planning meeting, when board members questioned the advisability of increasing patient volume, the medical department was the most vigorous endorser of the strategy! In the year following the planning meeting, Mott Children's Health Center, with the same amount of resources, had increased patient volume by 23% overall. In the medical department it was up 35%.

Many times a CEO singles out one central issue to motivate the organization to transform itself. Campbell Soup Company was considered in the early 1980s to be stodgy and content to rest on its laurels (in its case, successful, mature brands). The process of change for Campbell began in 1980, when management carefully looked at its position in the industry. No matter what the measure—growth, return on equity, number of new products—Campbell Soup was at the bottom. R. Gordon McGovern, the newly elected president and CEO, recalls, "We looked at companies like Heinz and General Mills and said, 'if they're doing it, why can't we?' "[3] Campbell Soup shifted its emphasis from commodities to value-added products with higher margins that address new life-styles and demographics. For example, from their Swanson dinners came the successful "Le

Menu'' line. Corporate growth was restored, and return on equity moved from 13.2% in 1980 to 16% in 1987.

Sometimes it is necessary to lay a hypothetical challenge in front of your planning participants to force them to think in new ways. I saw this work when consulting with the European subsidiary of a major U.S. manufacturer of industrial paints and coatings. Domestic operations in the United States had to develop an entirely new strategy in order to survive the abrupt industry downturn in 1982. The European and Mideast market had been less affected, and management there was less motivated to change. That is, until the executive vice president from the United States challenged the group to answer, ''What would you do here if your entire market disappeared, as it did to us in the States?'' Responding to this question opened up some conservative minds. Many ideas for new products, market segments and distribution channels were developed and put into an action plan.

No matter how successful your company, new issues are always emerging. So the question is not whether you have any, but if they are the same ones you had a month or year ago.

2. *Trends and Events.* Wayne Gretzky, the most prolific scorer ever in professional hockey, was asked how he scored so many goals. His reply: ''I skate to where the puck is going, not where it is.'' The next time you want your management team to recognize the need for change—for that matter, the need for planning—have them brainstorm every aspect of their industry that is changing or could be in the future. Cover everything: market trends, competitive moves, customer needs, technologies, manufacturing methods, employee needs. A long list usually motivates management at least to consider internal change. The next step is to list all possible implications of each of these trends. Visualize yourself already in the future with the trends in full force. What opportunities or consequences do you see? Let your imagination go.

Assign each trend and set of implications a measure of probability of occurrence (and staying power) and degree of impact on your business. These two measures can be plotted on a matrix. Develop strategies for, and monitor intensely, the high probability/high impact trends; monitor and develop contingency plans for the low probability/high impact ones. Also, watch the trends in the other two quadrants to make sure conditions do not change so as to increase their potential impact on your business.

This approach is used by many major corporations, particularly in long-range planning. For example, I had the honor of working with Merck & Co., Inc., in 1985 and 1986 to help them introduce a new corporate and divisional planning process. Merck is the largest pharmaceutical manufacturer in the United States and was rated by *Fortune* magazine in January of 1987, 1988, and 1989 to be the "most admired" company in the nation. With $5 billion in revenue and a 27% return on equity, the value of the company's stock in late 1987 (before the market crash) was $28 billion—greater than that of General Motors, which had sales more than twenty times Merck's.

One of the primary drivers of Merck's process, besides its issue-based approach, is its use of strategic scenarios. Scenarios and alternative futures are prepared at four levels: society overall, health care in general, the pharmaceutical industry, and the effect on Merck. One year, probabilities of occurrence were ascertained with the aid of a survey of 1,700 industry experts. In January 1988 J. Douglas Phillips, Senior Director of Corporate Planning at Merck, summarized its approach as follows:

> The pharmaceutical industry, and health care in general, was fairly predictable before the 1980s. But now, the direction of the health care delivery system in the U.S., in fact, all over the world, is increasingly uncertain.
>
> We identify the major trends and forces that are coming and assign probabilities of occurrence to them. We then translate this information into financial projections, with ranges of uncertainty for the pharmaceutical industry and Merck. In 1985, for instance, we called the current industry consolidation among the major players.
>
> We assign each development a trigger point, and prepare contingency plans. These cover our possible responses—how we should position the company, and what we should do differently, right down to the functional level. This way we are prepared for and can hopefully influence developments.[4]

A crucial event that changed the shape of health care in the United States in the mid-1980s was Medicare's decision to begin limiting its payments for most common ailments through its system of diagnostic recovery groups, or DRGs. Hospitals rushed to establish lower-cost outpatient clinics for many surgical treatments. Diagnostic testing shifted to outside laboratories, clinics, and even doctors' offices.

The trick in all this is to distinguish the true trend from a passing fad. Martin G. Letscher, marketing research manager at S. C. Johnson & Son, told members of the American Marketing Association in 1983 to look for six things that indicate a bona fide trend. He said the new development must:

- Fit with basic life-style and value trends (If it conflicts with them, it is most certain to be a fad.)

- Offer a variety of satisfactions including short- and long-term benefits to consumers
- Be flexible enough to be adapted to a variety of consumer or industrial segments
- Originate from unexpected or diffused sources, rather than an authority figure or style-setter
- Be supported by other related trends and developments
- Possess a legitimate underlying theme or reason for existence (Have you ridden any mechanical bulls lately?)

Be particularly sensitive to upcoming changes in the nature and buying habits of your customers and prospects. The consumer trend to fitness, for example, has led to an explosive market for exercise clubs and garments, and for "lite" foods and beverages. This was emerging in 1980 when I was working with a medium-size orange juice manufacturer. I noticed that while orange juice was perceived as a health beverage, particularly for its natural vitamin C, it contains more calories on an ounce-for-ounce basis than beer and many soft drinks. I made three varieties of a lite orange juice beverage in my kitchen, each with a different calorie count (one-third less, half, and two-thirds less). Consumer concept testing in focus groups was highly favorable, but the company was sold in a leveraged buyout to a group of investors. Procter & Gamble came out with its Citrus Hill brand lite juice in 1985 and positioned it as an all-day drink. Minute Maid did the same with its Lite & Juicy line.

A classic example of seeing a trend early and capitalizing on it is Domaine Chandon, one of the most impressive wineries in California. In 1973 it became the first joint venture in the United States with a premium French winery, Moët-Hennessy. Today it is a leader in high-priced champagne. The idea for the company was John Wright's, the company's founder and CEO. As a senior staff consultant with Arthur D. Little in San Francisco in 1972, he proposed a marketing study of the wine industry. Wright cited a depleted stock of champagne worldwide and correctly predicted the U.S. market for bubbly would explode. His report attracted the attention of Banque Nationale de Paris and, subsequently, Moët-Hennessy. It hired Wright to start up Domaine Chandon and run it. "I like to take the big picture," he says, "strategy, creativity, leadership."[5]

John Wright started a major industry trend. Now, years later, Taittinger and Mumm's have located in Napa, Piper Heidsieck in Sonoma, and Roederer in Mendocino. But Domaine Chandon's substantial lead, along with innovative marketing, largely accounts for its dominant market share. Plan for where the business is going, not where it is.

3. *Pet Peeves.* When was the last time you spoke to a group of customers and asked them to give you the vinegar-coated truth about your products, services, and policies? Understanding what bugs people most about your offerings and your competition's often can be the most valuable input to strategy development you can get your corporate hands on. Most major successful products and services eliminate or at least diminish a widespread pet peeve of a large block of customers. Think about it. What are pet peeves anyway but customer needs crying out to be filled?

Let's say you want to enter an existing industry. Look for flaws in existing products and solve them. Compaq Computer's meteoric rise in personal computers attests to this strategy. What Compaq essentially did in the mid-1980s was solve myriad small complaints that users had about IBM's line of PCs, while taking exacting care to retain IBM compatibility to win retailer acceptance. Rod Canion, founder and CEO, said in 1985, "For years, we've been hearing that when you elect to follow the IBM standard, you've essentially written off building anything innovative. We are living proof that, if you do it right, you can have it both ways."[6] Compaq is the fastest-growing company in history, reaching $111 million in its first year (1982) and $326 million in its second. It also was the only major personal computer company to post impressive growth in the midst of the industry's deep recession in 1985.

What is your biggest complaint concerning pizza delivery? When I ask this question in my seminars, the top one is invariably the pizza arriving long after it was promised. Enter Domino's Pizza with its thirty-minute guarantee. If it is late, even by a minute, $3.00 is deducted from the price (some franchises give you the pizza free!). The Domino's Pizza chain has grown at a minimum of 40% annually since 1978 and is currently second in size only to Pepsico's Pizza Hut.

Scan the entire industry chain for pet peeves, not just end customers. A competitive edge can frequently be established with industry middlemen. The president of a Midwestern U.S. wood window manufacturer I worked with designed an ideal product in response to a widespread, and apparently unsolvable, peeve of distributors. They had to carry two full lines of duplicate sized windows—wood and wood clad in aluminum—doubling their inventory and substantially decreasing their return on investment. The president's unique solution consisted of a wood window and a separate box of cladding that the distributor could put on in a matter of minutes. This reduced the distributor's inventory by 40% (as well as my client's). Distributors loved it and pushed the line. Six years later the company continues to enjoy this competitive edge. Sales are up more than 300%, and profitability is highly attractive.

You must, however, be selective in the peeves you solve. Be sure they are widespread, important (the highest-ranked ones by customers are the best to address), based on fact and not emotion, and, when solved, will generate a sizable customer benefit. For example, Federal Express tried to duplicate its Express Mail success with its two-hour ZapMail but misestimated the magnitude of the peeve. The service languished in the marketplace. Evidently, overnight service and FAX eliminated the bulk of the need. I speculate that if those had not existed at the time of its introduction, ZapMail would have been a success.

Such cautions notwithstanding, there is tremendous opportunity in product annoyances. People and companies want their burdens lightened, and they will pay a premium to any company that can do it for them. And the regenerative thing about progress is that every new solution creates new pet peeves. What things are just starting to bother your customers?

4. *Industry Traditions.* The operating policies and procedures of most companies are based on industry traditions that have evolved over many years. They tend to be self-perpetuating. Unfortunately, since structural changes generally occur gradually in an industry, these traditional approaches can become outdated without its being apparent.

With all due disrespect, some of the most profitable strategies you can implement require the trashing of an industry tradition. So, to fuel your creative imagination, brainstorm a list of all industrywide traditions that for one reason or another may no longer make sense. Forget that you may be violating industry taboos. On the contrary, look for things that will cause your competitors to say you are not playing fair. Dare to be different. Of course, you are only playing with ideas at this point and not committing to anything. But remember that the person who makes the rules has a much better chance of winning.

The investment banking firm Drexel Burnham Lambert grew from an industry also-ran to a major force with $350 million in profits in 1985. It struck gold in the market with high-yield, high-risk junk bonds, long shunned by other Wall Street firms. Drexel alienated them in the process. Those bonds fueled the takeover plays. In 1986, at a annual bash for major customers, Drexel showed a commercial starring Larry "J.R." Hagman, who held up a symbolic "Drexel Express Titanium Card." He told the corporate raiders, "Don't go hunting without it."[7] Drexel's and Michael Milken's legal problems aside, the development and promotion of junk bonds forever changed the investment banking industry and the takeover game.

Breaking with tradition is emotionally difficult. This is why industry-wide innovations frequently come from startups, small companies or large companies that are new entrants. They are not bound by a sense of how things have always been done. Take, for example, Iowa Beef Packing (IBP). This $6 billion powerhouse of the meat-packing business vaulted from obscurity to leadership by completely changing the rules. Instead of transporting cattle a thousand miles and slaughtering them in union-controlled Midwestern plants, it built its slaughterhouses near the grazing lands and operated them on a highly automated, nonunion basis. The rest of the industry laughed. But Iowa Beef's cost advantage gave it the competitive edge it needed to dominate the industry.

Major industry participants are capable of reinventing rules, if they are lead by an innovative CEO such as Robert L. Crandall, chairman of American Airlines. He has made his mark as a maverick of the airline business. Rejecting conventional wisdom, he launched (1) the first deep-discount fares (called Super Savers) to fill empty seats on unpopular flights, (2) the original frequent flier program, and (3) a two-tier wage structure. While all of these innovations have been copied by other air carriers, they helped American triumph in the chaotic period of deregulation.

Lotus Development Corporation went against industry convention in its launch of Symphony, its integrated software package containing spread-sheet, word processing, communications, data base, and graphics capabilities. It was the first major company to be explicit in disclosing proprietary information to other software developers so they could develop add-ons and what the industry calls "shells," which customize Symphony for specific markets such as health care of financial services. Previously, software companies didn't disclose until sales flattened. Mitchell Kapor, Lotus's President, likens this strategy to IBM's introduction of the PC. IBM disclosed its design to hardware and software vendors so they could manufacture peripherals and develop applications software.

Great athletes and great companies are a lot alike. The difference between a great athlete and a very good one is that the former changes the sport. Jimmy Connors and Chris Evert gave the sport of tennis the two handed backhand—the vast majority of teenagers playing today use this powerful stroking weapon. "Broadway Joe" Namath turned pro football more into a passing game than ever before. It hasn't been the same since. Dick Fosbury won the high jump in the 1968 Olympics by going over the bar backward. Today, all jumpers use the "Fosbury Flop." In each case, they left something behind. Great companies do the same.

5. *Company Traditions.* Innovating on a smaller scale than revolutionizing your industry is to break your own company's rules and regulations. Winning companies radically reappraise their strategy, policy, organizational structure, technology, et cetera. Continuously. As Tom Peters says in *Thriving on Chaos*, "The old saw, 'if it ain't broke, don't fix it,' needs revision." He proposes, "If it ain't broke, you just haven't looked hard enough. Fix it anyway."

High-performing business executives constantly challenge the assumptions that everyone takes for granted. As they study a situation, they analyze standard operating policies and practices by asking: "Why is it done this way?" or "Is this the best method?" or "How else might that be accomplished?" While constantly challenging company dogma in search of more profitable strategies, they listen for that one discordant note among the dozens in harmony. If their questions generate promising insights, these executives are ready to investigate new possibilities.

Sony in the United States, for example, pursued a strategic counter to the wisdom dispensed from Tokyo headquarters with its 8 mm videotape camera/player. The sales policy of President Norio Ohga in Japan prohibits discounts because they can hurt the company's premium image. Sony's U.S. subsidiary gives not only discounts but trade allowances and cooperative advertising money. These are the realities of doing business here. Well, standard U.S. sales tactics paid off. Their market share shot up to 30% the year after introduction.

IBM is surprisingly flexible in strategy, given its size and heritage. It broke many company traditions with the PC. It started a new venture in a remote location, used a substantial amount of components from outside suppliers, and marketed through dealers rather than direct sales people. In 1987 IBM began installing systems composed of hardware from other vendors. It had not done this in the past even if the equipment filled a gap in its system. This is all part of its effort to regain control of some large accounts that it is losing to Digital Equipment and others.

Sometimes it is desirable to introduce a new tradition without destroying the old. This is the most frequent reason why companies start new divisions and subsidiaries or develop entirely new brands. Marriott created a new division and brand name for its Courtyard chain, because a whole new corporate culture was needed to manage it. Walt Disney Pictures circumvented its sixty-year tradition of producing films for the whole family by creating Touchstone Films. Its first movie, *Splash*, was a box office hit.

Charles W. Moritz, chairman and CEO of Dun & Bradstreet, emphasized the need for breaking tradition in a 1987 speech at the national meeting of the Association for Corporate Growth:

> At the heart of D&B, there is a dynamism of change. Growth only occurs because of the willingness of human beings to change. In order to move forward, you have to leave some things behind. More often than not, what has to be left behind are the sacred cows of traditional thinking—those sacred cows of "But we've always done it this way."[8]

6. *Strategic Blocks.* These are defined as anything that stands in the way of increasing sales, profits, productivity, quality, whatever the issue. Try listing every obstacle you can think of to improving all aspects of your business. Each block, in turn, represents a target for ideas for eliminating or circumventing them. When clearly defined, most blocks are resolvable. In working with a large drug wholesaler, for instance, I asked the sales managers what was blocking them from increasing revenue by 50% the next year. The barrier, as they described it, was that the company's salespeople spent more than 70% of their time servicing existing accounts, and most of that time was spent handling customer returns, a widespread industry practice. We brainstormed alternative solutions and pursued these: Some of the duties were given to customer service, some were computerized, the returns policy was more uniformly enforced, and certain salespeople and managers were assigned strictly to the development of new territories and market segments. Revenue the following year increased 40%, as against the company's historical growth rate of 10%.

One of the most effective approaches to productivity improvement is determining bottlenecks. This works equally well in both a manufacturing environment and a service company. While leading a creative problem-solving seminar at a large telecommunications company, I asked a telemarketing representative what blocked her from a 100% increase in productivity. She said that her responsibility of having both to sell and to complete onerous documentation prevented her from handling more calls. The group worked out the details for a solution, the essence of which was to have the salespeople close the sale and then turn the customer over to a documentation clerk. The next day the telemarketer told me that she had mentioned the idea to her superior and was told that the strategy was already being tested in the company's Southeast region. We had developed it in thirty minutes.

The key to identifying strategic blocks is not to accept generalized answers such as "the competition." What exactly is it about your competition that is preventing your from gaining a bigger share? List all the separate reasons. Then creatively go after each by asking, "What do we need to overcome them?"

7. *Change Viewpoints.* Lack of progress in strategy development is many times caused by a problem of perception. As the saying goes, it is difficult to see the picture when you are inside the frame. This is one of the primary reasons consultants are hired. A fresh pair of eyes can often cut to the heart of a problem.

Changing one's viewpoint is a favorite technique of innovative executives. When no progress toward a solution is being made down one avenue of thought, they will approach the situation from an entirely different angle. If a marketing problem cannot be solved with one segmentation scheme, perhaps an entirely new one is called for. Or if a production problem is causing delivery shortfalls, maybe a broader systems view of the plant and distribution network is needed.

Role-playing is one of the most powerful ways to change your viewpoint. Try taking your customer's perspective. Make believe. If you were a customer, what would you want in terms of product design and service? Forget what you have to offer. This will help you to become truly customer-driven. I like to play a game I call "President du Jour." Ask people, "What would you do if you were president of the company for a day? For a year? In the long term?" Most people love to step up the challenge. I have heard some highly innovative strategy alternatives from lower-level employees. The approach is an ego builder as well, which can enhance morale.

Lastly, if you find one of your strategy meetings going slowly and you seem to be generating the same old ideas, try this out. Ask the participants to make believe they are someone who is noted for aggressive, innovative action. For example, what would Lee Iacocca do if he were CEO of your business? Or Jack Welch? Or one of the takeover artists, such as Carl Icahn, T. Boone Pickens, or Sir James Goldsmith? You are sure to get some radical ideas.

8. *Success Formula.* The company that has a firm grasp of its formula for success is already far ahead of its competitors in its strategic thinking. Management need only focus its resources on the key factors in the formula to gain a competitive edge. The challenge, of course, is to define the formula. Also, it can vary for each market segment and will change as the company grows in size and as the industry matures.

One way to define your success formula is to ask what the things are that your company has to do well in order to win in the marketplace and make a substantial profit. Be very specific. Do not settle for such ambiguous answers as high quality, excellent service, or competitive price. I asked Arthur Gensler, founder and CEO of Gensler and Associates in San Francisco, to define his company's formula as a way of understanding why his firm is so successful. It has consistently been rated by industry publications as the largest architectural design firm in the country, and for the last six years it has been named by peers as the firm they most respect. Art mentioned many success factors, but here are the most important ones:

- We provide the highest-quality design service matched exactly to our customer's style. We study their industry, their operations, and get to really know their business. There is no "Gensler style."
- We add value to our services by being expert on all aspects of design such as building codes, tax laws, the real estate market, et cetera. We are a total problem-solving resource to our customers.
- We take a very business-oriented approach to our projects, spending client dollars as if they were our own. Our fees are also reasonable, not the highest or the lowest.
- We smooth out the economic cycles by being national, doing a balance of both interior and exterior design, and taking both large and small projects. Most of our largest competitors won't handle small ones.
- We hire the best people for a lifetime—not a project—pay them a premium, and give them a lot of responsibility.

Gensler's success formula obviously works, because 85% of his company's revenue is from repeat business. The industry average is less than 50%.[9]

Once you have identified the success factors for your business overall and for each of your product/market segments, rank them in terms of importance. Then objectively compare this with a ranking of your company's strengths and weaknesses, and those of your competition. If your company's biggest strengths do not match the most important success factors, you need to take a hard look at your current strategies and the way you are allocating your resources.

The flip side of this technique is the "failure formula." In the same way, list the key factors that would make your company decline in revenue and profitability. Resources should be heavily applied to those of greatest potential impact and probability.

POINTS TO PONDER

If you react defensively when someone raises a new issue, or if you behead the messenger who brings bad news, you will be cutting off a tremendous source of insights into your strategic situation. Lewis Lehr, chairman and CEO of 3M, told *Nation's Business* in October 1984, "If you can't speak openly about your problems, then your problems shouldn't be attended to. And if, as a supervisor or manager, you can't listen to the problems, then you shouldn't be a supervisor or manager." When the unvarnished truth is exposed and the causes of problems begin to surface, there is a feeling that finally someone is turning on the light.

Executives have reported that doors to profitable strategies have been flung open when they used insight generation techniques such as I have just described. But I haven't even thrown my fast ball yet. What insights really do is prepare you for the creative leap, the topic of the next chapter.

3

Taking Creative Leaps

IF there is a place for fantasy in strategy development, this is it. In fact, it is impossible to be truly creative without taking creative leaps. As the saying goes, fortune favors the bold. The strategic insights developed from the techniques in Chapter 2 provide the platform. Now it is time to develop profound answers to vital questions.

PUT YOUR IMAGINATION TO WORK

The most powerful technique for developing breakthrough concepts is the creative leap. The thought mechanism used is the exact opposite of logical, convergent thinking. Logical thinking is appropriate for analytical problems that can be stated exactly and have only one correct answer, like totaling a column of numbers. In contrast, creative problems can be stated in many ways and have an infinite number of solutions—such as a strategy for a company. Exhibit 3–1 shows the difference between the two.

EXHIBIT 3–1

Two Types of Problems

ANALYTICAL	CREATIVE
One right answer	Many possible answers
Clearly defined	Needs defining
Logical approach	Open-ended approach
Solution exists	Solution will be new
Can be verbalized	Needs to be visualized
Deductive approach	Inductive approach
Left-brained	Right-brained

Vault Barriers

The creative leap is achieved by jumping to potential idealistic solutions first, then working logically backward to solve the problem in the reverse direction. Exhibit 3–2 shows how this works. In the words of Leonardo da Vinci, "think of the end before the beginning." In his book *Managing*, Harold Geneen captures it another way:

> A Three-Sentence Course on Business Management: You read a book from the beginning to the end. You run a business the opposite way. You start with the end, and then you do everything you must to reach it.[1]

Another benefit of creative leaps is that they avoid inhibited thinking. In fact, you can use one leap as a base from which to take another—a double leap. One idea stimulates another. Simply make your objective the suggestion of daring ideas, including those that may go against hallowed principles. The divergent thinking that results can scale mountainous possibilities, as well as restore the original entrepreneurial flair to an organization. So in taking leaps, leave logic behind. That is why brilliantly simple solutions to strategic problems are usually obvious only after they have been found.

The problem with most creativity techniques, however, is that they do not appeal to top and middle management. They are too complex, too time-consuming, or not directly related to solving business problems. Over the last ten years I have collected and developed approaches that mimic the way innovative executives think. Here are ten ways to take quantum leaps.

1. *Year 2000.* We are approaching one of those rare milestones in human history, a year with three zeros. The twenty-first century will leave skid marks on the 1990s. Visualize what your industry will be like in year

EXHIBIT 3–2

The Creative Leap

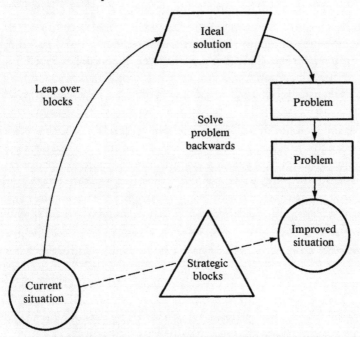

Visualize the ideal solution and fill in the feasibility afterward.

2000 and beyond and which products, services, and manufacturing methods will be winners. What competitive techniques will win in the new marketplace? Which technologies will be available? How will customers be served better than today? Get graphic. Be specific. Give as many answers as possible.

The purpose is not to develop a forecast. It is to unlock imaginations. Every time I ask a client's executives to take a mental leap to the end of the millennium, a bunch of wild ideas emerge. In them are some that smell of reality, even today. It is amazing how many no-tech or low-tech solutions emerge. The logical question is then: Can any be implemented immediately or within the next few years?

3M uses a similar technique in its strategic planning. Every year the general manager of each business is required to paint the best picture he can of his industry fifteen years ahead—challenges, threats, likely products, et cetera. In 1987 the process was called "Challenge 2002." (In 1988 it became "Challenge 2003.") Management claims the outcome is ideas and a fine guide for strategic planning.[2] The future will be invented by those who see it today.

2. *Ideal Company*. Ask your management team to describe in detail the ideal competitor in your industry. All aspects of the company should be covered, with feasibility and resource limitations set aside. Then ask: "If you could have anything this competitor has, what would it be?" or, "If you could acquire any company, which would it be, and why?" In 1983, after Chrysler had turned the profit corner, Lee Iacocca described his conception of the ideal automotive company: "It would combine German engineering, Japanese production efficiency, and American marketing."

Federal Express, one of the extraordinary business successes of the 1970s, is a good example of the "ideal company" framework. Frederick Smith, founder and CEO, had a vision of an overnight envelop and package delivery service that required a highly imaginative solution. All packages are air transported (140,000 in his original model, more than 900,000 in 1987) to a central location each evening (Memphis). There, airplanes switch packages within four hours, then take off and arrive at their final destinations by morning. This hub-and-spoke system has become the industry standard, with Airborne, Emery, Flying Tigers, Purolator Courier, and United Parcel Service operating similar wheels. "Absolutely, positively overnight" is the Federal Express slogan. It proves that people will pay a sizable premium for the ideal—in this case, forty-four times the price in 1988 ($11.00 versus a twenty-five-cent stamp). Ironically, Fred Smith's MBA project describing the concept earned him a C.

One top executive told me that he always sets high return-on-investment targets for marginally profitable divisions. He explained it is a sure way to get their managements to consider bold moves such as dropping product lines, closing plants, and so on, rather than more conservative strategies. As GE's John Welch stated in the speech I mentioned in the Preface:

> The challenge is: How do we make the quantum move—improve the cost structure, halve the overhead, invest in modernization—to get it profitable, to get into a competitive position where it can *fundamentally* win. The move has to be decisive and bold.

3. *Ideal Industry*. Take a step back and reconceptualize your entire industry. How could all players—your company, suppliers, distributors, dealers, and even competitors—make more money? The classic example is the invention of just-in-time (JIT) by the Japanese. Frequent deliveries of raw materials, little or no work-in-process inventory, and constant delivery of finished products to the distribution pipeline have numerous advantages: Everyone's inventory is substantially reduced (decreasing assets and increasing the return on them), enhancing flexibility and increasing customization.

Citicorp reinvented the way Americans select a mortgage loan in 1986. Its competitors aren't happy. Customers and real estate agents are, though. Its program, MortgagePower, has helped Citicorp, who wasn't even in the top hundred mortgage lenders in 1981, become the nation's biggest in 1988. Simply described, Citicorp has strung together three thousand real estate brokers, lawyers, and insurance agents into a thirty-seven-state referral network. To qualify for MortgagePower and receive a loan for an origination fee 1.5% below what one would get by going directly to Citicorp, the home buyer must go through a Citicorp agent. The agents, in turn, are paid by the home buyer a broker's fee of 0.5%. The positioning of the mortgage is not the lowest cost in the market, but a hassle-free one that will be approved (or not) within fifteen days, with very little paperwork. Everyone wins.

4. *Sweeping Solution*. One vice president of marketing called the technique of trying to find a total solution "The Whopper." Standing back from the problem and viewing it in a broader context is a continuing theme in making leaps. Finding a total solution for the situation often is simpler than trying to solve the individual elements. The CEO of a major food wholesaler told me to think of it this way: "It can be easier to cure pneumonia than to cure a cold."

I was working with the president of a major drug wholesaler, and we were not making any progress. I asked him to describe his ideal company. He responded with, "You mean if I could start all over?" I said yes, and the ideas poured out. So take out a fresh sheet of paper and design that ideal.

Sweeping solutions are not just for business. Imagine a city the size of San Francisco with 9 million people—Tokyo. One of its newspapers held an essay contest to come up with solutions to the lack of space for growth. A recent prizewinner was to put government offices on a ship and sail them out to sea, or keep them moored at the dock. Another idea was to pick up the capital of Japan and move it somewhere else. Both ideas are being considered. Tokyo, the seat of government since 1869, was after all rebuilt after the 1923 earthquake and again after the 1945 bombings of World War II.[3] The Japanese are noted for their "scrap and build" manufacturing strategy; for example, they start all over when it is time to incorporate major technological improvements in their plants. It can be expensive, but as they proved to the United States in steel and many other industries, new competitors entering your market are not constrained by present products, manufacturing plants, or ways of doing business.

5. *Perfect Product*. Both management and customers should be asked to fantasize about the products that could be provided to either existing customers or new ones, if there were no technical or fiscal constraints. To

stimulate ideas, team members are asked to review all the pet peeves developed in the previous step and to put themselves in the place of each person in the distribution chain: reps, brokers, distributors, dealers, and final customers.

A concrete mix that dries much faster and is much stronger than conventional types would be considered ideal by construction contractors. Greenwich, Connecticut, based Lone Star Industries invented one, brand named it Pyrament, and claims it is a bargain even though it costs twice as much as standard cement. Because it contains alumina (rather than the calcium silicate that is in Portland cement), it uses much less water, enabling it to dry in only four hours versus a week for the ordinary stuff. And Lone Star claims that just 7 inches of Pyrament will do the work of 10 inches of regular concrete. Army engineers are one group that is sold on it. Airport runways in California can be poured or repaired when a plane leaves New York and be ready for the plane's landing when it arrives at its destination.

Howard Head forever changed the tennis racket when he decided the ideal was considerably larger than what had been standard. In 1976, he introduced the aluminum Prince Classic, which is 110 square inches rather than the traditional 70. The oversize racket made it easier for novices to learn the game and gave advanced players increased power while reducing mistakes. Market share of the traditional-size rackets went from 100% in 1975 to 92% in 1978, then to 28% in 1983 and 1% in 1988.

There are many other products that were conceived in the ideal world: filmless cameras, disposable cameras, disposable contact lenses, smokeless cigarettes, no-calorie fat, and Miller's Genuine Draft Beer. One that I wish all microcomputer and word processor program manufacturers would sell is a CRT which displays a full 8½-by-11-inch page on the screen (Xerox and a few others do sell them).

6. *Perfect Package.* Want to wake up a sleeper of an old product? Repackage it. Ideally, make it the perfect package for the consumer or distributor, not just a new design for cosmetic reasons. Personal care and other consumer product categories are seeing quite a few innovations: toothpaste in a pump, Procter & Gamble's Liquid Tide (a new version of its powdered detergent), and micro-crisping microwave dinner packages that incorporate the dynamics of a conventional oven into its box to brown foods.

Industrial products can be innovatively packaged as well. David Kornblith, founder and CEO of Technology Chemical in Oakland, California, has beat out his competition in the industrial cleaners market by practically eliminating packaging ("zero packaging"). His competitors deliver cleaning solutions in 55-gallon drums, which have to be handled, stored, and cleaned for reuse. Technology Chemical offers to install a large tank outside the customer's facility free of charge, for use exclusively by his company. Then, both he and his customers save on the handling, and the tanks pay for themselves, in his words, "quite rapidly." Not to mention that it locks in customers.

So in your designing of perfect packages, strive for utility, simplicity, convenience, and protection or, perhaps, none at all. Look at the egg. How could millions of chickens be wrong?

7. *Ideal Service.* This technique is by no means just for service industries. More and more manufacturing companies are stimulating sales and reaping profits by providing innovative services along with their products. Steel service centers are one example, and chemical companies supplying applications engineering for their specialty products are another.

To assess your own possibilities, ask, "Which needs of my customers are directly or even indirectly related to my products?" Stand back again and view your customers as partners—if they do well, you do well. Don't think in terms of selling products. Sell the solution to all the customer's related problems. Analyze the entire way that customers purchase, stock, finance, handle, and consume your products to determine unmet needs and "total solutions," as discussed above.

ServiceMaster began as a supplier of cleaning products to institutions. It then contracted with hospitals, manufacturing facilities, and other organizations first to clean their premises, and later to provide maintenance, laundry, and related services. Chemicals are now a very small part of the business. ServiceMaster's return on equity in 1987 was an incredible 161%, one of the highest in the Fortune 500.

In an effort to restore a spirit of cooperation with food retailers, Procter & Gamble and General Foods both began in the early 1980s supplying product profitability software systems and data to retailers to help them maximize their income. (How these "Direct Product Profitability" models work will be covered in Chapter 10.) Those two companies plus Kraft, Philip Morris, Ralston Purina, and RJR Nabisco are now offering computerized shelf-space and promotion management systems.

8. *Ideal Information.* "To know what you don't know is the beginning of wisdom," said Socrates. What information do you need in order to win? It astonishes me that most of what management teams tell me they need is obtainable at costs ranging from low to reasonable: customer needs, the profitability of their product lines and services, regulatory scenarios, competitive information, and so on. First make a list of ideal information, then rank items in order of importance. Then brainstorm how to get them or at least some of each of the top-ranked ones.

To help it improve its credit scoring system for new credit card applicants, Citicorp has developed a unique approach to determining how deadbeats behave. Periodically, it takes a few thousand applications at random and okays them, except for people in bankruptcy. After a year or two it has the statistical fix it needs and more precise statistical control of future losses. Yuan Chia, manager of the division says, "A banker would have a heart attack watching us do this." But growth of the division has been spectacular, and profits are healthy.[5]

Gilbane, a major contractor of commercial buildings, offers its health care clients a "hospital equipment tracking program." It identifies specific utility needs and installation dates for the high-technology equipment hospitals use.

American President Companies has a computerized tracking system that enables customers to track each shipment from pickup to delivery, even if it involves an intermodal shipment involving APC ships, trains, and trucks. In 1987 it unveiled a powerful enhancement to the service called "EagleLink." Linda Cyrog, a vice president of American President Lines (APC's shipping division) described it to me: "It enables customers to 'talk' directly with our database by using a touchtone phone. They can request bill of lading, vessel arrival, cargo availability and other information on a specific shipment—and receive an 'uncanned' computer-generated oral report, available twenty-four hours a day, of the most current data on APL computers."[6] These and other services give APL a competitive advantage.

9. *Ideal System.* A great place to look for innovation possibilities is right in your own organization, specifically the way it works. Define the flow of activities in a particular area of the company, or the company overall, and design the ideal flow for maximum productivity and lowest cost. In the case of new product development (to be covered in Chapter 13), maximum speed is a key criterion.

The company's management information system is an excellent place to use this technique. Bill Jasper, president of Dolby Laboratories, told me his vision of the ideal computer system for his company in 1980 was one that connected its IBM 36 mainframe to everyone's PCs (made by Northstar Computer)—years before the term "networking" was jargon. IBM told him it couldn't be done. Jasper's response: "There had to be a way." He and his technologists bought some software and developed some of their own. "Within a year we were able to pull data off the mainframe into a PC spreadsheet and then play 'what ifs' with it. It came in bits and pieces—first personnel information, then open orders, et cetera."[7]

10. *Comic Relief.* Having fun is serious business. You can laugh your

way to ideas, and laugh yourself all the way to the bank. This is because hatching radically new ideas requires total breaks with tradition. One way to encourage them is, for a period of time during a creativity session, to request that all participants come up with wild ideas—ones that are as outrageous and/or funny as possible. No logical solutions are permitted. Humor activates the creative imagination. Indeed, the fewer funny remarks during a creativity session, the less flexible and original the group is.

The alchemy of humor works as follows. The right brain thinks up and reacts to jokes. If you analyze a joke with the left, it loses its impact. When people laugh, they get relaxed. When they are relaxed, they think better and more creatively. A joke can say the unsayable, so sacred cows can be addressed in a light atmosphere that otherwise would be impossible to cover. It gives people an opportunity to offer that "crazy" idea they have always had in the back of their minds, but wouldn't say it for fear of being considered foolish. In every humorous suggestion lies some element of truth. And last, all analysis and no fun makes for boring strategy sessions.

In the words of B. C. Forbes, founder of *Forbes* magazine: "Cheerfulness costs nothing, yet is beyond price. It is an asset for both business and body. The big men of today, the leaders of tomorrow, are those who can blend cheerfulness with brains."

Taking creative leaps is the best way to reinvent a product, service, organization, or entire company. The ideas that emerge may allow you to change the rules of your industry, as Citicorp did. Better yet, you may be able to invent a whole new game, like Federal Express.

4

Making Strategic Connections

SEEKING TOGETHERNESS

Good connections are an asset to any business person. But when trying to be innovative, connections—of thoughts, that is—are essential. Intuitive leaps are creativity in its purest form, but making connections between things that already exist can also yield excellent strategic ideas. This is particularly true in light of the following three aspects of the creative process.

1. *Quantity breeds quality.* The more ideas, the better the chances that a superb one will emerge during subsequent evaluation. As Einstein remarked, "I think and think, for months, for years. Ninety-nine times the conclusion is false. The hundredth time I am right."
2. *Ideas work in combination.* Many times, the positive aspects of two or more ideas can be combined in a way to eliminate each idea's negative characteristics. In fact, most successful strategies are a blend of many separate ideas.
3. *Unfeasible ideas are valuable.* Because they work in combination, it is vital to consider ideas that have only a glimmer of potential— even ideas already rejected. At this stage in Creative Planning, you

should not be overly concerned with the apparent unfeasibility of an idea. That will be covered in concept building.

CREATIVE COMBINATIONS

The objective in making strategic connections is to suggest as many options as possible concerning every facet of the business: markets, products, services, sales, distribution, manufacturing, finance, acquisition, divestment, cost reduction, and so forth. Both halves of the business should be addressed: the business that is and the business that can be. Here are ten approaches for making connections.

1. *Fertile Areas.* Start where you have the greatest probability of positive impact on your organization. For instance, review the list of prime insights you developed earlier. Can any solutions, even wild ones, be imagined to meet challenges, overcome strategic blocks, pacify pet peeves, or align the company with its success formula? Take your company's or department's list of strengths and weaknesses. In what ways can the strengths be capitalized on, or the weaknesses eliminated or reduced?

Using your financial statements, concentrate on the high payout areas: (1) cost and expense categories that constitute the highest percentage of sales and (2) assets that account for the largest portion of the investment in the business. A small reduction here can be far more productive than large percentage reductions of small categories of expenses and assets. Do the same for your areas of high profit and return an investment, whether they be products, services, markets, customers, or whatever. (Profitability improvement will be covered in detail in Chapter 10.)

2. *Fill Gaps.* When one or more companies in an industry offer two or more product types or sizes, there is always the possibility of positioning a third between the first two. What appears as an insignificant niche can sometimes develop into a significant opportunity. In terms of size, there are lakes, ponds and puddles. Puddles should be avoided, unless your company is quite small. It is best to find a small pond and increase its size.

A classic example of filling a gap is TWA's Ambassador Class seating, generically known today as business class. TWA saw an opportunity to devote a portion of its wide-body aircraft to a hybrid of first class and coach. Seat size, leg room, food quality, flight attendant service, and the like are all better than coach and less than first class, for a price that falls between the two. First class travelers have traded down, and coach travelers have traded up—particularly the business person, which is a high-profitability market segment.

Other examples of filling gaps abound. Nationwide Savings in San Francisco has done very well targeting the middle class. Mini-supercomputers, or super-minis, fill the gap between supercomputers and minicomputers. The suborbital plane on the military's drawing board is halfway between the space shuttle and the F-15 fighter.

Artful product/market segmentations such as these can be worth millions. It can be lonely in the middle—in terms of competitors, that is. So divide and conquer.

3. *Push Extremes*. In direct contrast to finding gaps, this and the next technique concentrate on exploding the boundaries of the current spectrum of products and services in an industry. The opportunities arise for three reasons:

- Demographically there is a polarization of the classes going on: The middle-class is shrinking, and rich and poor segments are expanding.
- People are becoming schizophrenic in their tastes and motivations; for example, many consumers simultaneously load their shopping carts with "lite" (reduced-calorie) foods and such densely caloric ones as gourmet ice cream.
- Blasting boundaries is always a reliable way to develop creative ideas.

Motorola reported in 1986 that it was making money at both ends of the spectrum: low-tech discrete components and high-speed microprocessors. In retailing, "value-added," with its high service and quality, is a winner along with a new "minimalism," such as automated tellers, gas stations with gas-only and self service, and the like. Food retailers make the most money on stores that have revenue of at least $50 million a year or less than $10 million.

Focusing on the high end segment in dollars or size, the Spiegel Catalogue accomplished a significant turnaround and growth by, as management calls it, "a shift from mass to class." Concentrating on a selective product line of high-priced goods generated healthy profitability.

Gourmet foods are a profitable segment. Now there is gourmet dog food, evidently for the discriminating canine (or owner). Ted Turner launched his first "Superstation," PPV, in 1976, and he has continued to be successful with the concept. Taking the high road is a profitable strategy, particularly when your company is the one that is the trailblazer.

4. *Lower Extremes*. The low road can also be profitable. However, moving downmarket can also be risky. The key is in the relation of your cost reduction to your customer's preserved benefit. What feature can be eliminated from current products or services that would enable a major decrease in cost and price, yet still fulfill a need?

The high growth of warehouse-type stores is an example. People buy things right out of boxes, but at such a low price that it seems acceptable. Not quite so extreme is the "category killer," as it is known in retailing. These mammoth emporiums carry such a huge array of merchandise in a product category that they wipe out competitors. Toys 'R' Us, Circuit City in electronics, Builders Emporium in hardware, and Price Club are general examples.

Other examples of pushing the lower extreme are Budget Gourmet frozen foods, microbreweries, minimills, and Weeboks (by Reebok) for children. In automobiles we have the super-low-priced Hyundai and Yugo, and Rent-a-Wreck. The Chrysler minivan ushered the stationwagon to its grave. The thirty-second television commercial was followed by the fifteen-second one, which can be 80% as effective for a bit more than 50% of the cost. Then we got the five-second commercial. There are natural boundaries on the low end. Things can go only so far.

5. *Make Combinations.* As was stated at the beginning of this chapter, this is the classic approach to creativity—things that already exist are linked together—a marriage of thoughts. Two standard new-product development techniques are "attribute listing" and "forced relationships." In both, matrices of product attributes, options, variables, and features are drawn up. Each box in the matrix represents a potential combination that could yield a new product variation. The food industry uses this technique often. Novel combinations of variables of product, package, process, and so on account for a large percentage of new product releases. Consider wine coolers, toaster waffles, milkshake breakfasts, chunky soups, and all the "lite" foods.

The birth of wine coolers is a revealing example. R. Stuart Bewley and Michael M. Crete started the industry by borrowing an old idea of combining wine and juice. Filling washtubs at beach parties with their special mixture led to their going commercial in 1981, during which they sold seven hundred cases. Sales volume in 1982 exploded. In June 1985 they peddled their company to Brown–Forman, the Louisville company best known for distributing Jack Daniels and Southern Comfort, for $55 million plus an earnout (it never paid additional funds). By August 1985 there were one hundred or more regional and national competitors, including the eventual market share winner, E&J Gallo, with its Bartles & Jaymes brand. (Bewley's and Crete's selling of their company is also a superb example of getting out at the top, before competitive proliferation demolishes profit potential.)

Wall Street's new flavor in closed-end funds in early 1988 was the high-income triple bond hybrid. *Forbes* called the sales pitch "right out of an old Howard Johnson merchandising manual. U.S. treasury bond funds, international bond funds, and junk bond funds are combined into one "super-duper combination."[1]

Procter & Gamble created a new combination detergent and fabric softener named Bold 3. The two ingredients are used together when washing clothes anyway. How did the rest of its competitors miss this obvious combination?

Affinity group marketing of credit cards was the hottest merchandising method between 1986 and 1988 for getting more plastic into consumer wallets and purses. Those that are tied to airline frequent flier programs (each dollar of purchase equals 1 mile) have done the best.

On a more technical level, the key to relational data-bases, the fastest growing segment of the software industry, is the power of the programs to relate two different files of data, so long as they have some element in common. Oracle Corporation is the largest of the relational data-base companies. By 1988 the company had doubled in ten of its eleven years of existence, reaching $282 million in revenue and $42 million in net income, for a 32% return on equity.

6. *Apply Concepts*. What works in one industry can be successfully applied, many times with a bit of modification, to another. This is one value-added feature of using management consultants that work in a variety of industries. An example of concept transfer occurred in the late 1960s when industrial manufacturers started applying consumer market segmentation techniques to industrial products. In the 1970s industrial firms borrowed again, this time from the aerospace industry, and started selling systems rather than components.

Raymond A. Kroc, founder of McDonald's, applied manufacturing principles to hamburger preparation. Computer retailers began selling private label microcomputers in the mid-1980s, just as supermarkets have been doing with food for years. First there was branded chicken, then branded beef, and now branded vegetables and fruits. Prepaid health care has led to prepaid legal services. Another health care spinoff is veterinary pet health and accident insurance—pet HMOs, if you will. Next came operations of the "Betty Ford Center" type for chubby canines. Born in the city of Boston and near the beach in Rhode Island were "car condominiums," or "autominiums," where one pays $10,000 to $100,000 to buy a parking space—forever.

Throwing concepts at your strategic situation can be lucrative. Look beyond your own industry for fresh ways of doing business.

7. *Related Areas*. The approach here is to start in one product/market segment and radiate into others. Ask creative people in your organization: "What's related to that which we are good at? What are our strengths and how can we capitalize on them if we want to get into new areas?" Ask customers: "What do our brand (or product) names mean to you?" "What related products and services would you purchase from our company?"

Robert Crandall, president of American Airlines, stated in 1984: "This industry needs every cent it can generate. We've got to be creative about using our huge asset base to develop new revenues. We're looking at businesses we can be in at low costs because some of the links are already in place."[2]

Sometimes the related ripe areas appear obvious. American Express came out with its Optima Card, the first one the company offered that extended credit to consumers, and it was highly profitable by the end of its first year. Mail order firms are starting up retail outlets. Retailers are going into mail order. The synergy occurs because each is a traffic builder for the other.

Be cautioned that not all related products work. B. Dalton phased out its computer software at four hundred of its 792 bookstores because sales were slow. People shopping for books are not necessarily looking for software. As of 1987, B. Dalton continued to sell software in its Software, Etc., stores. It now sells each audience separately.

Line extensions are always an opportunity, but be sure that you are not cannibalizing your own sales. John Greeniaus, head of Nabisco Brands, explains that his company prefers to think of new products as "franchise extensions" rather than line extensions. "The typical line extension gives consumers an either–or choice—Coke or Cherry Coke—but doesn't add much to a company's incremental sales. Nabisco's franchise extensions go after additional sales by trying to match eating patterns." Greeniaus goes on to explain that "the Oreo is an eat-at-home cookie, while Big Stuff, an oversize version, is positioned as a snack, munched on the go."[3]

George Bush, the writer John Lister contends in the November 28, 1988, issue of *Advertising Age*, was a line extension. "The run for the Rose Garden this year was an exercise in presidential packaging, and the secret of commercial success can be summed up in two simple words: repeat purchase." Lister goes on to make the analogy that the winner had the clearest national brand identity. Democratic brands sell well at the local level, as can be seen from the majorities in Congress. Dukakis was not able to pull off national distribution. Metaphors be with you.

8. *Entertain Opposites*. One of the most provocative ways to generate

ideas is to consider the opposite of conventional wisdom. This encourages new ideas and solutions by loosening habitual thinking. What's more, opposite thinking can help you turn a competitor's strength into a weakness, or your own weakness into a strength.

A company that exemplifies the use of this approach is Circus Circus, one of the largest casino/hotel companies in the world and, more importantly, the most profitable. Most casino/hotels go after the high roller and the upper income markets. Circus Circus's chairman, William G. Bennett, states: ''We don't cater to high rollers. We don't have any junkets (free air travel, rooms, and meals for high rollers). We absolutely don't believe in giving credit. And we don't even go after the convention business.'' What does Circus Circus do? It employs a unique marketing strategy developed by Bennett. As he tells it:

> One very important thing I learned while working for the Webb Co. in the 1960s was that people don't mind losing their money gambling nearly as much as they mind paying it out for high priced rooms and high priced food. Consequently, we decided to go after the middle income, family, high-volume business by featuring low priced rooms, low priced food, and diversified family entertainment.

William N. Pennington, former president and now retired, adds: ''There is no doubt that when we started out in 1974, we were the mavericks in the industry. And we still are. Our concept is totally different from other hotel/casinos.''[4] Double occupancy rooms in 1988 run $30.00 a night (the company's three main properties average an occupancy rate of 98%), the low-priced food draws in casino customers who are not hotel guests, and the company offers the two large circuses—for free. It is this exceptional price-to-entertainment value marketing strategy that has enabled Circus Circus to target and capture an ever growing market. Glenn Schaeffer, CFO, explained it to me as follows: ''Our primary goal is to build shareholder value. From 1983 to 1988 the company has averaged over a 20% return on equity, which it expects to continue along with 20% average growth in earnings per share over the next four years.''[5]

Another opposite is the anticredit card, the rage in Japan. Perhaps only the Japanese, with their devotion to saving money, could embrace this. It is the ''prepaid credit card''—a thin, magnetically coded plastic card that gives the holder the privilege of ''pay now—enjoy later.'' Consumers use them to prepay for cigarettes, taxis, groceries, and Japan's most popular hamburger, the Big Mac. Are the cards a hit? Well, the Finance Ministry has set up a task force to determine the danger of their replacing money.[6]

Some other opposites: Canfield's Diet Chocolate Fudge Soda, New

York Seltzer Water, Texas Cheesecake, Players cigarettes for athletes, Kool Aid television commercials in black-and-white, Jolt Cola for the hard core (has "all the sugar and twice the caffeine"), health maintenance organizations that make more money if you don't get sick. Bill McGowan has been known to ask everyone at MCI to think about the opposite of what AT&T, its giant long-distance competitor, does. Opposites attract—profit, that is.

9. *Collect Ideas*. Why reinvent the wheel? In addition to all the ideas that can be self-generated, why not collect those that already exist? This includes not only products and services but business practices, manufacturing techniques, and so on. At the 1984 international conference of the Planning Forum, Ed McCracken, a Group Business Development Manager for Hewlett-Packard, stated in a speech, "We have a philosophy of 'stealing' ideas from anyone inside the company or outside. Entrepreneurs don't have the NIH (not-invented-here) problem. We don't intend to, either. This is very important."

In doing a seminar for the City of Walnut Creek, California, I learned of its innovative program to share ideas with three other cities in California: Palm Springs, Palo Alto, and Irvine. A "venture team" from each city traveled together from city to city during a one-week period to witness different management styles, economic and planning strategies, technological advancements, and innovative services. Tom Dunne, Walnut Creek's city manager, told me, "the program propels thinking into the future and removes city staff from the daily schedule that stifles creativity."

An encouraging program on U.S. education occurred in 1987. Americans studied the lessons of Japanese schools, and vice versa. In Japan, IQs are estimated to be among the highest in the world, illiteracy is almost unknown, and 90% of the students graduate from high school. (Japan's weakest link is at the university level.) Teaching is a prestigious profession in Japan, and the pay compares favorably with commercial employment. The U.S. researchers faulted Japanese education for its "rigidity, excessive uniformity and lack of choice," while the Japanese reacted negatively to the proliferation of nonacademic subjects in the United States.

Supermarkets General's CEO, Leonard Lieberman, explained in a 1984 speech at a Food Marketing Institute conference: "We didn't invent all of our store formats. We copied them, and then massaged and modified them to fit our style. A significant strategic thrust need not be original or unique." He went on to say that "it would be willfully foolish to ignore the ideas of others."

Some companies are so good at studying their competition for ideas that they rival the CIA. The Japanese are renowned for this. They hire U.S.

consultants to smoke out innovations their competitors are working on and pick customer's minds for ideas. Eventually they copy the best ideas, add a few of their own, and find ways to manufacture the product more economically. So tap as many sources as possible for strategic ideas. Let others do the lab work for you.

10. *Make Modifications.* Finally, an attempt should be made to modify each existing product, service, process, and so forth by asking: "What changes would make it better?" "How else could it be used?" "Could it be made smaller, bigger, cheaper, more expensive?" All variables should be toyed with. You never know which may lead to a strategic advantage.

A POTPOURRI OF POSSIBILITIES

Strategy problems have multiple locks that require multiple keys. In these three chapters, I have explained myriad techniques for developing strategic insights, taking creative leaps, and making strategic connections. Each can provide a number of valuable ideas. But what counts is what you do with this raw material—which is all it is at this point in the creative process. It is now time to transform this raw material into strategic options.

5

Building Strategic Concepts

NOW you've created. Your team has unleashed its imagination and has an abundance of ideas from which to choose. If you think you are finished, you've underestimated the complexity of the creative process. It doesn't end with an idea, it begins with one. The raw ideas you conceived using the insight, leap, and connection techniques are only your port of entry to the development of a winning strategy. In the words of Walter Kiechel of *Fortune*, "Forget left brain and right brain. The real problem starts when you come up with a new idea."[1]

You are now entering the most crucial stage of Creative Planning, the handling of infant ideas. This is done in one or more concept-building sessions (the first half of Step Three in Creative Planning). How this twilight zone between inspiration and commercial reality is addressed will determine the final value of your effort. Too often, great ideas suffer crib death.

BIG ONES THAT GOT AWAY

Can you recognize a big idea when you see it? It is startling how many incredible success stories started out looking harebrained and were shot full

49

of holes by the prevailing pragmatists. Once the concepts were implemented, however, the laughter stopped.

- The giant Western Union turned down Alexander Graham Bell's offer to sell them his telephone patents for $100,000.
- Edwin Land tried to sell his instant camera to Eastman Kodak. Kodak turned him down, and Land went off to found Polaroid Corporation.
- A thirty-four-year-old engineer at Texas Instruments named Jack Kilby developed the first integrated circuit in 1958 and received this brush-off: "Young man, don't you realize that computers are getting bigger, not smaller?"[2]
- Steven Jobs and Steven Wozniak took their prototype personal computer to Hewlett-Packard and Atari, both of which reported "our plates are full" and turned it down. So Jobs and Wozniak founded Apple Computer.
- In the 1940s Chester Carlson offered his patent on xerography to IBM, RCA, and more than twenty other large companies, none of which perceived the magnitude of the opportunity. A small manufacturer of photographic paper named Halloid read about the invention, acquired the license, went into production, and sold the international rights to an English concern named the Rank Organisation, then a film and entertainment company.[3]
- Dr. W. E. Deming took his quality concepts to the Japanese in 1950 because American companies were not interested. Today, nearly thirty years later, quality is one of the most prevalent strategies being pursued by companies in the United States.
- America's major automobile tire companies rejected the radial design because it cost more than bias-ply tires. Michelin jumped to manufacture the higher-priced, higher-quality radials. It took years for U.S. companies to catch up.
- Trying to sell their weekly TV program, the creators of the Cosby Show were turned down everywhere. NBC finally purchased the rights out of desperation because it lacked new product for the coming season. The Cosby Show has been the most watched program in television history.

The list goes on and on. The point is: Avoid premature judgment. Give ideas time to develop.

NURTURING IDEAS

"No great thing is created suddenly," stated Epictetus.[4] Books frequently describe major inventions or business strategies as though they were conceived in their final form, ready to implement. Wrong. Raw ideas always take work before they can be implemented. Think of the last idea you had. Were you able immediately to put it into action in the exact form in which you conceived it?

The objective of the concept-building step in Creative Planning is to transform initial ideas into possible solutions. In the case of wild ideas, you are to make the illogical logical. Talk out ideas and take them further than was thought possible. Build and interconnect ideas. Give shape to imagination.[5]

Why not take the raw ideas and evaluate them against a variety of selection criteria? Because few, if any, would stand the test of close scrutiny. Perhaps the only ones to get accepted would be the all too predictable ideas that are extensions or mere modifications of what you are already doing. Nothing truly imaginative would survive. So often I have heard: "We had a brainstorming session which generated a long list of ideas, but almost all were impractical. It was a waste of time." It was, too, if you did not take the wild ideas and build them into concepts.

Concepts First, Options Later

In my work with clients, I make an important distinction between "concepts" and "options." A concept is a combination of ideas that have been molded together to offset each other's weaknesses to make them all more feasible. An option is one or more concepts that have been taken further in the creative process toward the threshold of respectability and have become worthy of strategic and financial evaluation. This may sound like semantics, but I have found that the moment ideas are called options, people stop developing and start judging. The crucial positive atmosphere is lost.

B. C. Forbes once said, "Diamonds are chunks of coal that stuck to their job." If there is any step in creative planning at which you should stick to yours, it's concept building. Too often there is a rush to "get on with it" and identify what to implement. As a result, the most important step in the creative process is glossed over or, worse, never undertaken. If there were a way to put speed bumps in creative planning, I would build them here.

CONSTRUCTIVE CONSIDERATION OF IDEAS

Our purpose then is to improve idea quality. Like an artist, we have lumps of clay we have to shape. Here are some suggestions.

1. *Create a positive atmosphere.* Innovative executives treat newborn ideas differently from other people. They realize that ideas are still in their infancy, by definition. Instead of harshly judging, they nourish them. This takes courage, one of the creative traits discussed in the Appendix. But it is their confidence in their ultimate judicial abilities that allows prolific thinkers to withhold criticism and give ideas room to grow. Remember, you have safety nets in the step following concept building, the critical judgment of options (Step Three–2), and again in contingency planning (Step Four–2). You will have ample time to weed out poor options.

Refer back to Exhibit 1–2, "Extreme Thinking Desirable." On that curve, concept building was shown to consist of 70% creative thinking and 30% realism. Invoke this ratio when facilitating. You are trying to introduce judgment in a gradual way, one small step at a time. At this point, positive thinking should far outweigh negative thoughts about an idea. I heard one senior executive in a concept-building session respond to criticism of an idea he thought had potential with the statement, "You've already used up your 30%! Have anything else to say?"

The most senior executives at the meeting need to be particularly careful about their responses. A new idea can be killed by a sneer, a wisecrack, a frown, or even a yawn. The role of the CEO in this is pivotal. He or she must demonstrate a willingness, even outright enthusiasm, to help develop ideas into concepts.

2. *Don't take absolute positions.* There are no rights or wrongs at this point. Approximations before precision. The problem is that we are taught in school to think precisely. Concept building requires thinking vaguely. The danger signals include judgmental listening, black-and-white thinking, yesses and nos. Shades of gray are sought. Multiple perspectives are encouraged.

Interestingly, this manner of thinking is the one type that is the most troublesome for designers of artificial intelligence (AI) computer systems to simulate. Humans often use fuzzy means to achieve logical ends. In fact, an obscure branch of mathematics has sprung up with the paradoxical name "fuzzy logic." It is being used to enable computers to cope with human reasoning and imprecision and to deal with such terms as "very," "somewhat," and "mostly." What researchers hope to achieve are computers that mimic that highest of human qualities—common sense.[6]

This type of thinking is anything but Aristotelian. Aristotle, the founder of classical logic, would have insisted that each idea be fitted into one category or another, with all middle ground excluded. But this thinking breaks down in both creativity and artificial intelligence.

3. *Employ benefit/cost analysis.* Set a firm rule that the positives of an idea must be discussed before the negatives. The typical sequence of cost/benefit analysis is inappropriate. Once the drawbacks (costs or otherwise) are hammered, there is no hope for even the best of ideas. Looking for positives ensures that all ideas get entertained.

Every new idea has both merits and difficulties, so identify value in even the wildest of thoughts. It made some sort of sense to the person who proposed it no matter what flaws were also evident. No idea is totally useless. Oscar Wilde once defined a cynic as "someone who knows the price of everything and the value of nothing." Ask not why, but why not? Perhaps you can extract the essence of an idea and conceive an entirely new one. As in basic brainstorming, use one idea to generate another. Remember the double leap discussed in Chapter 3. The craziest ideas can lead to the best solutions.

4. *Use idea advocates.* A way to ensure that ideas are viewed in a positive light is to use an approach I call "idea advocates." (I have also heard them called "idea champions" and "angel's advocates.") It is the opposite of a "devil's advocate," which we shall use later in the contingency planning step.

Assign a task force or an individual to develop an idea or strategic concept (a cluster of ideas, as will be described soon). The idea advocate's goal is to sell the positive aspects of the idea or concept to the rest of the planning participants: why it should be given highest priority and fully funded. This ensures the positive, can-do atmosphere needed at this stage of the process. The best way to assign idea advocates is to ask for volunteers. Seek out the originator of an idea, a strong supporter, or the person who would be responsible for implementing it.

With a health care client of mine, individuals from many levels of the organization were assigned to each of forty strategic concepts to act as their idea advocates. Some people had more than one. Then, in a half-day session of all participants, each advocate presented his or her case in five minutes, with two more minutes for questions and answers. Management felt that many more ideas eventually were pursued than would have been without this enthusiastic selling period.

5. *State negatives as problems to be solved.* The next step in concept building is to take each drawback in each idea and rephrase it as a problem to be solved. This establishes a climate where you can find out what the

flaws are in an idea without embarrassing its originator. This attitude is essential. It avoids prejudging ideas on rational grounds. Everything gets a chance to develop.

Consider the problem health maintenance organizations (HMOs) have with the consumer perception of their impersonal service (you don't get to select your doctor, or sometimes even see the same one twice). To preserve the essence of the HMO concept, yet make it appealing to a wider portion of the population, the preferred provider organization (PPO) was developed. Members of PPOs get to select a doctor from a long list of possibilities.

6. *Scale down the size of expensive ideas.* Strip out the costs and asset expenditures needed to implement an impractical idea, and often you end up with a valuable alternative. This is particularly true if you can reduce front-end costs, the investment needed to launch the idea. This also reduces one element of risk.

An acquisition of a major company in a related product segment was suggested at one divisional planning meeting I was facilitating. The idea was unfeasible because even the parent company could not afford the purchase. However, a smaller, niche-oriented company was then suggested as an acquisition candidate. The smaller company was found to offer most of the strategic synergies that the much larger one did, but was small enough to be purchased at the division level, which it was.

In the same vein, look for ways to test ideas inexpensively and easily. Can some concept testing be done with a variety of customers or prospects that will quickly shed light on the degree of attractiveness? But remember, concept testing only yields qualitative information. Projections from it should be done with extreme caution. Market research for yielding quantitative information is much more involved.

7. *Combine ideas for critical mass.* It has been said that the worth of an idea depends on the company it keeps. Many times two or more ideas are unfeasible separately, but when combined, form an excellent strategy (see Exhibit 5–1). Look for idea linkages where they naturally fit together. Weave them into strategic concepts. Only then begin to apply judgment slowly, in stages.

In working with a high-tech client, for example, the vice president of marketing came up with an idea for a joint venture with another firm in attacking a new market segment. This idea was shot down for lack of appropriate products. At a second strategy session, the head of research and development proposed an innovative new product line for this same market segment. That idea was also killed—until it was remembered that

EXHIBIT 5–1

Integrating Ideas

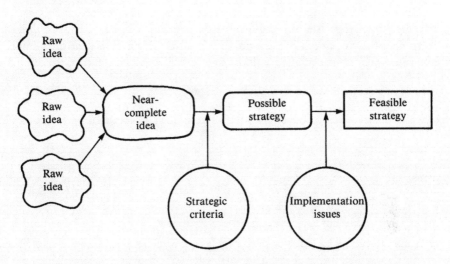

a way to attack this segment had been suggested, and shot down, at the previous meeting. Critical mass had been achieved. Both ideas were now worth doing. The two partial solutions were integrated into a new strategic thrust that opened up a major growth opportunity for the company. As in material science, alloys are stronger than the individual metals that make them up.

8. *Crystallize concepts.* This is the final step in concept building. Keep on suspending judgment, but not feasibility. Shape concepts slowly by clarifying the major steps of implementation. Add to them a rough estimate of the return expected in increased sales and profits, decreased costs, and so forth. What magnitude of investment is required? What is the time frame of execution and on to results? What are the key risks, if any?

Doing concept building in this way ensures that ideas cannot be dismissed out of hand in the interest of reaching a decision as to the direction of the company. You should be more concerned with screening *in* big ideas than with screening *out* bad ones. A quote from Peter Drucker's *Age of Discontinuity* reinforces this point:

> A top management that believes its job is to sit in judgment will inevitably veto the new idea. It is always "impractical." Only a top management that sees its central function as trying to convert into purposeful action the half-baked ideas for something new will actually

make its organization—whether company, university, laboratory, or hospital—capable of genuine innovation and self-renewal.[7]

So when straddling the line between fantasy and reality, don't be trigger-happy. The longer you keep viable concepts open, the more you learn about them, and the more flexibility you will have in your decision making—the subject of the next chapter.

PART

TWO

Make It Happen

6

Strategic Decision Making

YOU have reached the 50-yard line. Visionary thought must be followed by decisive decision making and speedy action. A company can have imaginative ideas, and even a superior strategy, yet still produce very disappointing results. Flawed execution of a brilliant plan is common. In the words of Theodore Levitt, editor of the *Harvard Business Review,* "Thinking things up is not the same as making things happen."[1] Remember, you have to outthink and out-implement your competition to win.

Making it happen begins by selecting the best ideas from all that you have. After imagination and concept building have flown as high and wide as possible, critical judgment becomes important. It is this evaluation and selection process that makes a worthwhile activity out of what otherwise would have been a frivolous exercise.

One senior executive called strategic decision making "the cold, gray dawn of the morning after—where reality catches up to the dream." It should not be so negative. I prefer to think of it as a yielding to strategic sensibility, a time to tighten up your thinking.

SYSTEMATIC SELECTION

The purpose of strategic decision making, Step Three–2 in Creative Planning, is to prioritize ideas according to potential for increased profit and

59

return on investment. This submission to logic is just the first of your reality checks, so keep the attitude relatively positive. The proper frame of mind is "guardedly optimistic." We slowly continue to introduce judgment, the "parent" in our personalities. Concept building was done with a mix of 70% creative thinking and 30% judgmental. Now we are at the 50%–50% point in Creative Planning, a balanced point of view. While we want to sort the wacky from the workable, we still want to improve ideas and concepts and move them forward. Recognizing great opportunities requires an open mind.

When dealing with a large number of possibilities, it is imperative that an organized process be used to choose which ideas to implement. Many an executive has shot from the hip, only to shoot off a kneecap.

Systematic selection improves the probability of making the right choice. It increases the possibility of transforming ideas and concepts into winning strategies. It also increases the planning team's confidence and commitment to the resulting strategy. The use of a structured process leaves members more satisfied than does the usual alternative: The person at the top makes all the strategy decisions either intuitively or with the help of some studies and ROI calculations. And we all know how important commitment is to the success of implementation.

The process of strategy selection that I have used successfully with clients consists of five stages:

1. Develop three levels of selection criteria.
2. Apply criteria in a progressive and more detailed fashion.
3. Do a preliminary ranking of concepts.
4. Combine concepts into final options.
5. Critically evaluate and select the best options for action planning and implementation.

Let's take a close look at each.

DEVELOPING SELECTION CRITERIA

Engineering tough decisions starts with the development of selection criteria specific to your business. Begin by brainstorming with your planning team. Quantity will lead to quality. With selection criteria in particular, it is the ones that you leave out that can hurt you the most. Next, group the criteria into as few categories as possible. Seven or eight is about the maximum that can be applied effectively to a long list of ideas and concepts.

Exhibit 6–1 presents a standard list of criteria useful in evaluating strategic options in most companies. However, even though I have used these many times, I find it imperative to go through the criteria formulation process. Each business is different. Also, your planning team must be convinced that the chosen criteria are the most appropriate for your business.

Criteria should be stated in a positive way. This makes them easier to use in a rating system, as will be discussed later in this chapter. But first let's review the criteria themselves.

EXHIBIT 6–1

Strategy Selection Criteria and Considerations in Using Them

1. *Financial Benefit*
   Market size, growth rate
   Market share potential
   Revenue potential
   Gross profit potential
   Your competitive advantage
   Cost reduction potential

2. *Low Investment*
   Capital investment needed
   Working capital
   Manufacturing capacity available
   Computer capacity available
   Research and development
   Test marketing
   Market introduction
   Market maintenance
   Management time
   Other resources needed

3. *Return on Investment*
   Operating profit divided by
      investment
   Discounted cash flow
   Payback period
   Impact on other aspects of
      business
   Defensive measure

4. *Strategic Fit*
   Fit with present strategy
   Leverages present strengths
   Fit with other high-priority ideas
   Eliminates a strategic weakness
   Degree of diversification

5. *Feasibility*
   Matches your strengths
   Talent for execution in place
   Resources available
   New technology possible
   Positive reception by customers
   Your organization will embrace it
   Manufacturing and distribution
      in place

6. *Low Risk*
   Chance of success
   Number of potential problems
   Magnitude of potential problems
   Competitive reactions probable
   Cannibalization on present
      volume
   Impact on present business

7. *Timing*
   Time period to see results:
      Short term—one year or less
      Medium term—in second year
      Long term—in three or more
      years

Financial Benefit

Let's face it, the real motivation for doing anything in business is to increase the company's financial performance. The two most fundamental ways are either to increase the top line (revenue) or to decrease the middle one (costs). The exact way to measure financial benefit will vary by the type of idea. Exhibit 6–1 presents some of the methods.

Low Investment

Ideas that can be pursued with little or no investment of any kind are few. The important thing here is to consider all the different types of investment that are required to launch and maintain a strategic option. Frequently, only capital investment is considered. You have to look beyond the initial ante. What about R&D, market introduction costs, ongoing working capital, and management time? If you are looking to launch a large number of strategic ideas, this last one may be the limiting function. It's not whether you win or lose, but how much you have riding on the game. Be sure to include all resources and, as a separate consideration, the management time needed to put the strategy into action.

Return on Investment

There are as many ways to measure return on investment (ROI) as there are books on the topic. Exhibit 6–1 lists a few. For idea screening, just pick one method and be consistent with it. Also, avoid analytical overkill. Rough calculations of ROI are all that is needed at this point. A top executive of a construction company, upon being presented detailed ROI calculations on still rough ideas by his finance manager, complained, "This is like killing cockroaches with cannonballs."

Strategic Fit

This can be one of the most important criteria you use. No matter how good an idea is, or even how much potential return on investment could be realized, if the idea doesn't fit your organization's skill set, it will probably fail. Your company must have the talent and systems (manufacturing, distribution, and others) to execute. Coca-Cola, for example, sold its Wine

Spectrum properties (Taylor and other labels) in 1983 and abandoned the wine business. It figuratively cried "uncle" to Ernest & Julio Gallo, the industry leader, which produces about 150 million gallons a year. Competitors suggested that Coke did not fully understand the wine business. Coke set unrealistic growth and profitability goals, created ill will with sharp comparative ads, struggled to get on restaurant wine lists, and couldn't manage distribution that was governed by both federal and state regulations. The Montreal-based Seagram Company purchased the Wine Spectrum and, in one move, catapulted to a strong Number 2 in the industry.[2]

A second aspect to "strategic fit" is how well ideas match your current and future (if it is to be different) positioning in the marketplace. As will be discussed in Chapter 11, you need to present a clear message to customers and prospects as to what your company does. A premium products company that releases an economy product may be not only be unsuccessful with it but may taint the image of its present line. Conversely, it is difficult for a low-price-positioned company to introduce a high-end line. The quality, even if it is real, may just not be perceived in the marketplace.

Feasibility

This criterion is related to all of the others. The fundamental question is: "Will the idea work?" Think of the essential things that have to happen and ask "Will they?" Can R&D develop it, manufacturing produce it, sales sell it, customers buy it, and your company afford it? Perhaps most importantly, will your organization embrace the change involved and execute with enthusiasm? Without being too cynical, think of the problems that may present themselves and ask if they can be overcome. Listen to outside opinion, but make your own decisions.

In 1983 Kellogg's market share in cereals had hit a low of 36%. The outside world was saying the company served a no-growth market and should diversify, as Quaker Oats and General Mills were doing. A prominent Wall Street firm called Kellogg "a fine company that's past its prime." Chairman and CEO William E. LaMothe said, "We loved that." He and his team became obsessed with winning the breakfast battle. They studied the market and found 80 million health-oriented baby-boomers, but market experts said, "They don't eat breakfast." Instead of listening, Kellogg widened its focus beyond kids to include twenty-five- to forty-nine-year-olds. With a line of value-added products for them, Kellogg built a market. The "no growth" ready-to-eat market grew from $3.7

billion in 1983 to $5.4 billion in 1988, expanding three times faster than the average grocery category. Furthermore, Kellogg gained five share points. Its domestic success and its ability to develop new cereals for foreign markets boosted profits 24% in 1987 and generated an outstanding return on equity of 33%.[3] Not bad for a "mature company." Once again, strategic innovation to the rescue.

Low Risk

What are your chances of success, and how much is at stake? If the idea fails, will it impact your present business negatively, or the other strategic ideas you intend to pursue? What might be your competitors' reactions to the strategy? This last one really needs to be studied, and ways of doing so are covered in Chapter 12. One way to assess risk is to ask: "Is it simple?" At the core of every brilliant innovation is simplicity. The more complicated an idea, the higher the risk. For example, critics of the United States' strategic defense initiative (SDI), commonly called "Star Wars," cite its complexity. They say that by the time SDI is implemented, it will be so bogged down in technical problems that it will make NASA's space shuttle difficulties in the mid-1980s seem trivial.

Timing

Estimate the time periods for idea development, implementation, and the realization of positive financial (or other) impact. "Short, medium, and long" term designations are usually all that is required at this point in idea evaluation. More detailed determinations can be developed in the next step, strategic action planning. From the standpoint of financial benefit, the best ideas are the ones that can generate returns the quickest. But there is more to timing than that. Larry Davis, president of DG Mouldings, the nation's leading manufacturer of prefinished moldings, says, "When rolling out a new strategy, we like to implement ideas that will show quick results." He suggests picking small ideas first. "The bigger ones can come later," he says. "Early success with the fast ones builds momentum and enthusiasm that the strategy is working."[4]

One additional criterion can be employed. The mark of a good idea is that, when you hear it, you say to yourself: "Why didn't I think of that?" It's cousin is: "Someone already must be doing this!" If you didn't, and they aren't, be sure to consider the idea in a positive light.

CUSTOMIZING THE CRITERIA

You can use the correct criteria for your business but still select the wrong ideas. Relative importance of the criteria is as important as which ones you use. For example, if your company is in a situation where it is imperative to get a positive financial impact quickly—such as in a turnaround situation, or when you are under a takeover siege—timing is everything. This should be your overriding criterion. Conversely, if you are doing well financially, you can afford to take the longer view and pursue growth-building strategies that may take longer to bear fruit.

If your company is cash short and financing is difficult or untimely (because of high interest rates or for other reasons), low investment would be your most important criterion. On the other hand, if you are cash-rich and a public company, your company may need to make a major investment so that you do not become a takeover target. Or else you should consider putting into place the manufacturing or distribution operations that will pre-empt your competitors from doing so.

In still another situation, your company may have a culture that resists anything new. If this is so, you need to pay particular attention to your organization's willingness to implement an innovative strategy, even if it makes obvious sense. Feasibility would be paramount in your decision making. The same holds true for the other criteria. The best way to use them, therefore, is to rank them in order of importance to your organization. Some of your executives may say they are all important. They are. However, some are more important than others. Discuss this as a whole group, and it will shed some light on the values and needs of your organization.

WEED 'EM AND REAP

It's now time to apply the criteria. Your objective is to make room for winners and at the same time weed out inappropriate ideas early in the process. The evaluation process has to be matched to the types of ideas, the resources committed, and available information. The biggest pitfall is to mismatch the evaluation method to the stage of development of the ideas. What happens then?

• Too many or too complex criteria in early stages of evaluation can prematurely kill off options with substantial potential.

- Waiting too long in the process to apply important criteria can waste management resources and time.
- Excessive quantification can lead to a complete bogging down of the system, or a belief that the forecast numbers are exactly right.
- The development of new ideas can be inhibited because it takes so much work to evaluate them.

The solution to these problems is to use different levels of screens. Three is a workable number:

1. *Coarse Screen.* To some degree, you already started this in the concept-building step by assessing and trying to make the ideas more feasible. Two criteria, with a maximum of three, is best. "Financial benefit" and "feasibility" are generally the most fitting. "Timing" is sometimes appropriate when you need quick results, as discussed earlier. Applying your two most important criteria can help you reduce the size of your idea list to a reasonable length.

2. *Medium Screen.* Here is where you apply all of your seven or eight strategy selection criteria in an organized way. Set up a matrix with criteria across the top and ideas and concepts listed down the left. Some rough quantification is done, resulting in a score of "high," "medium," or "low" for each criterion on each idea. A composite score can then be given to each idea—an intuitive average of all of the criteria. A numerical scoring system can also be used, complete with weighted criteria (from your ranking of them), but be careful not to get overly quantitative in your assessments. There are too many unknowables at this point. At the end of this medium screening, it is best to do a rough ranking of your ideas and concepts and to see if any can be further combined into strategic options.

3. *Fine Screen.* This is a detailed analysis of your highest potential options. Market studies, customer concept testing, technology and manufacturing feasibility studies, and reasonably detailed ROI calculations can all be appropriate. But don't become a prisoner of sterile analytical approaches. Ultimately, strategic decisions are about potential, probabilities, and people.

REMAIN OPEN-MINDED

The Eleventh Commandment at 3M is: "Thou shalt not kill a new product idea." Management may slow it down and may not fully fund it, but it will not kill concepts or their pioneers. One 3M observer noted: "If you want to stop a project aimed at developing a new product, the burden of proof is on the one who wants to stop the project, not the one who proposes the project.''[5] 3M and other innovative companies realize that it is difficult to forecast accurately the demand for a new product category. There are no reference points to rely on. Early attitudes or behavior of consumers may not be the most valid predictors of adoption behavior. The eventual market applications may not be fully understood. Scotch Tape was born as a fastener for industrial packaging. Sales volume didn't take off until an imaginative sales manager at 3M, John Borden, created a dispenser with a built-in blade. Small doors can open into large rooms.

At Merck & Co. in 1979, R&D had a difficult time convincing marketing of the huge potential of a breakthrough anticholesterol drug. Sales of cholesterol-reduction drugs were only about $100 million at the time, the biggest one being Bristol-Myers's Questran, which patients complained was difficult to swallow. Alfred Alberts, the Mevacor R&D champion, comments: ''Marketing people generally respond to what's out there, and the existing cholesterol drugs had not generated much of a market.'' Since Merck's release of it in 1987, Mevacor has done spectacularly, and financial analysts believe that it, plus its soon-to-follow cousin, Zocor, could add $1 billion of revenue by 1992.[6]

A Funneling Effect

The three levels of screening enable you to introduce criticism slowly. Exhibit 6–2 portrays this, along with the funneling effect on your number

EXHIBIT 6–2
Screening Ideas

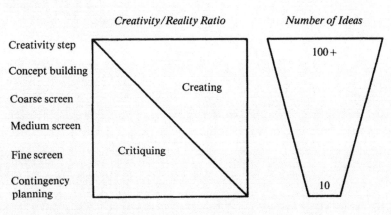

of alternatives. This process may appear slow, but it is essential to prevent the quick trigger finger.

What do you do with ideas that received "low" scores in the evaluation process? As in the concept-building step, you work on the negatives until they can be avoided or eliminated, making the idea attractive. And what do you do with the ones you still can't fix? Save them anyway. New information may turn up. Markets may change. New skills may be developed.

The Envelope, Please

At the end of the evaluation step, each idea and option should be classified into one of three levels of priority:

1. *High*—ones for immediate implementation
2. *Medium*—ones for further research
3. *Low*—additional alternative approaches to the situation

It is now time to develop a strategic implementation plan.

7

Formulating Strategy

THE output of the prior step in creative planning was a strategy in the raw, a skeleton of the company's plan. You have a prioritized menu of strategic ideas and concepts, but you lack a focus, a unifying theme, a vision of the future—along with a set of integrated action plans and a financial scorecard. The purpose of this chapter is to show how to formulate and write your overall strategic plan, and how to assess risk before committing valuable resources. Only then will your organization be capable of successfully implementing the innovations you have developed.

FORM COMES FIRST

Content without form is confusing. This is not to say that there is only one right way to write a strategic plan. There are many. But they all contain common key elements. Knowing these elements can help your strategic thinking as well. For example, defining your organization's vision and competitive positioning will crystallize direction.

Exhibit 7–1 provides a guideline for writing a strategic plan for your

EXHIBIT 7–1

A Format for Strategic Plans Plus Definitions

Executive Summary

Mission	The purpose of your company: what business your company is in, and what it will become
Vision	The ultimate destination you seek: a picture (images, metaphors, words) of a competitively superior company at some point in the future
Positioning	Why an enterprise exists today and what it stands for in the minds of its customers
Objective	What you want to accomplish and by when; comprehensive statements of where an organization wants to go and what it wants to become; measurable.
Strategy	How you are going to do it: statements describing the approaches to be used to achieve your objectives
Values	What your company stands for; its philosophies and its culture

Strategic Action Programs

A prioritized list of major programs to be implemented by your organization. Each program plan will contain an objective, action steps, resources required, timing and responsibility. Contingency plans are included when necessary.

Strategic Budget

A financial forecast for the company, including a summary of the dollars allocated for implementing the strategy and action programs, and the expected return on investment

Appendixes

Issue Assessments

The challenges and opportunities that were addressed, the major options for resolving them, and the selected strategies.

Strategic Analyses
A. Market
B. Technology/products and services
C. Competition
D. Operations
E. Organization
F. Financial analyses

company. The same format can be used for a business unit, a department, or even an individual. The exhibit also contains definitions of key terms. In planning, semantic confusion is rife. Objectives are mixed up with strategies, strategies with tactics, and so on. Let's now take each element of the strategic plan and discuss not only what it is, but how to develop it.

Mission

A mission statement should state a business's purpose. It should answer the question, "Why do we exist?" In addition, it should describe what business you are in. This should include a definition of the industry, products or services, markets, and any other major attributes. It could also include what the company stands for and how it conducts its affairs. The danger, as pointed out by Theodore Levitt in his seminal *Harvard Business Review* article (July–August 1960) "Marketing Myopia," is being too specific. His suggestion was to define your business more from the perspective of the market than from that of the products you produce. Ask how you should be changing, given the changing needs of the markets you serve. Also ask and answer what new types of business the company desires to enter.

The mission statement has to be specific if it is to provide some frame of reference for your strategizing. A good example is Otis Elevator's concise statement in the early 1980s of the business it is in: "Moving people and material vertically and horizontally over relatively short distances." This covers not only Otis's elevators but also its escalators and moving walkways.[1] The complaint most heard about mission statements is that they are all "God and motherhood," leaving you without much you can sink your teeth into. Even if that is true, don't worry. The next item will be more specific.

Vision

Every business starts out as a vision in someone's mind. Then, almost every time the management of a mature business successfully shifts its strategy, there is again a vision driving it. Unfortunately, what passes for vision in many companies is groping in the dark.

A vision, simply stated, is a picture of the company in a preferred future state. It goes beyond a linear extension of the present business. It incorporates all the changes in your business environment that may take place over the long run, plus a picture of your company thriving in it. The benefits of having a clear strategic vision are many:

• Better focus on opportunities while channeling the entire organization's effort
• Ease in making long-range decisions such as funding an R&D project or making a strategic acquisition at a high multiple
• Help in preventing haphazard capital investment or acquisition programs due to lack of direction
• Priming middle management so it can act faster than the competition
• Giving your employees a solid image. (According to Peter Russel's *The Brain Book,* adults who were shown ten thousand pictures remembered 99% of them correctly.)

The CEO, however, should not undertake this as a solitary task. In the words of John Akers, CEO of IBM, "The vision is certainly not the product of any one individual's mind. I think it's more the product of a collection of minds—my colleagues immediately around me, the 6 to 20 people who collectively help manage."[2]

To develop a vision for your organization, first wallow in the details of your industry's trends, including those of your markets, competitors, technologies, and other aspects. (Part Three of this book concentrates on these topics.) Then form a picture in your mind of what your industry will be like in the distant future, perhaps in five to ten years. This is similar to scenario building, discussed in Chapter 2, "Developing Strategic Insights." Develop two or three alternative pictures if necessary. Then summarize the key elements of each image on one sheet of paper.

Next, scan your list of high- and medium-priority strategic concepts. Get a feel for where your organization is headed if all of them are implemented. Then add to the picture whatever else your company will need to be doing to be a competitively superior organization within each industry scenario. Crystallize the common traits of your company that are necessary for it to thrive in all of the industry scenarios. Weave them into a picture of the ideal company. Last, distill out of this picture its essence. Try to think of a metaphor or something symbolic that points the way. Employees need a clear vision of where the organization is going, and if you can give them one, you have an exceptional motivating tool. Answer the question: "If all of your major strategies were successfully implemented, what would the company look like in three to five years?"

Frequently, visions begin in a fuzzy way and are refined over time. In June 1988 Apple chairman John Sculley took a six-week sabbatical while the company was booming. He spent time jogging, philosophizing, and dreaming about what he hopes will be a twenty-first-century high-tech renaissance, with Apple as one of the primary change agents.[3] "In some way, I want Apple to be the living laboratory for the model corporation of this new century," Sculley wrote in his 1987 book *Odyssey*. The people I have interviewed at Apple all mentioned the company's renewed push "to change the world." Sculley goes on in his book to say: "Don't give people goals, give them directions." In this regard, many successful leaders have been called "great simplifiers"—able to give birth to a theme or a slogan that can galvanize the entire organization.

Be aware that your vision may need revising from time to time as the external world changes and your company goes through stages of growth. Kent Dorwin, senior vice president of strategic planning at Charles Schwab, calls it "re-visioning." Schwab's change in vision and strategy will be covered a little later in this chapter.

If you are having trouble "seeing" a clear vision of your company, use the closed-eye exercises presented in the Appendix. Relax your body and picture in your mind where you want your company to go. Be optimistic. Then picture where you are today. Closing the gap requires positioning, objectives, and a strategy.

Positioning

It is important to translate the vision of your company into what it stands for to your customers—your company's positioning. This should highlight what is unique about your organization and distinguish it from competitors along the dimensions that are the most important to customers. The corporate positioning you choose should be derived from your corporate strengths, your competitive advantages, your current reputation, and your ideal reputation. If you are trying to put on a new face, your positioning has to embody those characteristics as well. But be careful to stay realistic.

Actually, there are three levels of positioning: corporate, market, and product (or service). Here we are dealing with your overall corporate positioning—your company's identity, look, and feel. Market and product positionings are an extension of your corporate one and are treated in detail in Chapter 11.

Reebok's meteoric rise in the sports footwear business is a classic case of positioning: comfort with fashion and a dash of function. With this, the company has reached the $1 billion mark, selling one-third of all athletic shoes in the United States. "When I first came into the athletic footwear business in 1979," Reebok chairman and CEO Paul Fireman says, "athletic shoes were basically uncomfortable. When we asked people about their shoes, we found that most liked them typically four to six weeks after they played in them—about the time the shoes were ready to be used for painting or mowing the lawn.'' Reebok took the soft garment leather and cushioning from its super-successful aerobics line and put it into tennis shoes—and revolutionized the industry. To crystallize its positioning, Reebok's advertisements introducing its first tennis shoe guaranteed it would be the most comfortable tennis shoe ever, or the company would give a full refund plus a can of tennis balls. It sent out 128 cans.[4]

Objectives

It is now time to get specific. Your objectives are what you want to accomplish, how much, and by when. They are the desired outcomes you seek, for example, to close the gap between your vision and the current situation. The key word to keep in mind is "measurable." Here are some examples of both good and bad objectives:

Objective Statement	*Comment*
To increase profit from $40 million in 1988 to $60 million by 1990.	Good, clear, measurable
By 1990, become the market share leader.	Good, as long as market share statistics are available and accurate
We will strive to minimize our costs and maximize productivity	Poor: no standards or time frame specified

A useful time frame for strategic planning is what you want your company to achieve in three years. Depending on your industry and your current financial situation, this could vary from one year to ten, but three years is the most common. It helps to have one overall objective for the corporation that can be stated in a single sentence. At its best it is a combination of financial and strategic elements. For example, one might be: "By 1992, we will reach $1 billion in sales, have a 17% return on equity, and be the market share leader in our industry segment." Subsidiary to this, you should have more detailed objectives dealing with the annual increases in financial performance sought, market share milestones, and other specifics.

The importance of having a unified set of objectives for the whole organization cannot be overstated. Chrysler Corporation, in its pre-Iacocca days, had a goal-setting program, but there was no unifying theme. Production wanted to build automobiles and didn't care if they were not sold because they were built to inventory. Engineering wanted to design state-of-the-art cars, even if marketing could not sell them. Operations adored the Hamtramck plant, built by the Dodge brothers. Lee Iacocca changed all that. Ignoring the traditions of the old Chrysler, he told engineering to design cars people wanted to buy. He ceased manufacturing until inventories were down, and he tore down the inefficient Hamtramck plant.[5]

There is one last thing to watch for in setting objectives. Don't confuse them with strategies. Many executives have pushed full steam ahead on a strategy, while missing the real objective. I worked with a professional services company that was about to launch an expensive advertising campaign to improve the firm's image. In discussions, I found that their objective was not really to improve the image of the company but to get new clients. The objective should have been to obtain X number of new clients over the next twelve months, with improving the image of the company as one strategy *option*. But there were other strategic alternatives, many of which were much less costly (targeting market segments, more effective sales management, and so on). These were successfully implemented along with a considerably scaled-down image campaign.

Strategy

You know what has to be done. Now how do you do it? This is what strategy is all about. It is one or more statements of how you are going to achieve your objectives. Strategy should be more than broad, directional declarations and general policy statements. Rather, your overall strategy statement should pull together into one seamless picture your high-priority options for both what you are going to do with your existing business and how you will attack new businesses.

While being explicit, your overall strategy also must be straightforward and understandable. Tom Peters suggests, for example, that "managers might try explaining their business plan in one hour to a group of part-time or temporary workers on the night shift in the distribution center." A different sort of test is to see if you can do it in five minutes to a group of middle- and lower-level managers. Ideally, you will have a single, central strategy from which your entire plan flows. In architectural terms, your overall strategy is the artist's drawing of the building, the major elements of your strategy the blueprints, and your action plans the construction schedule.

Wyse Technology, started in 1981 by Bernard Tse, became the world's second largest computer terminal maker behind DEC in 1987. It had profits of $18 million in 1987 on sales of $260 million. The company's overall strategy is to supply well-designed, low-cost terminals. The main elements of the strategy are:

- Wait for someone else to establish the technology.
- Jump in only when high volume exists.
- Manufacture in Taiwan, where labor is cheap and there are good, low-cost suppliers nearby.
- Keep marketing costs to a minimum by selling only through distributors and other resellers, never through direct sales or via retailers.
- Add enough attractive features, such as European styling, larger screens, and better resolution, so that price is not the only selling point.[6]

Unfortunately, Wyse tried to use the exact same strategy on personal computers. While they represented 25% of the company's sales in 1987, personal computers were a major contributor to the company's financial problems in 1989.

Strategies have to be updated regularly, far more so than visions, and even objectives. Markets shift, competitors change, your company acquires new capabilities, just to name a few reasons. One strategy shift that seems to be working, for example, is MCI's. William McGowan founded the company on August 8, 1968. During the mid- to late-1980s the company transformed itself from the Kmart of the long-distance industry into a full-service, lower-priced alternative to AT&T. In 1987 it rolled out 800-number service, in 1988 worldwide direct dialing (the only company besides AT&T), and its billing system remains far ahead of Sprint's in timeliness and detail. After a loss of $488 million in 1986, MCI earned $88 million in 1987.

A company that has gone through a constant state of strategy development in pursuit of the founder's ultimate vision is Charles Schwab & Co. Kent Dorwin, senior vice president of strategic planning, explained it to me as follows (see Exhibit 7–2):

> Charles Schwab's strategy was purely one of low price in the 1970s. Chuck created the category with a plain vanilla, no-frills service. Then in 1980, the direction of the company shifted to automation—high-tech, low touch. The management style continued to be highly entrepreneurial, with a focus on transaction execution, direct response marketing tactics, and performance measurement.
>
> The purchase of the company by Bank of America in 1983 was a transition point. The firm's strategy shifted to expansion of the branch network system in order to provide convenience and high-quality personal service. This was followed by a slight price increase in late 1984.

EXHIBIT 7–2

Charles Schwab & Co., Inc., A Historical Perspective: "Chapter 1"

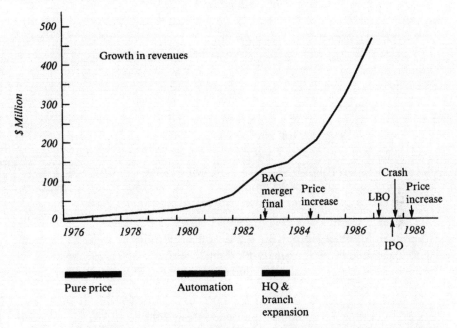

By 1986, the strategy focused on offering the broadest possible product service—CDs, mutual funds, IRAs, et cetera. Revenue and profit expanded dramatically. This was followed by another transition year, 1987, in which Chuck bought back the company from B of A through a leveraged buyout in April, took it public in September, and was faced with the stock market crash in October.

In early 1988, we added more services and announced a commission price increase of 10%. This makes us what I call a "tweener," positioned right between the high-priced wire houses and the bare-bones discounters.

Throughout 1989 we will reposition the company once more. We intend offering an investment system for active independent investors, expanding into services for corporations, acquiring some smaller competitors, within the discount niche, and implementing some strategies which are confidential at this time.

From the beginning, it has been a natural continuum of strategic shifts, each moving the company to a new level of growth. Our fundamental goal is to broaden Schwab's positioning and strengthen the product offering. We will create the perception that Schwab is *the* place for independent-minded investors to satisfy the majority of their needs.[7]

An important thing the Wyse, MCI, and Schwab corporate strategies have in common is that they communicate not only what the company will do but why it will win—the company's competitive advantage. It is not enough to have a master plan. You have to be able to answer: "Why will my company earn higher returns and grow faster than my competitors?" If you can clearly and candidly answer that, you are on your way to a winning strategy.

Values

The chances of success for your strategic plan can be greatly improved if you crystallize the management philosophy needed to put it into action. A philosophy, or corporate culture, as it has come to be called, is a set of values that are conveyed to employees, customers, suppliers, investors, and the public. Corporate culture will be covered in detail in Chapter 15. But let us look at a few examples of strategic values, starting with Dow Chemical. Founder Herbert Dow's fundamental strategy was simple: Start with cheap and basic raw material, then develop the soundest, lowest-cost process possible. His values included:

- Don't copy or license anyone else's process. In his words, "Don't make a product unless you can find a better way to do it."
- Build large, vertically integrated complexes that are the most technologically advanced in the industry.
- Locate near and tie up abundant sources of cheap raw materials.
- Build in bad times as well as good.
- Maintain high cash flow so the corporation can pursue its vision.[8]

Here is a set of corporate values which I helped a major conglomerate develop for guiding its diversified portfolio of businesses:

- Pursue increased return on equity and profit, not just sales growth.
- Focus on market niches that will generate high profitability and growth.
- Develop unique, specialty products and value-added services that are clearly superior to the competition's.
- Increase asset turnover (sales divided by assets) as a way to increase return on investment.
- Avoid highly capital-intensive and cyclical businesses.
- Exploit interdivisional opportunities.
- Encourage an entrepreneurial attitude throughout the corporation.

These values, once communicated to the division management, were used as a guide in allocating resources to the various businesses, making divestitures and acquisitions, and selecting action programs for its strategies.

Strategic Action Programs

This is where you get down to details. You have to think big, but see small. Now that you know "what," it is time to figure out who, where, when, how, and how much. Many managers insist their strategy was correct, but it simply was not implemented properly. Strategic action planning can prevent this from happening.

Action planning should not be overly formalized or it will involve excessive paperwork and constrain flexibility. But it does need structure. A straightforward form can be developed. On it, you can, for each of your high-priority programs:

- State its overall objective and the benefits to be achieved by completing it.
- Break it down into program steps, listing them in the order that they have to be completed.
- Show the major resources needed to complete each step, including financial, human, and physical.
- State whose responsibility it is to complete each step. It may be more than one person, but a single individual should have final responsibility.
- Show the completion date for each step and the overall program, being careful, in your excitement, not to commit to too much all at once.

Find an enthusiastic champion for each of your high-priority programs. People, particularly creative ones, "seem to work best if they are event driven," says Jay Elliot, vice president for human resources at Apple Computer. He cites the introduction of Apple's Macintosh: "Everybody knew it was to be shown at the annual shareholders' meeting, so nobody could expect extra time."

A proper balance has to be struck between too few and too many programs. Prioritizing reduces confusion. But I would rather have too many programs than too few. In 1984, Bill Marriott states that people felt Marriott Corporation could not continue to grow at 20% per year: "There's always been a considerable amount of skepticism, and we've always been able to do it," he says. "It's always been our strategy to have enough new things going on and enough things going on in each area, to make it all work."[9] The Marriott Corporation grew at the rate of 24% a year in 1986 and 1987 while delivering a 20% return on equity.

Strategic Budget

John Welch of General Electric says that his primary job is "resource allocator of money and people."[10] This is the heart of strategic decision making. Your company will be tomorrow where management spends its time and money today.

The purpose of the strategic budget is to show how funding and other assets are allocated to the existing business and to each major new strategic program. It should also provide a financial forecast for each program, a roll-up for the entire company, and return on investment calculations where appropriate. Again, do not get too detailed in your financials. Summary figures are sufficient for strategic planning. An exact assignment of resources to departments, functions, targeted accounts, and the like should be saved for the annual operating plan.

Plan Appendixes

Many corporate strategic plans start with detailed descriptions of market trends, competitor assessments, strategic issues, and other analyses. This information is extremely important in the conception of the strategy. It is far less so in its presentation, though. By the time a busy top executive or a board member wades through all of this material, you have lost their interest. I recommend that this information be put in the appendix of your plan. Better yet, you could put all of it into a support document that can be made available to interested readers. Your strategic analyses should certainly be saved. However, I have found that the shorter the plan, the more thoroughly it will be read and used to manage the future of your company.

FORMAT FLEXIBILITY

The format in Exhibit 7–1 is universal, but it can pay to have various versions of your plan for separate audiences. Treat them like different products for different markets—market segmentation. Here are the aspects of your plan to highlight for different audiences:

- *Board of Directors*. They want to see the big picture—where the company is going, the major resource allocations, the returns expected from large investments, and the financial forecast.
- *Corporate Management*. If you are a division manager presenting your plan, top management wants to see everything a board of directors would,

but in more detail. Also, point out the major business issues and how they will be resolved. But don't take the attitude of one division manager I worked with. He wanted a "teflon plan," one that would slide past corporate management and not raise any questions.

· *Lower-Level Employees.* They need to understand the overall direction of the company, the corporate values, and what people are expected to do to implement the plan. This will be covered in the next chapter.

· *Your Banker.* He wants a financially oriented presentation showing how the funds you have borrowed will be paid back as agreed, with a substantial cushion for contingencies.

· *Venture Capitalists.* Their first priority is to see the track records and capabilities of the management team, because it is people that make new ventures succeed. Their second is your competitive advantage—why your company will do better than the competition. And third, what return the venture capitalists will get on their investment—they demand 30% to 60% compounded annually.

CREATIVE CONTINGENCY PLANNING

There is a saying that no-risk managements run no-win businesses. You can't avoid risk if you are reaching for dramatic profit growth. But you can reduce it. If you don't, you may end up in the next edition of *Misfortune 500*, written by Bruce Nash and Allan Zullo in 1988.

If there is a time for pessimism, for picking nits, it is now. You are about to take out the corporate wallet and fund your strategy. Now is the time to head Murphy off at the pass. Murphy's law ("If anything can go wrong, it will.") was first enunciated by Ed Murphy, an engineer, in 1949. It teaches us to expect the unexpected, be prepared for something to go wrong, and in planning, to look for strategy backfires. Paul Hawken, author of the highly successful book *Growing a Business,* says, "If you plan to start your own business, plan to fail—it's one sure way to succeed." He explains: "If you conceive a business where twenty serious mistakes could occur, and then you create safeguards to deal with them, you are creating a survivor." The same goes for the strategies of major corporations.

The Power of Negative Thinking

Here is where you can benefit from the "doubting Thomas" on your management team. Let him and his kind tell you why your plan will not work. Join in and brainstorm all the reasons why the plan might fail. Explain it to selected front-line people to get trench-level feedback. Encourage them to find holes in it, such as why your organization cannot execute, or a competitor will retaliate, or your advertisement will be misunderstood.

Mistakes of this last kind are particularly prevalent when domestic companies do business overseas. The classic was committed by the venerable Pepsi Co. with its famous slogan, "Come alive with Pepsi." When the company introduced it in Germany in the 1970s, the translation that hit the billboards was "Come out of the grave with Pepsi." In Thailand, the same slogan translated to "Bring your ancestors back from the dead." These gaffes could have been prevented if employees in those countries had been consulted. So make a list of contingencies—the longer the better. Be creative in a negative way. It will pay positive dividends.

The Morning Line on Your Plan's Pitfalls

For each of the things that could go wrong in your plan, assess them from two standpoints: (1) the probability of occurrence, and (2) the impact on your strategy and financials. Ratings of "high," "medium," and "low" will suffice. Then plot them on a matrix as shown in Exhibit 7–3. The

EXHIBIT 7–3

Contingency Planning Matrix

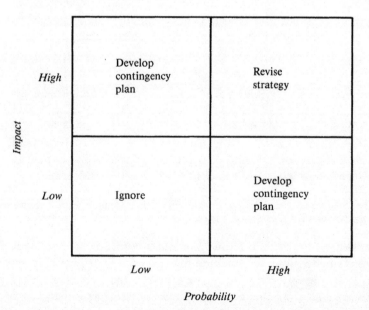

precautions to take are shown. Develop ways to reduce the impact or probability of any "high-high" items. You just can't live with those odds. They are especially disastrous in an entrepreneurial company, where a single mistake can sink the ship.

Formulate complete contingency plans for anything that is both medium or high in probability and of any significant impact, and develop a short-form plan for low-probability, high-impact items. Answer this question: How will you salvage the situation if the problem does occur? Next, stipulate what the early warning signals are for each potential problem, the "trigger points." Then set up a surveillance system by giving select people responsibility for each high-impact contingency. Have them briefly report on their status periodically. Alert the whole management team if anything significant occurs. Avoid problems by anticipating them.

There is only one way for contingency planning to work, however. There has to be a forum for constructive dissent. The messenger has to be heard, not shot. For instance, the fatal launch of the Challenger space shuttle could have been prevented. Allan McDonald, Morton Thiokol's representative at the Kennedy Space Center, was a twenty-six-year Thiokol veteran. He stated his fears and those of several company engineers that the cold weather might damage the seals on the boosters. They never came to the attention of NASA's decision makers.

Back to the Positive

You must not let your management team's attitude remain negative very long. You can't risk thwarting the enthusiasm that has been built up. So when contingency planning is complete, make the transition back to the positive. Here are three ways:

1. Emphasize that looking for trouble is a limited event in the process and is now over.
2. Feel confident that you have considered and planned for all possible occurrences that could derail execution.
3. Launch the plan on a highly positive note, the subject of the next chapter.

8

Enthusiastic Implementation

WE'VE COME A LONG WAY MAYBE

The proof of your strategies is in their implementation. This is where the action is. It's time for superior execution. This is the way for your fantasies to come true.

There are seven major things you as a CEO, department manager, or project leader must do to ensure enthusiastic implementation by your people:

1. Communicate your vision
2. Encourage flexible implementation
3. Lead the change
4. Demand departmental planning
5. Provide resources
6. Monitor results
7. Continue improvement

CURTAIN TIME

Leadership is a performing art. The art is communication. Without it, it is unlikely your plan will be implemented. It won't be understood. Irving S.

Shapiro, former CEO of Du Pont, insists in his book *America's Third Revolution:* "The main task of the CEO is communication." Terrence Deal and Allan Kennedy, co-authors of *Corporate Cultures: The Rites and Rituals of Corporate Life,* claim that "Good communication is the key. There should be no mysteries. If you leave things unsaid, people will invent their own explanations." The rumor mill will grind away.

In general, the more your employees know about the company, the better. But communication is crucial when undertaking strategic change. Donald F. Craib, Jr., CEO of Allstate Insurance Group, says:

> If our strategic planning efforts are going to be successful, people will need to know *what* they need to do and *why* it is important. Employees must be motivated to make the plan succeed, and they need to feed information back to management to ensure quality control and higher sales. If this does not happen, all the strategic planning in the world will not produce a profit.[1]

Too often, top management assumes that its decisions will be implemented without question or discussion. Then it is at a loss to understand why its ideas were misinterpreted, or not acted on, or even sabotaged. Here are some suggestions for getting your organization to execute effectively.

1. *Strategic Launch Session.* Gather all upper and middle management personnel for a half-day or a full day to explain the company's overall objectives and strategies, new values and philosophies, and action plans. If bold new strategies are involved, uncouple the organization from the company's previous ways of doing business. Peter Drucker recommends continual "organized abandonment" of outworn products, services, and strategies. Explain how they were appropriate for the past but ineffective for the future. Also, get feedback on any other barriers that have to be vaulted. End the meeting by having everyone commit to getting the job done, with enthusiasm and excitement about pursuing the vision. Then fasten your seat belt.

2. *Companywide Communication.* Focus your message on a few critical items and convey your strategic plan to everyone in the company. Larry Davis, president of DG Mouldings, tells how he and his top management team did it:

> We removed sensitive financial and personnel pages from our finished plan and presented it:
>
> • To all salaried people in the corporate office, explaining the role of each administrative function in implementing it

- At our various manufacturing facilities, focusing on quality and productivity goals
- At our national sales meeting, emphasizing sales of our various sales forces in our target marketing strategy
- To our major suppliers, so that they would understand our future raw material requirements and product development programs (Our suppliers became much more attuned to our needs and even performed some free R&D for us.)
- To our major customers, as a means of test marketing our strategies

DG Mouldings has grown and increased profits substantially since launching its plan. "The only drawback is that everywhere I go people ask, 'how are we doing on our plan?'" Art Ramey, vice president of marketing and sales, reports. "I now have a thousand bosses! But their commitment and enthusiasm are worth it," he adds. "The results paid great dividends to all of the people involved—almost all got promotions by the time the plan was completed."[2]

James Treybig, CEO and cofounder of Tandem Computers, in a 1984 speech at the international conference of the Planning Forum, harped on "sharing their five year plan with everyone in the company." He explained how he and other senior executives presented their corporate plan at each of their ninety facilities in the United States and twenty-nine countries over the course of a few years. This contrasts sharply with the approach of most high-tech company managements, who guard their plans with utmost secrecy. Treybig explains: "We were initially afraid our competitors would get a hold of our plan. However, we found that our competition already had it anyway. The only people who didn't, prior to our presentations, were our own employees!"

J. Douglas Phillips, senior director of corporate planning of Merck & Co., described an innovative approach in 1988. His department wrote what he calls a "sanitized version" of the company's strategic plan, which was distributed to every employee in the company. "We know that the document will find its way into the hands of our competitors, but we feel it is crucial for all of our employees to have a common understanding of our strategy so we can all pull together in the same direction."[3]

3. *Once More with Feeling.* Getting a new strategy implemented requires a continuing series of reinforcing messages—both informal and formal. Fred Smith, CEO of Federal Express, has been known to stop crowded elevators between floors at headquarters to talk with employees. Patrick Haggerty, the late chairman of Texas Instruments, would at times enter the plant late at night, climb up on a table, and tell everybody to stop working and gather around. He'd then talk about the

company, its challenges, and ways employees might help in finding solutions.[4]

At Tandem Computer, an element of the corporate strategy is featured in each of its monthly newsletters, a weekly television program is broadcast to all plants in the United States, and management takes questions, live, over the phone. "Next week we'll go through asset management," exclaims James Treybig, CEO.

4. *Dramatic, Symbolic Events.* Outrageous behavior can be used as an organizational tool. It certainly will get your employees' attention. Charles L. Hughes at the Center for Values Research in Dallas advocates being "systematically outrageous" to get points across. Say, for example, one of the values in your plan is a renewal of trust. To make the point, you decide to remove the time clocks. Hughes recommends, "Why not dramatize the change by having all the time clocks piled in the parking lot, then letting people demolish them with sledge hammers? It will make the change more symbolic and create a lasting impression."[5]

Communicating a dream to your organization and then leading the jubilant cheer when success occurs are paramount. A fine example of a great communicator and cheerleader is Sam Walton, the seventy-year-old chairman and CEO of Wal-Mart Stores. The dynamic salesman opened his first Wal-Mart store in 1962. Today he has 1,144, plus eighty-six Wholesale Club stores, fourteen discount stores, and two giant Hypermarkets. He often visits as many as six of them in a day. At his 1988 annual meeting, attended by seven thousand (including 1,200 employees), he implored, "Can we do 21 billion [dollars in revenue] this year?" "Yes," the crowd responded politely. "I can't hear you," he barked out with a smile. "Yes we can!" the crowd bellowed. Five years before, in 1983, Walton promised to do a hula dance on Wall Street if his employees could top 8% profit. They did. And he did.[6]

You might protest that conducting an annual meeting like a pep rally or television game show—or hulaing through the financial district, for that matter—is not your style. Regardless, enthusiasm, spark, and flair must have their rewards. Walton was rated in the October 24, 1988, issue of *Forbes* magazine as the richest man in the nation with an estimated net worth of $8.7 billion.

At one of my client companies, the managers had never before prepared strategic action plans and didn't believe that the objectives of the first one they developed were going to be enforced by the CEO. About two weeks before a deadline date on an important project, a manager casually mentioned to the CEO that progress had slipped. The CEO told the manager he could have whatever resources he needed to make the deadline and made a big point that all commitments were to be met. A new value was established in the company in that single act.

The four approaches just described will strategically align your organization's elements as shown in Exhibit 8–1. No longer will they be working at cross-purposes. Everyone will be pulling in the same direction. But at the same time people need freedom to continue creating.

AMPLE ELBOW ROOM

Meeting objectives is important. On the other hand, if you follow your plan blindly, it may be worse than having no plan at all. John Sculley stated in a 1987 speech to the Contra Costa Council in Concord, California: "The ones who will be successful in business will be those with extraordinary flexibility, those able to deal with the conceptuality of business. There will no longer be the dependability that things will happen the same, year in and year out."[7]

Change is a constant. What if the economic, market, or competitive scenario you chose is wrong? You need both strategic and operational flexibility in implementation. Lower gasoline prices persuaded Lee Iacocca to cancel Chrysler's plan to scrap its old rear-wheel-drive New Yorker in 1982. Sales of that car, one of the company's most profitable, rose to 43,000 in the first half of 1983 from 29,000 a year earlier. This demonstrates Iacocca's ability to seize unplanned opportunities. Be open to surprises.

EXHIBIT 8–1
Strategic Alignment

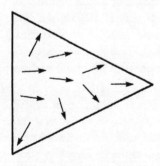

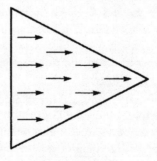

a. Partially Aligned   b. Fully Aligned
   Organization   Organization

To stay ahead of change, encourage local experiments that are variations on the chosen strategy, within bounds. A strategic plan should allow for change and flexible implementation, and should even encourage it. Don't criticize your planner when revisions to your plan are necessary. Expect them. They may even turn out to be positive. If all companies followed their plans to the letter, you would never have heard of Compaq, Sun Microsystems, or many other plan-busters. To guard against adverse changes, on the other hand, keep your new investment programs as flexible as possible for as long as possible. Freeze them only when necessary. Start small, kill small. This reduces risk and increases nimbleness. Even giants must react quickly in the 1990s.

CREATING CHANGE

Managing strategic change is not easy. What makes it challenging is that senior management has a dual responsibility. It must keep "the business as is" running smoothly while facilitating the transition to the new modus operandi, "the business that can be." "Changing GM's corporate culture was like teaching an elephant to tap-dance," says H. Ross Perot. "You find sensitive spots and start poking." But he may have poked too hard. Roger Smith, GM's CEO, says, "The experiment in change got out of hand." Perot is now starting up a competitor to Electronic Data Systems, the company he sold to GM.

Before a strategy for change can be developed, receptivity and resistance to it have to be assessed. First, involve those who are to be affected, even if only to work out some of the details. Second, do not condemn the strategy and tactics employed previously. Change must be positioned in a context that is positive: What was done before was appropriate for its time. Third, the organization must usually learn new skills; give it time. And fourth, change should be implemented as gradually as possible in transition states.

Change occurs on three levels: (1) strategic, (2) organizational, and (3) operational. Each has to be dealt with separately. For a company to become more market-oriented, for example, it requires more than for management to target a few segments and employ new promotional programs. Old behavior patterns must be altered in terms of the company's relationship with customers (elevating their importance; listening to their peeves, needs, and ideas; customizing products and services for each type of customer; and so on). Operational systems must be revised so the organization can give customers what is necessary on a day-to-day basis. The entire way business is done may have to be transformed, which will have a ripple effect throughout the organization. One of the best ways to do this is through the creation of operational plans.

DEPARTMENTAL PLANNING

Each component of the organization needs to translate corporate objectives and strategies into ones for their own units. The vehicle is strategic departmental planning. Strategic thinking is no longer a skill required only by top management. Dimitri d'Arbeloff, the CEO of Millipore Corp., a leading manufacturer of high-tech filtration systems, got rid of most of his corporate planners in the early 1980s. Operating managers are now expected to do their own planning. "We just had to be there at an operational level rather than at a top-down corporate level."[8]

An Untapped Resource

Companies often seek to stimulate creativity among their lower ranks through quality circles and productivity teams. But the middle layer of most organizations, representing a tremendous creative resource, remains largely untapped for ideas and innovative approaches. A way now exists to give this layer of people an opportunity to contribute. Furthermore, the middle manager's role is changing dramatically. Having been major casualties of corporate restructurings and acquisitions, there are now fewer of them. Those remaining are expected to make a greater contribution. More than ever, they are responsible (and get paid for) the strategic as well as operational performance of their people.

Here is a summary of the process to use to align a department with the mission of the overall organization. It parallels the top management objective and strategy setting process, but it should be driven by the corporate plan and the plans of other departments in the company.

Step One: Define the Department's Situation

In any planning, the external and internal environments must be understood before you can generate alternatives. Here are a variety of approaches for defining the situation at the departmental level. Some or all should be used.

1. *Translate the Corporate Plan.* The corporate mission, objectives, strategies, and values must be explained to everyone in your department. Only then can these people conceive of ways for your department to support the overall plan. A recent situation I experienced shows how the process works. The president of a high-tech client of mine presented the overall corporate objective and ten subsidiary ones to the company's department managers. He then asked the managers to work with their people to develop a department objective that would correspond to each corporate one. We then held a meeting. Each department head presented his objectives, and we discussed them as a group. Managers were expected to suggest improvements to the plans of the others. This gave everyone a chance to see how each department's objectives tied in with one another. Conflicts were resolved on the spot.

2. *Understand Thyself.* Within a department, have each member stand up and present his or her responsibilities, accomplishments in the last period, and challenges in the coming one. Then have all members brainstorm the department's SWOT: strengths, weaknesses, opportunities, and threats. Listing issues and challenges for the entire department is also valuable. Last, rank these in order of importance.

3. *Internal Customer Analysis.* Some departments, such as marketing, sales, and customer service, deal primarily with outside customers. However, every department in the company has internal customers. First, list the people or departments that are beneficiaries of your output: services, reports, documentation, new product designs (going into manufacturing), and so on. Next, from these customers' perspectives, define the "products" or services you give them, each customer's buying factors (how they judge the quality and quantity of your output), and, as objectively as possible, how your department rates against each factor. After your first draft of this analysis, you should do some internal marketing research by asking some of your customers to rate you. You can do the same for your department's internal suppliers.

4. *Competitor Analysis.* You say, "Our department doesn't have any competitors." Consider indirect ones, such as: internal or external customers doing your work themselves, or work being done by a corporate staff person, outside contractors or consultants, or by another department or facility. I helped the management of a manufacturing facility in a large chemical company go through this analysis, as well as the customer one, and we developed an entire internal marketing plan and operational strategy around our findings. The objective was to ensure that the plant continued to be a prime supplier of products to the company's marketing divisions so it would not become a candidate for liquidation or sale.

Step Two: Generate Alternatives

You are now ready to take leaps and make connections. Refer to Part One of this book. Brainstorm the following: ideal services to other departments; ideal information systems for your department and its customers to work at maximum effectiveness; and the ideal department, including size, structure, and philosophy. Also use the President du Jour and Comic Relief techniques. The best ideas will emerge if you keep the mood of the meeting upbeat and fun.

Steps Three Through Five

The rest of the departmental planning process mirrors the one described for use by top management. The best ideas are culled out, using criteria developed specifically for your department. An overall department plan would contain your department's mission, objective, strategy, values, action programs, and budget. Gantt charts and PERT diagrams are frequently necessary, particularly for complex projects. And implementation requires the same approach as discussed in this chapter. The perspective of the department manager is different from that of the company's CEO, but the principles of planning are the same.

MAKE RESOURCES AVAILABLE

When new programs are to be implemented, the way resources are allocated also changes. Resources consist of funds for expenses, capital expenditures, working capital, and time—of executives, managers, labor, nonemployees (such as wholesalers and reps), test equipment, manufacturing processes, and other items. As discussed in the last chapter, your overall plan should contain a strategic budget that looks out three to five years. The breakdown in the link between the strategic budget and the one-year operating plan and budget occurs in two ways: (1) the two are not integrated because the operating budget is prepared months after the completion of the strategic plan, or (2) as soon as a mild profit squeeze occurs, strategic items, which are discretionary in the short term, are underfunded or dropped altogether.

The best way to ensure that the strategic budget and the one-year operating plan are integrated is to do a double link. As shown in Exhibit

8–2, first make sure strategic action programs are prepared and their first year coincides with the operating plan. Second, after your annual budgeting process is completed, compare it with your strategic budget. Many annual budgets do not include funding for the strategic programs committed to earlier in the planning cycle. The reason is that the strategic plan is prepared in an environment that focuses on strategies, while the annual plan focuses on quarterly profit.

You have two options at this point. Either revise the annual budget or change your strategic objectives and programs. Don't do what many companies do—ignore the lack of integration and then at the end of the year complain, "Obviously, strategic planning doesn't work because we didn't do what we said we were going to do."

SO FAR, SO WHAT?

There is another way to ensure that your ambitious strategic action plans are implemented. Review them on a regular basis. To say "implementation tends not to happen by itself" is an understatement. Here are some benefits of monitoring your rollout:

- Accountability makes responsibility deliver. "What gets measured gets done," the saying goes.
- Reviewing the progress of strategic programs on a regular basis provides

EXHIBIT 8–2
The Double Link

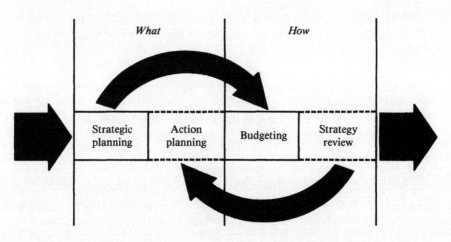

for celebration of things accomplished, learning why others weren't, and making adjustments.
- Strategies sometimes get off track when being implemented by lower-level managers. "As the Tower Board reported," said President Reagan in March 1987, "what began as a strategic opening to Iran deteriorated in its implementation into trading arms for hostages. This runs counter to my own beliefs, to administration policy, and to the original strategy we had in mind."[9]
- Strategy review sessions should include time to enhance existing strategies and provide an idea forum for totally new ones.

Here are some suggestions for managing the feedback loop.

Quarterly Implementation Meetings

Meeting every three months to assess implementation progress ensures execution of your plan. Three months is enough time between meetings to get things done, while not so long that people forget the plan and it collects dust on the credenza. These meetings, generally a day long with all key management team members attending, in essence cover what's happening, what's not happening, and what should be done about it. When I facilitate these sessions for clients, I have each participant accentuate the positive and present to the rest of us:

- What strategic programs are on or ahead of schedule, and why
- Which are behind schedule, and what are the bottlenecks
- How the program will get back on track, and what the rest of us can do to help
- Any new developments either inside or outside the company that should be considered in the company's overall strategy or specific programs
- What their new or revised commitments are

The generation of new ideas and refinements to strategies are encouraged throughout the entire meeting. At Chrysler, Lee Iacocca still uses today the quarterly review meetings he put into place as a sales manager and executive at Ford. Every first-of-the-quarter week at Ford came to be known as "crunch time." "If he's a good manager," Iacocca says, "four times a year he has to come into the barrel and report." This, he says, increases self-accountability. "The discipline of writing something down is the first step toward making it happen," Iacocca adds. And quarterly meetings, he says, force dialogue, improve teamwork, raise superiors' awareness, motivate, and foster creativity. "I've never found a better way to stimulate fresh approaches to problem solving or to generation of ideas," he concludes.[10]

Persistence

Conviction is essential for success. Just because a strategy or program is taking longer to implement than expected, or positive financial results are delayed, there is no reason to pull the plug. Many things look like failures in the middle. In the mid-1970s, when Fred Smith was trying to get Federal Express off the ground, his business plan had to be modified continually because the break-even point could not be reached. Once Smith persuaded his employees to pawn their watches for a short-term bridge loan. Later, some of his venture capitalists tried to replace him with another manager. His management team threatened to leave if Smith went—a form of the "people pill" some top managements are using today as a takeover defense. The positioning of "absolutely, positively overnight" helped put the company on the growth track and in the black.[11]

CUC International, winner of the Association for Corporate Growth's Emerging Company Award in 1988, is another example. The company is a leader in electronic shopping. Walter Forbes, chairman and CEO, says the company went from eleven years of failure to a winner over the 1984–88 period, during which it had compound growth rates of 110% in revenue and 384% in earnings. For an annual membership fee, its 10 million members are offered products and services via home computer or telephone at the guaranteed lowest price. These include travel and an array of goods found in mail order catalogs. CUC intends to offer new and used automobiles next.

Skill at Abortion

Persistence is needed, but at an extreme it crosses that thin line into obstinacy. You can become overly committed to failing programs and throw good money after bad. It has been said that the trouble with experience is that you only get it after you need it. Leonard Liberman, CEO of Supermarkets General, says, "Of course we have to procreate heavily, but I give more credit to our willingness to experiment and skill at abortion. Some of our firsts that didn't work include a catalog desk, insurance sales, and travel services.''[12] Knowing when to abort a project is as important as knowing when to launch.

Robert J. Carbonell, chief of Del Monte and vice chairman of RJR Nabisco, says: "If something isn't working, we're prepared to move 180 degrees in a hurry." Tom Peters insists that one can let $20,000 get dragged into a $2 million catastrophe when people are afraid to admit defeat.[13]

Encourage Admission of Mistakes

At Johnson & Johnson, people are encouraged to take risks, creating a corporate culture where even mistakes can be a badge of honor. Management realizes they are an inevitable byproduct of innovation.[14]

Harold Geneen, in his book *Managing,* says: "One of the essential attributes of a good leader is enough self-confidence to be able to admit his own mistakes and know they won't ruin him. The true test is to be able to recognize what is wrong as early as possible and then to set about rectifying the situation." He goes on to admit, "I made my share of mistakes at ITT and they did not ruin me."

When it was discovered that Chrysler Corporation had disconnected the odometers on some 60,000 test cars it sold for new, Lee Iacocca held a press conference and flatly said: "Did we screw up? You bet we did." He placed two-page ads in national newspapers explaining the error.

John Cleese, the insightful British comedian of *Monty Python* fame, has produced a training tape, "The Essence of Creativity." In one scene a boss says: "No more mistakes and you're through!"

Dealing with a Sizzler

The opposite of making mistakes is having a strategy turn out to be almost too hot to handle. Sun Microsystems' CEO, Scott McNealy, told reporters in October 1986 that the company blasted through its five-year business plan twice a year to keep pace with reality. "This is not a place for the weak of heart, because we are riding a rocket ship here." At the time, even McNealy was on a waiting list to acquire one of the company's hot new technical work stations.

Sudden interest was created for Canfield Company's Diet Chocolate Fudge soda when the *Chicago Tribune* columnist Bob Greene wrote in 1985 that it "is like biting into a hot fudge sundae." Alan Canfield, the

CEO, wasn't impressed with the immediate consumer reaction. He figured a turbulent month of sales would be the end of it. Wrong. Within a month the third-generation family business was practically unrecognizable. The company sold about $80 million of Diet Chocolate Fudge in the two years following. But it scaled up production capacity in a rational way.

Many small companies strive to live out their fantasies, only to find that they turn out to be nightmares. Joshua Hyatt wrote in *Inc.*: "A hot product is like a dangerous and sophisticated weapon. Instead of learning how to use it, many small companies end up wounding themselves—sometimes fatally."[15] Mistaken managements overinvest in production facilities or assume that one winner makes them infallible and overinvest in the next product; others just live beyond their means. Often, what's hot quickly becomes what's not. Wham-O almost went under with the crash of its fad product, the Hula Hoop. Coleco went into Chapter 11 because of overspending after its short-lived hit with Cabbage Patch Dolls. So before launching your plan, ask: "What if we succeed beyond our wildest dreams?" Be sure to have a strategy for it.

CONTINUOUS IMPROVEMENT

As in sports, the only thing harder than winning is winning again. Repeating the big win requires that your organization constantly improve itself. The Japanese call it *kaizen*, the spirit of constant improvement. The concept drives everything they do, from design to manufacturing. At no time do Japanese firms sit back and get comfortable. They systematically strive for higher levels of product and organizational quality and performance. The managements of American companies must do the same.

Creative planning can be one of the key vehicles that drives constant improvement in your organization. Tom Peters says to "make constant improvement strategic . . . each manager [and eventually nonmanager] should have a personal and group constant-improvement plan."[16]

On a strategic level, top management should be pursuing corporate improvement on a number of levels simultaneously. Exhibit 8–3 presents a menu of strategic actions to increase profitability and/or increase growth, on either a short-term or a medium term-basis. Corporate superstars always have something going on in each quadrant. James Burke, CEO of Johnson & Johnson, sees innovation as an unending process. Francis Aguilar, a professor at Harvard Business

EXHIBIT 8–3

Menu of Strategic Actions

	Increase Profitability	Increase Growth
Short Term	Cost reduction Customer profitability Price increases Working capital controls Organizational focusing	Sales productivity New promotion strategies Line extensions Market positioning Target market segments
Medium Term	Quality improvement Productivity improvement Reorganization Divestitures CAD/CAM/Automation	New products New markets Licenses Acquisitions People development

School and author of several books on J&J, says: "What Burke does is crucial—he continually energizes the system."

Parts Three and Four of this book address additional ways for building your business. But before I get into those topics, I will address one more skill you will need to develop and implement your plan: leading creative teams.

9

Leading Creative Teams

"IF you are looking for a word that we live by," says Ford CEO Donald Peterson, "that word is 'teamwork.' "[1] Teamwork was the key when he transformed Ford from one of the most autocratic and politicized corporate cultures in American industry—and a company with a hemorrhaging bottom line—to the winner of the automotive industry.

Inspiring employees to excel requires a unique type of leadership that goes beyond just motivating. When executives and lower-level employees are properly tapped for ideas and brought into the decision-making process, peak experiences occur. Peak results follow. Lack of teamwork yields the opposite.

BRINGING OUT THE WORST IN EACH OTHER

It is surprising how many senior executives only give lip service to teamwork. Robert Lefton and V.R. Buzzota, in their study of twenty-six top management teams (twenty of them from Fortune 500 companies), found little in practice. What they did find was autocratic decision making, polarized communication, poorly run meetings, little coordination, hardly any emphasis on execution, and quite a bit of childish behavior.[2] Unfortunately, it was not the creative side of children that was observed, but the back-biting, name-calling mode.

Many top executives mistakenly believe the participative approach to strategy development and problem solving weakens their authority. They don't want to change. Many of them lack the skills to be objective participants in high-level team sessions. They attack group members, don't listen to the positions of others, and take sides. Worse still, they spread their lack of team building skills down the ladder. Middle managers mimic top management, including the management style of hostile attitudes and chaos. Technical and other lower-level employees are hardest hit. They wonder why companies hire them for their intelligence and creativity, then fail to draw on it.

Supervisors and foremen get caught in the middle. Orders come down to get workers involved in problem solving and to ask them to do things, not tell them what to do. These managers worked hard to get where they are, and now they are being told by management to give up some of their authority. At least they perceive it that way.

This chapter will first cover some basics on teamwork and participatory management, and will dispel some misconceptions along the way. Then it will tell how to lead groups, both small and large, through the Creative Planning process. Last, it will cover how to lead high-performance creative teams on a continuous basis.

EXECUTIVE EXTRAORDINAIRE

The higher you go in an organization, the more you need people skills more than technical talent (see Exhibit 9–1). In every study I have ever seen of executive qualities, the one near or at the top is the ability to build and lead a management team. This is demanded at middle- and lower-management levels as well. Tom Peters, for example, says:

> First and second-line supervisors must learn to be facilitators and cheerleaders, not cops or naysayers. You can order people to come to work, but you can't order them to be excellent in what they do. Excellence on the production line or office floor is a matter of a 100 percent voluntary commitment. Getting that commitment is what identifies the superior manager.[3]

EXHIBIT 9–1

Skill Shift in Climbing the Ladder

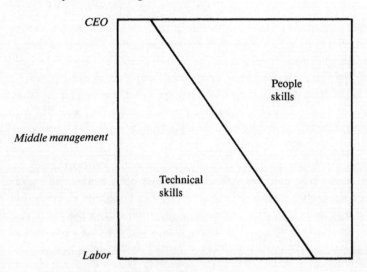

All levels of management have to learn to be facilitators. Not only will it leverage the organization, it will significantly reduce the single biggest reason managers fail: poor interpersonal skills.[4]

Tough and Tender

Does this stuff sound too soft for your management style? General Electric's John Welch is a tough competitor when it comes to winning in business, yet he is a strong believer in participatory management. He says:

> We have found what we believe is the distilled essence of competitiveness. It is the reservoir of talent and creativity and energy that can be found in each of our (300,000) people. That essence is leveraged when we make people believe that what they think and do is important—and then get out of their way while they do it.[5]

People tend to dichotomize styles of leadership. Participatory management doesn't mean that you give all your decision-making power over to your team. It means you involve members in trying to make the whole department or company work better. While you solicit your subordinates' ideas as well as their judgment, you retain the right to make the final decision.

Sometimes the authoritative Vince Lombardi style of management is still called for. One of his Green Bay Packers, once explained about Lombardi: "When he says 'sit down,' I don't even look for a chair." Another player remarked, "He's fair. He treats us all the same—like dogs." In certain rare times, you may have to be a Vince Lombardi. Be both tough and tender, but mostly tender.

More participation is desired at all levels and in all functions. A survey of *Sales and Marketing Management* subscribers in 1983 revealed that the two elements of their company sales meetings they would most like to improve were an increase in sales force participation at meetings and a wiser and more efficient use of the time.[6]

The intense desire for participation is not restricted to business. In Detroit in October 1988, a group of Catholic priests held protest meetings and considered suing their bishop because a number of parishes were being closed. Their chief complaint was they were not involved in the decision making. Said one rector, "I agree that something needs to be done about decreasing membership, but the way it was handled, it was a little too much from above."[7]

Henri Lipmanowicz, vice president of economic and strategic planning at Merck & Co.'s international division, states the requirement succinctly: "What is needed is a strategic dialogue, not just communication. And it needs to happen vertically, horizontally, and even diagonally." Communication can be in just one direction. Dialogue calls for communication in both directions.[8]

LEADING THE CREATIVE
PLANNING PROCESS

Three results are possible from strategy sessions: planning pandemonium, puffery, or performance. The purpose of the next few pages is to show how to achieve the third.

The Creative Planning process was summarized in Chapter 1. Generally, a minimum of five meetings, one for each step, is required to create an innovative strategy for a company. A kickoff orientation meeting is also very helpful. If the organization consists of a number of separate divisions, more meetings or entirely separate planning programs can be necessary.

Sometimes fewer than five meetings can be enough. At the request of clients, I have done it in two, three, and four sessions. If two are involved, I split the process down the middle. In the first meeting, we discuss the results of the participants' strategic analyses (Step One), generate ideas (Step Two), and build concepts (Step Three–1). The participants then work alone in small groups to collect information to help evaluate the concepts and mold them into options. The second meeting starts with judgement of options (Step Three–2), covers planning (Step Four), and ends with commitment (Step Five). The addition of kickoff and launch sessions, even if brief, helps considerably.

In an extreme case, I was contacted by the CEO of a past client who needed a strategy in two days in response to a major unexpected new product introduction by a competitor. We met one-on-one for an entire day and went through all five steps with the information available in his mind or at his fingertips. Spending roughly two hours per step, the streamlined creative process worked well. What we lacked in participation and time, we made up for with intensity. The president continued to verify his assumptions after the rollout.

To the Woods

John Sculley wrote in his book *Odyssey*: "Managing creativity has nothing to do with sitting around a table and brainstorming. The atmosphere is too rigid. We almost never do anything important in any of our offices." Strategy sessions can be conducted on the company's premises, but that is not the preferred location. They certainly cannot be held in the CEO's office. This domain can have an inhibiting effect on many participants. If you are to stay on the company's premises, move the sessions (at the very least, the creativity one) to a location other than where normal staff meetings are held. Environmental conditions play a big part. First, you are trying to stimulate the team to think differently. Second, moving the meeting signals that something new is expected. I once held a top management creativity session in the company's factory conference room. We had to get out of the conservative atmosphere of the boardroom, which had on its walls pictures of former CEOs who had been extremely authoritative.

Off-site meetings are best for Creative Planning sessions. The environment is different, more relaxed, and free from disturbances. Everyone can concentrate for the one to three days they are there and can interact informally and socially as well, an important element in building rapport and exchanging ideas. At the end of a three-day boardroom session with a major European firm, one officer suggested holding the next meeting off-site. The managing director thought for a moment, then said: "To the woods." It couldn't have been put more succinctly.

Strategy sessions should involve everyone who has a significant effect on the business unit's or company's future. At the corporate level, this should include the chairman, president, and heads of all key functions: marketing, sales, finance, operations, research, engineering, service, quality, human resources, legal, and others. One person may come up with a germ of an idea, but someone else, perhaps from another department, may be needed to develop and improve on it. At the department level, it would include all supervisors and senior professionals. But limit the size of the group sessions to ten to twelve people, with a maximum of about fifteen. If more people attend, voicing an opinion becomes a public speech, constraining open, free-wheeling communication. How to handle larger groups will be covered later in this chapter.

Facilitating the Process

I once heard that planners are like seagulls. They fly into a company or division, stir things up, drop their "loads" all over the place, and then fly out to their next destination. This need not be. Planning facilitators can be heroes if they organize and energize the planning sessions, and foster teamwork. Who should be the planning facilitator? Someone has to guide the management team through the thought process of strategy development. I have been purposely vague about who the meeting leader actually is, because there is a choice. It can be the CEO, a planning executive, or a consultant. The choice is important. The success of Creative Planning depends largely on the skills of the facilitator. This is no assignment for a second-rate mind, or even a first-rate thinker who is lacking either facilitation skills or a good understanding of the process.

Since the CEO knows the company well, he or she may decide to facilitate the meeting. Most certainly the CEO identifies with the organization's goals and possesses the authority to shape the thinking of the management team. However, you should be aware of the potential drawbacks that could hinder your effectiveness. You may be biased about what could or should be done. You may lack the facilitation skills to draw out ideas, or you may not feel comfortable with creativity techniques, yet. Perhaps your greatest disadvantage is the difficulty of switching roles from CEO to idea catalyst many times throughout the sessions.

While an insider has detailed knowledge of the company, he or she may lack objectivity and have a hidden agenda. An outsider brings a fresh perspective, additional skills, experience from other companies—and au-

EXHIBIT 9–2

Role of Facilitator

- Explain the Creative Planning process to participants, sell its benefits, and instill confidence.
- Maximize everyone's participation, particularly reticent people.
- Develop detailed agendas for each meeting, and prepare each person for them.
- Help everyone with their strategic analyses.
- Give kick-off speeches at each meeting to establish objectives, review process, and set tone.
- Help the group synthesize diverse information and viewpoints.
- Ask provocative questions and draw out ideas from everyone.
- Offer ideas of your own, including witty, even outrageous ones to loosen up group.
- Support ideas of others far more than your own.
- Provide assistance in developing ideas into concepts, and then options.
- Keep meetings moving; prevent gross digressions and overkill on points.
- Listen closely to capture everyone's ideas so you can write them on chart paper.
- Maintain balance between adherence to method and disorganized confusion.
- Don't let any session end on a note of defeat.
- After each meeting, follow up with the participants for further ideas, to keep them thinking.
- Adapt the Creative Planning process to the needs and capabilities of the company and participants.

---

tonomy. He or she might be more effective at facilitating the sessions thanan internal person.

Encouraging Suggestive Behavior

It's been said that nothing is tougher to create than creativity. The facilitator's responsibility is to guide the group through the five steps of Creative Planning so that it generates imaginative strategies. The objective is to multiply the power of the individual minds beyond what could be achieved by working separately with each participant. Exhibit 9–2 summarizes the facilitator's responsibilities. When generating ideas or lists of issues, pet peeves, et cetera, the four rules of brainstorming apply. Invented by Alex Osborn in the late 1930s, they are:

1. Allow no criticism of points made
2. Enthusiastically call for wild ideas
3. The more ideas the better
4. Encourage improvements and combinations

A fifth rule is: All participants are equal during the session. This is important when working with people from widely different levels.

Classical brainstorming allows for no discussion, just the rapid firing of ideas. In strategy conception and development, I find that a small amount of discussion during brainstorming sessions can be highly beneficial. However, the facilitator must be careful not to let discussions exceed 10% to 20% of the total time. Depending on the open mindedness of the group, once the line is crossed, brainstorming degenerates into a judgmental session. Exhibit 9–3 depicts this phenomenon.

Effective participation cannot be overemphasized. Why? It is human nature to want to work harder on our own ideas than on those of others, including our boss's. In Abraham Maslow's hierarchy, his pyramid of human needs, the pinnacle is "self-actualization." Creating, leaving a mark on one's environment (in this case the company), is the ultimate

EXHIBIT 9–3

Discussion During Brainstorming Sessions

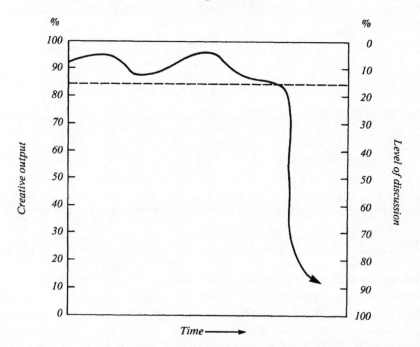

reward. Pay isn't the payoff. The joy of business is in the creation. Creativity breeds commitment. And it is commitment, not authority, that produces results. So a strategic planning process that taps management's creativity and doesn't have it just filling out forms or preparing forecasts can be a powerful motivator. Creative Planning harnesses this force.

Maintaining planning as a line function rather than a staff function has another benefit. It is management that brainstorms and judges ideas, not planners from corporate headquarters or outside consultants. This eliminates the "not-invented-here"(NIH) syndrome that is so pervasive in many organizations. The "was-invented-here" (WIH) factor takes over. As a result, plans are implemented.

Ringisho

The Japanese term for building consensus is *ringisho,* another challenging responsibility of the facilitator. Before Compaq Computer executives give the green light to a new product, they hammer out a consensus on everything: design, manufacturing methods, price, and marketing strategies. Rod Canion, CEO of Compaq, says:

> You always have disagreements. But at Compaq, instead of just arguing over who is right, we tear down positions to reasons. And when you get to reasons you find facts and assumptions. Then you try to eliminate the assumptions and come to agreement on the facts. Almost always, when you get your team to agree on the facts, you agree on the solutions.[9]

Scott McNealy, CEO of Sun Microsystems, has two points to make regarding consensus. On decision making: "Consensus if possible, but participation for sure." On management cooperation: "Agree and commit, disagree and commit—or just get the hell out of the way."[10]

Managers frequently have to be trained in how to run meetings effectively before I can pass the facilitator baton. The person in charge needs special advice.

The Leader's Role

Whether CEO or department manager, dedication to planning must start at the top, or it will not start at all. The leader must recognize the need for Creative Planning, want to maximize the performance of the company or unit, and believe in tapping the brainpower of the team. The leader is watched constantly, so he or she must provide the role model. At the same time, he or she must not dominate the sessions, and if facilitating, not overrun them. But he or she has to attend. The responsibility for strategy can't be delegated. Other suggestions include: Wear a thick skin when outmoded company traditions and pet peeves are brainstormed; throw out a wild idea or two during the creativity session to set the example; endorse previously rejected ideas; keep alive unfeasible but potentially good ideas in the concept-building step; insist that everyone think strategically; commit resources to longer-term projects as well as short-term ones; and lead the charge when it comes to execution.

RETREATS INVOLVING LARGE GROUPS

I once heard it said that large meetings to collect ideas are many times held to share the blame. In a multiday retreat, this is at least better than nothing but speeches and more speeches, which are not remembered a week later.

Large numbers of executives are frequently assembled to undertake planning or problem solving. At the company's annual management conference, or a marketing or sales meeting, or a retreat specifically for planning, the danger is heightened conservatism. Injecting creativity into the situation is more complex than with twelve or fewer people. It's not just stage fright. Thoughts of departure from tradition are repressed.

Major Company's Annual Conference

I was requested to facilitate a multidivisional corporation's three-day management conference at a desert resort. We stayed with the company's previous format: mornings devoted to business, and afternoons to golf, tennis, and other types of interactive recreation. The first morning the CEO gave a "state of the company" address, and each of the fifteen division presidents presented a brief overview of his or her unit's objectives and strategies. We began creative planning the second morning with two objectives: (1) to improve the corporate plan, and (2) to explore interdivisional opportunities among the fifteen divisions. The meeting went as follows:

- The forty executives were broken up into eight groups of five each and given ninety minutes to "roast" the existing corporate plan and think up possible improvements. They used a streamlined process of thirty minutes for each of three steps: insights, leaps, and concepts.
- After they finished, seven new groups were formed and spent ninety minutes addressing potential interdivisional opportunities using the same three-step process.
- The third morning, each group leader (fifteen in all) presented a summary of his or her group's findings to all of us. The CEO and I led everyone present in a discussion to blend the best ideas and identify action items.

Group leaders were chosen for their abilities to handle the group dynamics (assisted by a written facilitator guideline) and to deliver a good presentation. The CEO's other requirement was to hear from any outspoken executives who had been known to grumble off the record about the corporate strategy.

The participants carved up a few sacred cows and in the process generated a few hundred ideas. Four of the most important concepts that emerged from the first eight presentations were:

- Concentrate the company's management efforts on those divisions that possess long-term prospects for attractive financial returns, and divest the others. (Specific divisions were listed in the first category, implying those in the second.)
- Develop tighter resource allocation among divisions, as well as an annual "report card" on the ROI of investments.
- Institute a "super incentive" plan that compensates division top management for the attainment of long-term goals.
- Create a corporate venture group and develop innovation budgets for the divisions. (Specific new venture ideas were listed.)

Corporate issues were faced head on, and potential solutions for each were conceived. Camaraderie and communication between division managers were established where little had existed before. A new respect for top management was developed. And many division managers were amazed—the corporate office had asked for their opinions.

The second set of presentations highlighted fifty possible interdivisional opportunities, even though top management prior to the conference felt this was a barren area. But the ninety minutes had only whetted their appetites. It was decided separate conferences were needed to treat opportunities for division cooperation in three areas: marketing/sales, technology, and operations/purchasing.

Interdivisional Marketing Conference

The chief marketing/sales officer from each division (plus a few marketing-oriented division presidents) assembled for a two-day meeting with me as facilitator. Most of the first day was devoted to having each officer make a presentation on his or her company's product lines, customer categories and markets, channels of distribution, advertising programs and budgets, trends in markets, and issues and challenges. Then we started creating. Because there were nineteen participants, we used breakout groups, as had been done in the corporate planning meeting.

Thirty programs were committed to by the group. Each was assigned to the pair of marketing executives at the divisions involved. Results from many of the easier opportunities were seen within twelve months. A number of larger ones were realized within two years. For example, a building materials division, which had strong distribution through home centers, assisted another division, which sold through dealers. An attack of the home center market enabled the latter division to double its sales and profits within eighteen months. The latter half of the second day was devoted to brainstorming by the whole group for solutions to each division's major issues and challenges. Anywhere from two to ten ideas emerged for each. It was as if each participant had eighteen marketing consultants at his disposal sweating their brains free of charge.

Interdivisional Technology and Operations Conferences

The same format was used in meetings of the chief technologists and operations officers from each division. Between the two, fifty opportunities were identified, then screened down to fifteen high priorities. These programs always produce results. One Fortune 500 company with which I worked had ten divisions in high performance materials such as graphite composites, ceramics, and adhesives. One division, however, was in biotech. We didn't think the other technology executives had anything to contribute to the biotechnology division's major challenge. But we were wrong. Once the problem was described in detail, a dozen ideas emerged. Once again, it was proved that outside viewpoints can be highly valuable in creativity sessions.

CREATIVE TEAM BUILDING

Teamwork is defined as people working together effectively toward a common goal, for a common benefit. It is as essential to execution as it is to strategy development. It is the primary way you can increase profitability—through the creative cooperation of your people. Cooperation between people is most often needed in three places in organizations:

1. *Within Units.* This includes the smallest one-on-one task force to the largest company, institution, or government. Usually a manager and his direct reports are involved, but cooperation could also entail entire divisions and companies.
2. *Between Units.* The interfaces of most organizations are where teamwork is sorely lacking. These include between divisions, departments, task forces, and the corporate office and its divisions.
3. *In Parallel Organizations.* These are temporary units that exist outside the organization chart. Parallel organizations include task forces, project teams, quality circles, productivity teams, innovation teams, and others.

Team Is the Hero

The characteristics of effective teamwork include wide participation, a shared vision and purpose, consensual decision making, interdependent roles, an informal and trusting atmosphere, acceptance of individual responsibility, and a "can-do" climate. Team players have to get away from "I, my, me" talk and speak about "us, our, and we." Arnold "Red" Auerbach, the inspirational leader of the Boston Celtics, said in an interview with *Harvard Business Review:* "It's like Larry Bird always says before a big game: 'I'll be ready and the other guys will be ready and we're going to win this thing.' Not 'I'm going to win it.' Larry Bird gets as big a thrill out of making the pass as he does making the shot."[11] The team is the hero.

Team leaders and players need empathy. "I understand how you feel" and "How can I be of help?" are the proper attitudes. Insensitivity toward others derails teamwork—and careers. Cooperation, not competition, is the key. "Working together we can succeed" should be the watchword.

Enhancing Teamwork

There are a variety of ways to increase teamwork within a group or between groups. The Creative Planning process, properly facilitated, will go a long way in accomplishing this. Here are some additional techniques.

1. *Admiration Sessions.* Donald Peterson masterminded a radical shift in the culture of Ford from an autocratic management to a cooperative one. One of the techniques used at Ford was to get executives and managers together and have them state what they most admired about each other. The purpose, Peterson states, was "to get people to get along with one another." Spending time trying to see the positive in a person or situation can build relationships.

2. *Introduce Each Other.* This is a great way to have team members get to know each other. It is also an excellent tool to use when facilitating a small to medium conference. At a conference, have participants pair up and interview each other for five to eight minutes on their professional and personal backgrounds. Then have each make a two-to-three-minute introduction of his or her partner as if he or she were Johnny Carson. Pair up the people who will have to work together the most in the future or who have been having conflicts. Instant rapport and respect will be established between pairs, and the whole group will develop an understanding of everyone's background. Encourage humor, and you have a tremendous ice-breaking tool with full participation in the first half-hour of a conference.

3. *Roast the Culture.* Executives at 3M are known to roast the company's new product development abilities so they don't start believing all of their company's great press and get overconfident. Roasting the culture in your organization can lead to insights on where it needs to be overhauled. Continue using the Creative Planning process to identify needed changes, formulate an action plan, and execute. One way to foster this is to ask everyone to evaluate the organization overall and the unit (or units) specifically on a variety of factors, including trust, responsibility, cohesiveness, loyalty, drive, creativity, productivity, mission, and strategy. Another question to ask is which sport the organization is playing: basketball, football, baseball, crew, tennis, golf, or boxing. The answers can be quite a surprise.

4. *Communication Mapping.* It can be highly revealing to compare how the organization actually operates with written procedure or hearsay. Interview everyone in a particular department—or in a number of them, if interdepartmental cooperation is being assessed. Find out from each person who they communicate with and for what reasons, where communication breaks down, where it is successful, how decisions are made or not made, where mistakes occur, and other relevant topics. With this information you can literally map out the communication patterns and decision-making mechanisms in an organization. Present the results to everyone involved, and then brainstorm how to improve teamwork, cooperation, and com-

munication. Usually systems can be streamlined, saving costs, while at the same time their effectiveness is improved.

5. *Interface Teams*. When two or more departments or divisions have to work together, it can be helpful to form a team of a mix of personnel from both units. Proctor & Gamble has done this in response to changing markets, new classes of consumers, and the growing strength of retailers due to advances in their information technology. P&G revamped the brand management system it created decades ago. Cooperation, not competition, is now emphasized between brands and category managers. Strategies for Tide, Cheer, and Bold, for example, will be developed jointly, where just a few years ago P&G's philosophy was that it would grow faster by competing against itself. Brand managers used to be Czars.[12]

6. *Conflict Resolution*. Growth or concentration leads to change, and change creates conflict. When two departments or divisions are at odds with each other, have representatives of both use the Creative Planning process to resolve the situation. First, brainstorm the issues from both sides, and identify the causes of the issues. Second, model the ideal relationship on an element-by-element basis, as well as overall. Third, create a picture of what is feasible, and facilitate agreement. Fourth, develop an action plan with responsibilities. Fifth, implement it and periodically check back on results. The same process works when only two people are entrenched in conflicting positions.

A PEAK TEAM EXPERIENCE

On April Fools Day in 1985, Villanova University's basketball team demonstrated what can be accomplished when all of the right elements of teamwork come together. It defeated Georgetown for the NCAA championship. That was noteworthy because to quote *Sports Illustrated*, "It was the most fascinating upset in the 47 years of the NCAA championship game." Before the game, reporters were saying that "in a game between two Catholic institutions, Villanova didn't have a prayer." The Hoyas, led by Patrick Ewing, were number one and had the best defense in the country, allowing opponents all season to make only 39.8% of their shots attempted. Villanova almost didn't make the tournament draw.

In the locker room, Villanova's coach Rollie Massimino told his team they would have to play a perfect game in order to win. They went out and shot an NCAA record 78.6% from the field. In the emotion-packed second half, when nerves are known to shatter, Villanova shot 90%. The only shot the team "missed" was blocked by Ewing.

"So how did they do it?" asked the *Los Angeles Times*. "Simple. They came into the big game equipped with the following: poise, tempo, defense and support." They had two other things: a zealous belief in themselves and a dream. After Mass before the game, Massimino asked his players to retire to their rooms for fifteen minutes of solitude to think about two things: "One, to play not with the idea not to lose, but to play to win. Second, I wanted them to tell themselves they were good enough to win, that we could beat anyone in a one-shot deal." The dream was that of three of the players who, when asked as freshman in 1981 to scribble a goal on a piece of paper, each wrote, "Final Four." They underestimated themselves in their four-year plan. They should have written, "NCAA championship."

The day after the game, an article in the *Los Angeles Times* opened: "Rocky still lives in Philadelphia." Scott Ostler, a *Los Angeles Times* sports columnist, wrote: "I hate to say I told you so, because I didn't. In fact, I may have mentioned something about how Georgetown was going to cram the pumpkin down Cinderella's throat. Cinderella, my foot. Pass the pumpkin." The win was particularly sweet for me. I graduated from Villanova's school of engineering in 1969 and was an athlete (swimming and rugby) for the school.

Teamwork can do amazing things. It is a recurring theme in corporate success and will come up again and again in this book.

PART

THREE

*Insightful
Strategic
Analysis*

10

Profitability Improvement

TOP management is often scorned for not being able to see the forest for the trees. On the other hand, I find many executives can't see the trees for the forest. Once they get to the top of their companies, they restrict themselves to the big picture and avoid the details. But what about the trees?

The details top management receives from below are often of limited value. Information for developing and implementing a strategic advantage is absent. But it is essential. Steve Jobs told *Fortune* in 1988: "A lot of macro insights come after you've spent time on microscopic detail."[1] Fred Smith, in an interview with *Inc.*, explained it another way: "I think it is the ability to assimilate information from a lot of different disciplines all at once—particularly information about change, because from change comes opportunity." And on vision, Smith says: "The common trait of people who supposedly have vision is that they spend a lot of time reading and gathering information, and then synthesize it until they come up with an idea."[2]

Creativity begins with perceptions. Part Three of this book will give you ways to look at your business that will provide fresh knowledge and spark ideas. You will be shown how to perform imaginative, selective analyses and how to rethink your basic assumptions. Both the forest and the trees have to be understood. Ideally, everyone in the organization would have one eye on the forest and one eye on the trees. The big picture is particularly important for middle and lower management if they are to make a significant contribution to the company's future.

BUSINESS IS A NUMBERS GAME

There is an old saying that if you can't measure it, you can't manage it. This holds true in strategy as well as in day-to-day decision making. The problem is that in most companies the management really doesn't understand where they make money. It may think it does, but its outmoded accounting and control systems supply meaningless numbers.

This chapter will discuss managing your business—and the parts within it—on the basis of gross profit, operating profit, return on investment (ROI), and cash flow, and how the four ways differ. It will show you how to identify the strategic variables in your company that, if managed properly, will enable you to increase the profitability of your firm dramatically. And it will give you a variety of ways to approach a subject that is on every manager's mind these days: cost reduction.

WHY ROI?

Few executives would disagree that the most important measure of their business's overall performance is some form of ROI. It is a conceptually appealing tool. ROI relates profits to the level of assets needed to generate them—whether financed by an entrepreneur's seed capital, accounts payable, bank debt, public equity, or the parent company's investment.

ROI was first used by Du Pont in the 1920s to compare objectively the performance of the company's various decentralized operations. It was an elegantly simple concept—assets should be related to earning power. In the mid-1970s Wall Street began shifting away from comparing businesses on earnings per share and toward return on equity (ROE), a form of ROI. ROE is net earnings divided by stockholders' equity. It has proved to be the most reliable determinant of a company's market-to-book ratio, and therefore its stock price. Growth in earnings is a distant second.

Exhibit 10–1 demonstrates the relationships. The ROE of the Standard & Poor 400 has averaged 13% over the last ten years. This is also the after-tax cost of capital of the average large company. In addition, the stock price of the average company sells for book value (stockholders' equity

EXHIBIT 10–1

ROE Determines Stock Price

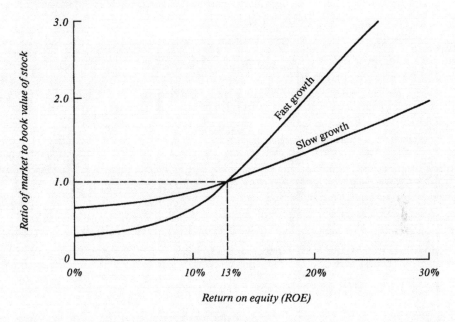

shown on the balance sheet divided by the number of shares outstanding).

Fast-growth companies with an ROE above 13% sell at a premium. Below 13%, fast-growers usually sell at a discount to slow-growers. Yes, you read this right. If a firm is not earning its cost of capital and is growing quickly, it will run out of money faster than a stable slow-growth firm. Therefore, Wall Street penalizes it. Growth for growth's sake is dangerous. As you will find out in Chapter 18, it is the most common reason for turnarounds.

STRATEGIC VARIABLES

With such emphasis on corporate ROE, it only seemed logical for me to extend the ratio's use down into the components of companies and business units, which I began to do in the late 1970s. It proved to be a powerful strategic tool. Isn't watching gross or net profit good enough? Flatly, no. Take a look at Exhibit 10–2, the ROI Matrix. It is a simplified portrayal of the income statement and the balance sheet, side by side. Every aspect of your business involves all four quadrants.

EXHIBIT 10–2
ROI Matrix

Income Statement	Balance Sheet
Gross profit (Sales less direct costs) **G**	Working capital (Current assets less current liabilities) **W**
Expenses (All "below the line" expenses) **E**	Fixed assets (Facilities, equipment, capitalized leases) **F**

$$\text{ROI} = \frac{G - E}{W + F}$$

Cash flow = G − E − (Increase in W + F)

What components of your business am I speaking about? I call them strategic variables, those controllables that affect overall profitability. Product lines and market segments are the most common. Regardless of a business's overall ROE, I almost always find a wide range of product line and market segment ROIs. The most widely used formula for ROI is "return on net assets employed" (RONAE), which is operating profit divided by total assets less current liabilities. The returns usually range from negative to some over 60%. The ranking by RONAE usually shows no relationship to the ranking based on gross profit or even net profit. The reason is varying levels of overhead expense associated with the strategic variables, and asset turnover (sales divided by net assets).

Let me give you a simple, striking example. I worked with a food machinery manufacturing company and as part of strategy development helped management determine the RONAE of its two product lines— food-processing and food-packaging equipment. Prior to the analysis, accounting records indicated that each product line generated $1 million in profit. Management theorized that the packaging line would show the higher RONAE of the two, because it was half the revenue of the other, giving it twice the profit margin on sales. The CEO was about to invest in it heavily.

Starting with the income statement, we asked all general administrative personnel (marketing, sales, engineering, production management, and accounting) to estimate the percentage of time they spent on each of the two product lines. Those percentages were multiplied by each person's salary in order to apportion these expenses below the gross profit line. Other overhead items were handled the same way. One large item—the $400,000 factory overhead adjustment—was found under close inspection to be 90% attributable to the packaging line. The products were much more diverse and difficult to manufacture than the more standardized food-processing equipment.

On the balance sheet, most factory equipment was directly chargeable to one or the other of the two product lines. Some shared equipment was allocated according to time in use. The building was allocated based on square footage used. Inventory, receivables, and payables did not require allocation, just sorting.

The outcome of the analysis shocked management. The food-packaging line was found to be losing $500,000 per year, and the food-processing line was making $2.5 million at an attractive ROI. As a result, expenses and assets were slashed for the food-packaging division.

Incremental Versus Fully Absorbed Allocations

I can visualize the reactions of accountants upon reading the example just cited. One trap in making allocations, accountants are quick to point out (and rightly so), involves the use of ROI for identifying product lines for streamlining, divestment, or liquidation. Selling or closing down a product line (market segment, brand, or the like) is a complex decision. This is where incremental ROIs must be used.

In eliminating part of a business, only variable costs and assets are usually cut. The remaining parts of the business must absorb the fixed costs, decreasing their ROIs, perhaps to poor levels as well. Another divestment pitfall is assuming that the sale of the dedicated assets will generate the book value equivalent of cash, which can be reinvested at a higher ROI. Perhaps it will be found that the assets involved are unrecoupable, "over the hill" dollars. The incremental ROI of the poorly performing unit may actually be quite high based on the salvage value of the assets used, in which case it should continue to operate (but should not expand).

Survey Results

In 1983 I decided to determine to what extent ROI was being used in this manner by surveying the heads of planning at twenty large corporations. Five reported they were calculating ROI at least annually for each product line in their company's divisions. Two more said they were developing the system in the coming year. Three reported they calculate ROI for product lines, but only in selected divisions—in the largest division, in a recently acquired one, and in capital-intensive divisions. Three firms said they did it only on an ad hoc basis—when major capital expenditures are anticipated, for example. Five of the companies said they didn't do it but, upon hearing of the concept, said they would look into it. The remaining two companies had a negative attitude toward the concept because they believed (mistakenly) it wouldn't tell them anything new.

The planning officers who did analyze and use ROI's of strategic variables in decision making offered a lot of suggestions. The three most important were:

1. *Break the Allocation Barrier.* The biggest hurdle to jump, they all said, involved allocations. As one vice president of planning of a multibillion-dollar corporation put it: "Accounting is structured for reporting purposes rather than decision making. It is not good enough for making proper allocations." (Robert Kaplan came to the same conclusion in his July–August 1984 *Harvard Business Review* article entitled "Yesterday's Accounting Undermines Production.") The solution to the allocation problem offered by respondents was to maintain two sets of books—one for accounting, and one for strategy development and planning. There is a saying that accounting is too important to be left to the accountants.

2. *Use Numbers Intelligently.* A second caution cited by respondents was that you cannot manage just by the numbers. Substantial interpretation and judgment are needed to use them wisely. The vice president of a major food retailer commented: "Our product line ROI model is not a magical black box. It puts a finger on potential opportunities and problems which then have to be dealt with individually." Recall the issue of fully absorbed versus incremental ROIs.

3. *Two-Digit Planning.* The respondents cautioned against getting

caught up in the details when making ROI estimates. The reaction of most accountants to this approach is that it can't be done. It can't, if five- to seven-digit accuracy is desired. But that is not needed for strategic innovating and decision making. Do you really care if a product line or market segment's ROI is 2% versus 3%? The same goes for ROIs in the twenties and thirties. Most top managements would be thrilled to know which strategic variables in their companies are negative, between zero and 10%, 10–20%, 20–30%, and over 30%.

ROI RESTRUCTURING

ROI Restructuring is my process of determining the ROI of the different parts of your business and strategically managing based on it. Implementing the approach in your organization entails four steps.

Step One: Identify Critical Strategic Variables

Every business has many strategic variables: products, market segments, distribution channels, technologies, manufacturing facilities, delivery systems, brands, suppliers, and others. But usually only two or three are crucial to increasing profitability. The creative challenge is to identify which have the most impact on your company's total return on investment, hence return on equity. Exhibit 10–3 shows how you must conceptually slice up your business. Brainstorm with your management team a list of potential key variables. As in any creativity exercise, do not attempt to assess their relevance at this point. Next, discuss these variables with executives in each area of the company: finance, marketing, sales, manufacturing, purchasing, engineering, and others. Ask if there are any items in either the income statement (particularly below the gross profit line) or the balance sheet (the major items being accounts receivable, inventory, fixed assets, and payables) that differ from the average for a particular strategic variable. Those with differences from the average are the strategic variables to investigate.

For example, the product lines of a large drug wholesaler varied in gross margin, but not in any other respect. What turned out to be crucial in terms of ROI however, were market segments. Each type of customer (hospitals,

EXHIBIT 10–3

ROI Slices of Your Business

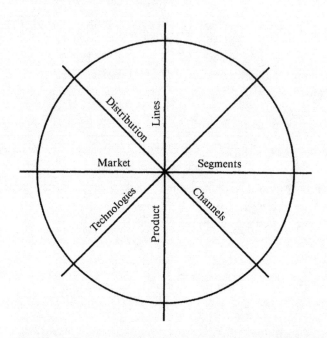

independent drug stores, drug chains, discount stores, and so forth) had specific pricing levels, product mixes, sales and delivery costs, payable terms, and inventory requirements. The ROIs varied tremendously and became key to the company's expansion strategy.

Step Two: Assign and Allocate Costs and Assets

Focus only on the most important figures. Identify those revenue, expense, and balance sheet items which are sizable relative to the others. These are the ones you want to allocate as intelligently as possible. An expense that is less than 1% of sales can be handled in a much more straightforward manner.

Aren't standard accounting allocations good enough? Generally no. For example, accounting systems typically record marketing costs in aggregated accounts by nature of expense such as salaries, advertising, and promotion. If they are allocated to product lines and markets, it generally is done by some arbitrary measure, most often in proportion to sales.

Allocations should be made the way a savvy industrial engineer would approach the problem if he understood both accounting and the ROI Restructuring method. Start with a fresh sheet of paper and take it item by item, from the top. Get inside the numbers. Concentrate on the biggest items first. Exhibit 10–4 presents some suggestions.

Major supermarket chains use a direct product profitability (DPP) model to give them the net variable profit of each item in the store. Proctor & Gamble began offering the approach in 1982 and used McKinsey & Co. to develop the algorithms by analyzing fourteen retail chains. Supermarket managers find DPP superior to gross profit for decisions on products, shelf space allocation, and coop advertising. All costs that have a variable element are charged against the gross profit of each product, in each size. This includes allocations of transportation expense from the warehouse, shelf stocking, utilities, space cost (rent, depreciation, fixtures). The same is done for assets, which are charged to items based on the cost of money. Inventory is broken into three categories: what's in the store, what's in transit, and the accounts payable offset. The only costs not allocated are those that are truly not related to a product: the store manager's salary, courtesy booth and people, headquarters expense, the laundry bill for uniforms, et cetera. Even the paper and plastic bags are allocated, based on how many of a particular item fits into them.

Step Three: ROI Ranking

A rough-cut analysis should be shared with management to get its comments and criticisms. Be open to refining your assumptions and allocation factors when new viewpoints emerge. As in any innovative approach, participation is the key to use for results. The best format for presentation is to show in summary form the strategic variables of your business ranked from highest to lowest on the basis of ROI. In this ROI Ranking, as I call it, include in columns the most important financial indicators, such as revenue, gross profit (and percent), operating profit (and percent), net assets (and asset turnover), ROI percent, and cash flow. I can see the late Clara Pella on the board of directors of a company asking: "Where's the cash?" Cash flow is an important figure that I haven't yet discussed. One of the advantages of having ROIs of your variables for multiple years is that you also have all the data for easily estimating cash flow. The formula is:

Cash flow = After tax income − Increase in net assets

EXHIBIT 10-4

Allocation Methods

INCOME STATEMENT ITEMS	TECHNIQUE
Gross profits	Accurate figures generally available at most companies. Double check such items as standard cost, inventory costs, transfer pricing.
Manufacturing overhead	Make sure this account is not a catchall. If significant in size, review allocation methods to ensure they are not arbitrary.
Research & development, marketing and sales, and administration expenses	Have each employee fill out a form spreading his or her time between product lines, market segments, etc. Use salaries as the basis for allocating compensation and benefit costs. Also, trace all major nonsalary expenses to product lines and market segments.

BALANCE SHEET ITEMS	TECHNIQUE
Cash	Deduct cash from assets in determining net assets employed
Accounts receivable	Assign directly to customers, then consolidate by market segment (customer groups) or order size, etc. Can be allocated to product lines by the product mixes purchased by the market segments.
Inventories	Attribute directly to product lines and then to market segments via product mixes consumed.
Manufacturing equipment	Charge special-purpose equipment to product lines, then to market segments. Allocate common equipment based on units produced, percentage of time utilized, or other measure.
Manufacturing facilities	Attribute to product lines based on square footage. Allocate common facilities on basis of assets employed, salaries, or some other representative measure.
Payables	Assign to product lines by source of supply. Allocate to market segments by product mix consumed.

This formula for estimating cash flow assumes that prepaid expenses, accrued liabilities, and depreciation do not materially change from period to period, a fairly safe assumption that can be easily verified.

Imagine knowing the cash flow of product lines, market segments, and other variables in your business. It would certainly help in resource allocation and in developing corrective measures to cash flow problems.

Step Four: Using ROI Rankings

Here is where imagination comes in. Ask three simple questions:

1. How do we expand the areas of high ROI?
2. How do we improve and then expand the medium ones?
3. How do we fix the low ones or, if we can't, streamline or divest them?

Taking action on the ideas that emerge can revitalize your company's financial performance, increase ROE, and drive up the price of your stock. Entire business strategies can be built around the insights that occur. Areas in the company that may not have received much attention can be stressed, and areas responsible for internal bleeding can be plugged.

A major food wholesaler maintained separate books and tracked ROIs on each of its three divisions: grocery products, frozen foods, and dairy/delicatessen items. It was easy. Separate warehouses and delivery systems were needed for each. A key question, however, was whether it made a higher return on national brands or its own private labeled goods, which all three divisions distributed. Analysis showed that gross margins for its private labeled goods ran 2% higher in two divisions and 0.5% in the third because of purchasing economies. Inventories and payables were also much more favorable, thanks to the terms of their long-term supply contracts. The ROIs of private labeled goods turned out to be almost twice those of the national brands. A key strategy for the company became stressing the sale of its private labeled goods through a variety of marketing mechanisms, including regional radio and television advertising. Since its private label name was the same as the corporate name, it received free institutional advertising as well. Revenue and profitability increased substantially over the following two years.

A floppy disk manufacturer sliced up its business along the lines of technology and found that it made a much greater return on its downstream technology of burnishing and packaging the disks. Manufacture of the blank disks, called "cookies" by industry insiders, not only generated a low return but could easily be subcontracted.

A juice manufacturer in Europe was about to liquidate its small bottle product line—the type of product you find in delicatessens. It had a 15% gross profit margin, as against 20% for liter bottles and 25% for aseptic cartons. However, analysis showed that the ROI of the small bottle line was 55%, while the other two lines had ROIs of only 15%. There were two reasons for these surprising results. First, the manufacture of the bottles was subcontracted, so no fixed assets or raw material inventory was invested (while the company operated large plants for its other lines). Second, the co-packer of the small bottles was located in Italy, where ninety-day payables terms are customary, and the bulk of the sales of the small bottle line was in Germany, where fifteen- to thirty-day terms are prevalent. The business unit was a cash machine. Upon discovering this, management developed a promotional campaign for the small bottle line, and today it is a big winner for them.

Profitability, not gross profit, is the name of the game.

CREATIVE COST REDUCTION

To remain cost-competitive today, cost reduction has to be constantly pursued even if you have an excellent ROE. Domestic and foreign competition forces you to have a profitability improvement strategy that continually takes bites out of your cost structure.

Retrenching is a top priority in all types of organizations, not just in manufacturing firms. For example, the World Bank is the international lender of communal funds from richer nations to poorer ones. In May 1987 it announced it had reorganized operations to cut its staff by 5%, saving $50 million a year. It did so because of complaints that it was inefficient and unresponsive.[3]

In television, where creativity often reigns, all companies are battling to keep costs down. "The game used to be spend in pursuit of a hit, but hits don't guarantee profits anymore," says MCA's television group president, Robert Harris. Lorimar–Telpictures Corp. has implemented a broad cost-containment program; Twentieth Century Fox Film Corp. has gone through major staff reductions; and even Universal Studios, known in the industry for its "deep pockets," is cutting back. Universal's lowest-cost hour-long program is *Simon & Simon*, at about $1.2 million per episode. The costs jump to $1.6 million for shows like *Murder, She Wrote*, and *Miami Vice*, which use big-name guest stars and elaborate stunts. Expect less action, and fewer actors and actresses, on television.[4] Even Apollo and Zeus, those two fearsome Dobermans on *Magnum, P.I.*, felt the budget cut. They used to earn $1,000 per week, but they are not regulars any more.

Organizing for Cost Reduction

Cost and asset reduction should be a part of any Creative Planning process. But when it is to be approached as a program on its own, I recommend that everyone in the company be charged with the responsibility. The essence of any cost reduction program is ideas. Ideas come from people. So wide participation in the program is essential.

1. *Top Management.* Senior executives should employ the ROI Ranking approach to identify major target areas. No longer should fat be confused with muscle. At this level of the organization, the cost and asset reduction options to consider are product line pruning, shifts in marketing strategy, organization streamlining, plant consolidation, and division divestiture. Top management's second responsibility is to participate on a Cost Improvement Committee, with a few second-tier managers also joining in. This committee reviews the ideas and proposals from the level below.

2. *All Exempt Employees.* Interdepartmental teams should be formed (perhaps of randomly selected employees) and assigned to cost and/or asset reduction goals. These surgical teams should be required to meet at least once per week on company time to brainstorm project ideas and solutions. The Creative Planning process is the ideal one for them to use, only this time focused on identifying and rectifying areas of waste, inefficiency, and ineffectiveness. The strategies the teams develop should be proposed to the Cost Improvement Committee for approval before the teams implement them.

3. *Hourly Employees.* You have two basic options at this level. You can implement a suggestion system program or form productivity teams of production and other hourly workers. If a suggestion system is used, make sure that foremen and supervisors benefit in some way from their workers' contributions. They in turn can assume the responsibility for reviewing ideas, once they have had some training in how to judge them. Moore Industries, a Sepulveda, California, manufacturer of control instrumentation for the process industries, instituted a program called "IDEAS" in 1988. IDEAS stands for "Improvement Demands Everyone's Awareness and Suggestions." In the first five weeks, management received 125 ideas,

and 167 more in the three months following. "Bursts of ideas come in after someone on the manufacturing floor is handed $200 in cash," Steve Wood, director of planning and the developer of the system, reports. Moore Industries uses three levels of rewards: (1) a token item just to say thanks for the idea, and a star next to the person's name on a display board, (2) gift certificates for four passes to the movies, dinner for two, et cetera, for anyone whose idea will be used but doesn't result in cost savings, and (3) $200 in cash plus an allocation of 25% of the first year's cost savings to the company's profit-sharing fund for cost-saving ideas (so everyone benefits).[5]

A second option is to use the quality circle format, but to focus most of the participant's efforts on cost reduction and time-saving ideas. A reward system of some kind should be put into place, offering both money and recognition. Don't underestimate the power of the latter. Toyota illustrates the incredible power of participation. In 1951, when it first started using quality circles, management received 789 suggestions and adopted 23% of them (0.2 per employee). In 1983, Toyota averaged 31.8 suggestions per employee, 1.6 million in total, and implemented 96% of them.[6]

Revamp Your Industry's Cost Structure

Sometimes it takes a total restructuring of the way the industry works for a company to achieve a major cost advantage. Medco Containment Services, Inc., by far the most profitable pharmaceutical mail order firm in the world, did just that to drug distribution. Medco had $500 million in sales in fiscal 1988, and more than $21 million in net income. Financial analysts forecast the company's net income to grow at the rate of 50% annually over the next three years.

Chief financial officer James Manning explained to me: "We offer significant savings to employers by reducing the cost of prescriptions to their health plan subscribers by 20 to 25%. We order large quantities of pharmaceuticals from manufacturers, receive prescriptions by mail, process them through our sophisticated computer system, and send the drugs directly to the person's home." Medco's focus is on "maintenance drugs," those used by a patient for a chronic condition. The company has a special program for prescriptions for acute conditions through a relationship with 50,000 pharmacies across the United States via a Medco plastic card.

The way Medco changed the economics of the drug distribution and retailing industry is shown in Exhibit 10–5. A big reduction in the cost of delivered pharmaceuticals to consumers is achieved by avoiding the costs

EXHIBIT 10–5

Medco's Cost Containment Edge (cost to employer per day of dispensed drug, before the employee–employer split)

COST ELEMENT	MAJOR MEDICAL THROUGH DRUG STORES	MEDCO THROUGH MAIL ORDER
Pharmaceutical	$0.68	$0.44
Administration	0.14	0
Dispensing fee	0	0.05
Waste	0.06	0.02
Utilization	0	0.07
Total Cost	$0.88	$0.58

of the conventional drug distribution system, including the necessary markups of wholesalers and retailers. A small offset to these savings is the cost of processing prescriptions on a centralized basis and the expense of mailing pharmaceuticals to peoples' homes.[7]

Take a close look at each step in the value chain of your industry—product and service development, sourcing, manufacturing, distribution, sales, and customer service. Are there any ways to significantly reduce the cost or assets of these steps by breaking industry tradition? If so, it could enable you to achieve the following objective.

Become the Low-Cost Producer

The top managements of many high-quality manufacturers are insisting that their companies become their industry's low-cost producer. General Electric, Procter & Gamble, Compaq Computer, Citicorp, and many others follow this philosophy. As will be discussed in Chapter 12 on understanding the competition, management must study the cost structure of all its competitors to make sure it has the lowest.

One way is to mandate it. Anthony J. F. O'Reilly, the CEO of H.J. Heinz, has long been warning his managers, "The party is over," and threatens to quit manufacturing! The company is selling brands and tastes, he insists, and with strong quality audits, its products could be manufactured by others who have excess capacity. O'Reilly reports: "We discuss this with our factory managers, and it creates a new level of constructive tension."[8] I'm sure it does.

Downsize the Company

In lieu of eliminating all manufacturing facilities, many companies have consolidated facilities by as much as 50%. Heinz, for example, shut down sixteen major plants between 1978 and 1986 while increasing revenue 8% annually and, more importantly, net earnings 15%.

Caterpillar, Inc. bounced back from huge losses in 1984 to respectable profitability in a soft industry by slashing its work force by 40%, closing nine domestic plants, and doing more manufacturing overseas. Management figures it reduced costs by 25%. It is shooting for 15% more by 1990, mostly by a sweeping modernization program in its thirty remaining factories worldwide.

Even the U.S. Army is downsizing. A twelve-member government commission in 1988 rolled out a plan to close eighty-six military installations, partially close five, and realign fifty-four more. The Defense Department Commission on Base Realignment and Closure estimates the savings would reach $5.6 billion over twenty years.

Expense/Asset Ranking

I am always amazed when I see the CEO of an organization begin a cost reduction program by putting out the edict for employees to cut back on office supplies and subscriptions. These two cost elements invariably amount to less than 1% of total costs. A commonsense approach is to list all costs and expense categories from highest to lowest. Do the same for assets. Concentrate on the largest items. A 5% reduction in a cost that is 20% of sales will add a full 1% to return on sales. A 20% reduction of a cost that is 1% of sales will add only 0.2% to ROS.

Slash Overhead

After eliminating inefficient plants and other assets, the next place to look for economies is overhead. An *Industry Week* survey published in July 1988 found 78% of the respondents to be seriously concerned about overhead costs, and 92% making determined efforts to cut them. Factory burden rates frequently run 25% of direct labor costs, and sometimes reach the 350% level.[9] It takes management to manage management. As a result, overhead people propagate themselves. Known as "organizational creep," the more people your organization hires, the more it needs. And worse, the more bureaucratic it becomes.

Countless major organizations have dramatically cut back the size of their formerly bloated corporate offices. Staff people are farmed out to the divisions that most use their services, are taken off the payroll and used on a consulting basis, or are laid off. Only the most essential departments, and in small size, are retained. Exxon went through a wrenching restructuring and pumped up profits. The head count was reduced 30% in two years because of organizational cutbacks and divestitures. CEO Lawrence G. Rawl says, "People worked like beavers to generate reams of information." It was a burden rather than a strategic weapon. Some managers spent all their time preparing reports. Rawl confesses, "I didn't read them at all, and I don't think anybody did." Now at Exxon, a less formal management style speeds up decisions.[10]

Evaluate your company's overhead with the aim of significantly reducing it. Keep in mind that top management people must do it, or a raider will do it for them. The best approach to an overhead head count cutback is through task analysis: (1) identify the roles of each person, (2) assess the importance of each task, (3) design how it ideally should be done, (4) define the cost and benefit of it, (5) determine where the task should best be done (at corporate, in a division, outside the organization), and (6) make decisions.

There are many more methods for reducing costs and improving profitability. Additional ones will emerge in the remaining chapters on such topics as low-cost market positioning, competitor cost analysis, manufacturing productivity, cost of quality, organizational streamlining, corporate restructuring, and turnaround management. Operating lean is the order of the day in all areas of institutions.

11

Market Positioning

THEODORE Levitt, editor of the *Harvard Business Review*, stressed in his book *The Marketing Imagination:* "There can be no effective corporate strategy that is not marketing oriented, that does not in the end follow this unyielding prescript: The purpose of a business is to create and keep a customer."[1] To be in business, you have to be able to deliver something needed by customers, and be able to persuade them to buy it. If you can do so at a cost less than the price customers will pay, you make a profit.

Competitors complicate this simple model. Their presence requires you to have a distinctive competence, a reason customers will buy from you rather than them. The usual way is to demonstrate to customers that your products and services are a better value than your competition's. The second, more challenging way, is to create new customers—or entirely new markets—by identifying and satisfying unfulfilled needs. The purpose of this chapter is to show you how to do both, and thereby win in your marketplace.

EVERY ORGANIZATION NEEDS IT

I cannot think of any organization, whether or not its mission is to make a profit, that does not require effective marketing. Some recent newcomers to the marketing game include hospitals, accountants, lawyers, sports franchises, public utilities, even religion. For example:

1. *Hospitals Expand Branding.* American Medical International in late 1986 was the second investor-owned hospital system to undertake a branding campaign (Humana was the first in early 1986). Its television campaign tells consumers that the quality of its doctors sets it apart from other health care providers. Its theme: "Our doctors make the difference."

2. *Law Firms Position Themselves.* An advertisement in a New York subway in 1985 read, "Had an accident? We come to you in your home or hospital. No fee unless successful. Se habla español." Corporate law firms are doing the same. Paul Erickson, a former chief operating officer of a major law firm and now a consultant, explains: "Today, law firms have to position themselves and each of their individual practices. As in investment banking, heavy hitters are needed in the practices you want to stress. This brings up profitability of practices, allocation of resources, and other marketing issues."[2]

3. *Peter Ueberroth, Marketer.* Borrowing a technique he used to promote the Los Angeles Olympics, Ueberroth began in 1986 a program of national sponsorship of Major League Baseball (MLB). The purpose was to help teams in smaller markets find enough fans to be profitable. In the program, national firms sponsor the game of baseball, not individual teams.

4. *College Admissions Marketing.* With well over half a million fewer eighteen-year-olds in 1985 than there were five years earlier, university recruiters stepped up their direct mail and other promotional efforts. Hundreds have enshrined themselves on videotape, the usual format being a ten-minute overview that sugar-coats campus life. Some are pretty objective, though, such as the U.S. Military Academy. Its movie includes an upperclassman shouting at a nervous plebe (freshman). I guess this qualifies prospects as well.

Organizations of all types are finding they must become aggressive, creative marketers to survive in the hot competitive, cost- and quality-conscious environment of the late 1980s and early 1990s. Those without a well-thought-out strategic marketing plan may not be around in the mid-1990s.

MARKETING INNOVATION

What aspects of the marketing function can benefit from an injection of creativity and innovation? All of them. As shown in Exhibit 11–1, strategic marketing has three distinct phases, each with a different charter:

EXHIBIT 11–1

Strategic Marketing Management

Focus	MARKETING STRATEGY	MARKETING MANAGEMENT	MARKETING IMPLEMENTATION
	• Identify niches • Market positioning • Plan priorities	• Channel selection • Marketing organization • Marketing mix	• Marketing communications • Sales • Service
1. Challenge	*Where* to compete	*How* to compete	*Compete*
2. Time frame	Long	Medium	Short
3. View of environment	Constantly changing	Stabilized	Constant
4. Opportunities sought	New products and markets	New ways to attack	New customers
5. Communication flow	Bottom-up/ Outside-in	Top-down/ Bottom-up	Top-down/ Inside-out
6. Impact of creativity	*Highest*	*Medium*	*Lowest*

Copyright © 1988 Strategic Action Associates, Walnut Creek, Calif.

1. *Marketing Strategy. Where* to compete and *with what* are the challenges. One or more market niches are targeted with existing and new value-added products, a strategic marketing plan with priorities is formulated, and your products and services are uniquely positioned. The time frame is long and the environment is assumed to be changing. Of the three phases, this one requires the greatest amount of creativity.

2. *Marketing Management. How* to compete is the question. Channels of distribution are selected. Then a marketing/sales organization is put into place, and the marketing mix (price, type of advertising and promotion, et cetera) is determined. Creativity is particularly needed to match the marketing organization to the opportunities being pursued, and to keep the strategy flexible and responsive so emerging opportunities can be capitalized on.

3. *Marketing Implementation. Who* specifically to go after, and getting them to purchase, is the task. Advertising and other marketing communications vehicles are employed, the sales force is trained and directed, and customer service strives to keep customers happy. These are normally top-down directed activities. They don't leave a lot of room for creativity. However, superior performance even at the implementation stage requires innovation.

These three activities overlap and are highly interdependent. Finding a niche and positioning, for example, go hand in hand. You have to identify your most attractive markets, yet the attractiveness of your market depends on the positions you have, or could develop, in them. Or the markets you target (at least in the short term) should be determined partly by where your distribution is strongest, but you should develop your most effective distribution capability in your most attractive markets.

As we discussed in earlier chapters, imaginative thinking is not linear. It is holistic in nature. You can break up the problem into pieces and look at them separately, but the true breakthrough ideas of which business coups are made come from reassembling the pieces in a new way. Speaking of business coups, lets look at how a company located in northwest Houston goes about its market planning.

MARKET PLANNING AT
COMPAQ COMPUTER

Compaq Computer Corporation is known for its unique line of high-performance personal computers for the business market. But what this company is really expert at is marketing. It targets a market, identifies customer needs, translates them into superior product concepts, develops the products, launches them into the market, and provides outstanding product support. The planning process at Compaq Computer demonstrates many qualities that are worth emulating at other companies, high-tech or not. Fred Cutler, director of strategic marketing, described its highly effective system to me in July, 1987 this way:

> Our system is really product/market planning rather than strategic planning. The reason is that we have an extremely tight focus on a single market: users of PC hardware, possibly broadened to be called PC workstations because some of our units are approaching minicomputer capability. Furthermore, we have one method of distribution—through dealers—not through OEMs or direct sales. We do have people looking at related product areas such as peripherals, but it is a minimal effort. We consider the defocusing effect of any of these other areas very strongly.
>
> This consistency is central to our strategy. It gives us a competitive advantage over IBM and Apple, because we play against their weakness—their breadth, their lack of focus (they are also in peripherals, software, et cetera). As a result, we are less bureaucratic. We can make decisions and move faster. We have to be better than IBM, not

just an alternative. We have close to 10% of the worldwide PC market and our goal is to have 20% to 30%. To do this we have to constantly improve our position as a performance/technological leader.

Our overall planning process is market-driven. We use a three-year planning system that is updated every six months. Step one is to assess customer needs: what they do with, and want to do with, a PC. This defines the kinds of products possibly needed. Then we define alternative concepts in one-paragraph descriptions with line drawings and screen them with focus groups. As these proceed through our process they become more definitive with specific features, how they work, and their weight and size.

Year three in our plan portrays these rough concepts. Year two details the concepts and engineering feasibility. Year one presents next year's products which still have to be fine-tuned with additional customer feedback. In addition, our plans describe the competitive environment, technology trends, market and economic situation, changing needs of customers, and our financial forecasts.

Once concepts are developed, they are handed off to the Product Marketing Group, six to nine months before introduction. They handle final refinement of the product, pricing, and the market introduction strategy. After the product is introduced, another marketing group takes over: Product Management. They handle sales optimization, cost reduction, and product support.

There is a strong intent to have flexibility and informality as part of our culture. As I said, this is one of our primary strategic advantages.[3]

Compaq Computer is an outstanding example of a company that found a niche and filled it. And refilled it again and again as market needs presented themselves and technological capabilities kept expanding. Let's now discuss how to go about finding *your* niche.

A NICHE HUNT

The object of niche marketing is to focus your business resources on one or more opportunities (the fewer the better) that give you the most profitable growth. What makes this possible is that you are avoiding a thundering herd of competitors. Finding a niche entails identifying and then successfully targeting a specific class of customer with a single product or family of them. This combination is commonly called a product/market segment, and each such opportunity is defined by two parameters:

1. A customer group, with a need, or needs, to be satisfied

2. The product and/or service to be supplied, with the benefits they will convey

The best way to search for niches is to break down your overall market into individual segments. Michael Porter in his book *Competitive Advantage* stresses the need for imagination in the segmentation process: "Identifying segmentation variables is perhaps the most creative part of segmenting an industry." He goes on to say, "Segmentation must go beyond conventional wisdom and accepted classification schemes. The greatest opportunity for creating competitive advantage often comes from *new* ways of segmenting, because a firm can meet true buyer needs better than competitors or improve its relative cost position."[4]

Your objective is to develop a segmentation scheme that is unique to the industry. Adhering to the creative principle that quantity yields quality, your initial objective should be to slice up your market in as many ways as possible. In this way you can identify unfilled niches—roads less traveled. Or if the traffic is already heavy, new ways to serve customer needs in the existing ones.

Industrial Market Niches

Market segmentation is an approach that has been used extensively by successful corporations serving commercial markets since the early 1970s. Yet I am constantly amazed at the number of medium-sized and even large companies that treat all of their customers and prospects the same—with the same product line, marketing strategy, distribution channels, and promotional support. Let's start with the most common segmentation schemes and work toward the more creative ones.

The most frequent way companies selling to other businesses break customers down is by size. Large accounts receive more attention. Key accounts, or house accounts as they are sometimes called, are frequently sold through direct sales efforts from the home office. Medium-size accounts are the responsibility of the company's sales force or an outside sales rep network. Small accounts are often handled by distributors.

Geographical segmentation is the next most often used method. This is usually a necessity simply because various territories or countries are served by different outside sales organizations. Calculating market share and evaluating your competition on a geographic basis can be enlightening. In working with a national food service manufacturer that sold to fast food chains, restaurants, and hospitals, we were able to determine that this manufacturer's share of the Northeastern U.S. market was substantially below its average in other territories. A concentrated push in that region helped the company steadily increase revenue and profit.

A simple increase in sophistication can be achieved by segmenting customers by industry. Frequently, each industry has different product needs, quality requirements, price sensitivity, and growth prospects. In working with a medium-size supplier of temporary personnel, for example, we found that prospects that passed on the cost of temporary personnel to their own customers—consultants, accounting firms, law firms, architects—were the least price-sensitive and therefore the most profitable. Also, supplying personnel with particular industry experience (so that they had specific skills, understood the terminology, et cetera) gave this firm a competitive edge.

Technology capability is an important variable. Certain classes of customers are technology leaders while others are followers. In the 1970s and early 1980s petrochemical companies purchased the most technologically advanced and accurate electronic and pneumatic control systems, while food manufacturers got by with far more rudimentary ones. In the late 1980s, however, food companies began installing the state-of-the-art digital control systems, complete with "smart transmitters," in an effort to increase manufacturing productivity and flexibility.

Another way to identify niches is to segment your commercial market by your customer's buying factors: product performance, quality, service, delivery, price sensitivity, and others. Different strategies can be designed for each segment. Many times the segments are horizontal—they cut across industries. U.S. textile mills did this in order to deal with an onslaught of foreign competition. While modernization efforts increased the industry's productivity more than 20% between 1982 and 1987, making it cost-competitive with Japan and Italy, it is still at a 30% to 40% disadvantage with newly industrialized countries (NICs) for such products as lightweight shirting. Domestic mills, therefore, are concentrating on markets requiring high-end materials like industrial fabrics, and products such as sheets and towels, which require little direct labor. They are also focusing on markets where quick delivery and service give them an edge.[5]

Identifying common customer applications that are not being fully served, or not with an ideal product or service, can lead to opportunities. Digital Equipment Corporation virtually invented the concept of the "departmental computer" with the introduction of its MicroVax line. It is a small minicomputer that can be linked to others or to a large central processor. DEC put price pressure on IBM, Hewlett-Packard, and other minicomputer companies whose systems were larger and more costly to manufacture.

Gensler and Associates, the leading architectural firm in the United States, described in Chapter 2, got its start by attacking an underserved customer application. Professional architects viewed interior design as a necessary evil. Art Gensler says that in the 1960s designers working on the inside of a building would ask, "when do we get to do *real* architecture?" Gensler's firm brought professionalism and enthusiasm to the interior segment and later expanded into building exteriors as well.[6]

Isolating your "ideal customers" can lead to profits. Try defining win–win prospects, those that (1) most need what you have to offer and (2) are potentially the most profitable to you. Be specific. A major commercial building contractor I worked with had a marketing policy of serving a limited number of ideal customers. It defined them as major corporations that (1) have a small or, preferably, no in-house construction staff, (2) are growth-oriented so that they provide a steady volume of work, even in poor economic times, (3) are financially strong, (4) are motivated more by quality of construction rather than by cost, (5) prefer negotiated fees rather than open bidding, and (6) are susceptible to the company's relationship selling approach. The company's strategy is to be its customer's surrogate in-house construction department. They usually get 100% of their clients' business, not the norm in the commercial contracting business.

A simple and often overlooked source of target market segments is right in your company's own order book. Frequently you can catch a new one that is just emerging. It could be a totally new type of customer or a new application by an existing customer. DG Mouldings is the national market share leader in prefinished mouldings and trim for homes. In one of its planning sessions I was facilitating, a sales manager mentioned that it had just received an order from a picture frame manufacturer. Art Ramey, vice president of marketing, pursued all major producers. He convinced the picture frame industry of the value of plastic over wood and metal. Five years later picture framing was a very attractive niche for the company in which it had significant market share.[7]

Consumer Market Niches

Niche hunting in consumer markets involves similar approaches. In fact, segmentation was employed in consumer marketing decades before it became accepted in the industrial products sector. The two primary segmentation vehicles consumer marketers use are demographics and life-styles (also called psychographics). Most consumer products are aimed with one of these two segmentation schemes, or a combination of the two. Demographics includes such factors as age, sex, household income, family size, education, occupation, nationality, geographic location—just about any aspect of the population that can be quantified. Life-style factors, though, are qualitative. They deal with the way people act, their values, their attitudes, their needs, how they make purchase decisions, and other aspects.

Many successful companies focus their entire organizations on a specific demographic group. For example, the American Express card was developed to be the best possible credit card for upscale, affluent business people. It was designed with a number of unique features for the traveling professional such as no preset credit limit, and mailing bills with copies of actual receipts so customers could substantiate expense reports or tax records. The business segment has been very profitable for American Express. In contrast, Sears, Roebuck has a demographic problem with its Discover card. Despite the fact that 19 million cards have been issued, use is low. Discover card users do not spend anywhere near the levels of American Express card-holders.

The one constant about demographics is they are always changing. Take age patterns for instance. The post–World War II Baby Boom generation has matured. The U.S. Census Bureau reports that as of July 1, 1986, the fastest-growing segment of the population is the middle-age group, ages 35–44, which grew 29% since 1980. The second fastest-growing is the eighty-five and over group, followed closely by the 75–84-year-olds. Home health care is one market that is exploding, in part because of the growth of the older generation.

Changing demographics and life-styles create problems as well as opportunities. Take, for example, the direct selling industry companies such as Avon, Fuller Brush, Amway, and Shaklee. With nearly 55% of all women now working outside the home, hardly anyone is around to buy anything. Besides, selling door to door without immediate delivery is not easy in this era of convenience and instant gratification.

PLANNING FOR GROWTH

Thus far I have presented various ways to slice up your market in search of possible niches. But how do you decide upon what to attack, and your priorities? Map out your markets by preparing product/market segmentation charts. Use different market segmentation schemes such as by customer geographical region, industry, size, buying factor, and any relevant others. These should show how much of each of your (and your competitors') products are sold to each market segment.

With your segmentations in hand, assign one of three categories of attractiveness to each product/market segment: high, medium, or low. Here are some criteria that indicate you should focus resources on it:

- You have high sales volume, market share, and/or profitability in the segment.
- You have a strong or developing reputation in it.
- A number of your products serve the same segment.
- You expect the segment to grow (although growth invites competition, so you'd better not be late for the party).
- Customers in the segment have unmet needs, and you have identified the solution.
- There is a single major competitor serving the segment possessing one or more weaknesses that can be exploited.
- A large number of competitors serve the segment, no one of which is dominant.
- Other criteria for selecting opportunities and allocating resources, as discussed in Chapter 6, "Strategic Decision Making," which indicate it is an opportunity.

The selection of product/market segments is as much an art as it is science. In applying the above criteria, many times you have to arrive at tentative conclusions and test the strategies on a small scale first to see if they work. Market research can tell you only so much. Over time, however, you should be able to prioritize your targets of opportunity quite solidly. Your goal is a time-phased, market-driven plan of implementation. With your market segment priorities in hand, the next challenge is to develop a way to stand out from the competition.

MARKET POSITIONS

At the essence of your marketing strategy—in fact, of your overall corporate strategy—is how you want your company and products to be perceived in the marketplace. It is the most crucial element of the way you distinguish yourself from your competitors. All other aspects of your marketing effort should flow out of it—advertising, merchandising, direct mail, public relations, pricing, packaging, and sales. Study the market leader in any industry, consumer or industrial. You will find two things. First, its image is clear, concise, and hard-hitting. Second, it is in tune with the most important buying factor of a majority of customers. Here are a few examples of clear, successful positionings:

- Federal Express: "Absolutely, positively overnight."
- Joel Hyatt: "We took the fear out of legal fees."
- 7-Up: "The un-cola."
- Lite Beer: "Everything you ever wanted in a beer and less."
- Air Cal: "First class leg-room at coach prices."
- Nyquil: "The 'nighttime' cold remedy."

In industrial markets, many successful postionings revolve around such intangibles as quality, reliability, and service. The ads IBM ran in the 1950s are still remembered today by most business people: "IBM means service." In a senior executive seminar that I was leading, an executive vice president of a major firm told us that IBM should change its name to "International Business Service." It sounded good until someone pointed out the acronym: IBS. Somehow, it did not fit.

What was the number one issue in corporate computer systems in the late 1980s? Total compatibility, allowing different machines to talk with one another. Who first filled the need and became the industry's sensation? Digital Equipment Corporation. DEC's ads in 1987 positioned it clearly: "DEC has it now. Enterprise Computing. The corporate-wide computing strategy for every part of your business strategy."

The Positioning Process

The process of positioning your products and services is highly creative, because you have to synthesize input from outside your company and from within. The starting point is to determine the strengths and weaknesses of your company's image vis-à-vis the competition. To do this adequately, you need to undertake some in-depth research with your customers, your competitor's customers, and such other audiences as the investment community, industry experts, and the industry press. Have them

- Describe your company in one or two sentences, particularly the image they have of it.

- Do the same for each of your company's key competitors.
- List and rank the most important things customers take into consideration in selecting a supplier—their buying factors.
- Compare your company with the competition on each of the most important buying factors.
- Explain the primary reasons customers would consider switching suppliers.
- Describe any unmet needs or pet peeves they have concerning any or all suppliers.
- Ask them to fantasize about the ideal supplier and the image it would have.
- Have them tell about any trends in the marketplace or technology that would change any of the above.

These questions and the creative techniques described in earlier chapters will help you to form a composite picture of how your company and its products are perceived in the marketplace. The next step is to perform an internal analysis to clarify how your employees view your company. Start with the CEO, then officers and managers, and then a selection of employees at lower levels. Be sure to include some employees from any department that has contact with customers: sales, service, billing, accounts receivable, and others. Use the same questions you asked of your customers, and add a few more:

- What are the company's values? What do we stand for?
- What are our company's success factors?
- What are our goals and objectives?
- Why do customers buy from us rather than the competition?
- When do we lose orders to the competition?
- How should we be perceived by our customers?

Step three is to contrast what your customers said with what your employees think. This is best done in a meeting with the top management team in a format as described in Chapter 9. Review how your company is perceived. Then brainstorm what the ideal positioning would be in the market for a company selling your type of products and services. If there are substantial differences, you should discuss and decide what positioning you should target, and the strategies and action plans needed to close the gap. In most cases, companies need only to refine, clarify, and communicate better their existing position. In some cases, however, the image of a company and its products have to be overhauled.

Reposition When Necessary

DG Mouldings, the company I mentioned earlier in this chapter, repositioned itself in order to maintain its record of profitable growth. In the late 1970s it was perceived as a supplier of plastic mouldings for use with low-cost wood paneling for homes and manufactured housing. When the demand for wood paneling dropped dramatically, management developed a strategic plan which called for repositioning prefinished mouldings as a decorator item. Art Ramey states, "We pulled our products out of the lumber department in home centers and began merchandizing them as stand-alone decorator products or as complements to wallpaper. All wallpaper has three background colors, which we match—blue, almond, or white. We rarely merchandise with paneling any more." This repositioning, combined with the development of a wide variety of trim parts for door, window, and other building materials manufacturers, has made the company the world's largest prefinished mouldings manufacturer.[8]

Many high-cholesterol foods are trying to be repositioned in the late 1980s to change the direction of their sales. For example, beef consumption dropped 33% between 1975 and 1985. The Beef Industry Council launched a huge campaign in 1987 with the theme, "Real food for real people." The National Pork Producers Council, not to be left behind, portrays pork as "the other white meat." Whether these attempted repositionings can reverse the sales trends remains to be seen.

ENTRY POSITIONING

What is needed to penetrate an existing segment or to create an entirely new one? Primarily it is a unique positioning seen by customers as a significantly better value for the price. This is where imagination comes in. It's a tall order to become unique and superior for the price, but it is a must. Even major corporations have learned this the hard way. Procter & Gamble wanted to muscle into the growing orange juice category in the early 1980s with its Citrus Hill brand. It even had a new patented manufacturing process that improved the taste and aroma of orange juice—slightly. But consumers did not discern the quality improvement. P&G's entry strategy came down to promotion muscle and dollars, with unprecedented levels of couponing to consumers and discounts to retailers. The end result was mediocre sales and red ink for the company and most of its competitors. When P&G finally did develop genuinely unique positionings with its Lite and calcium-fortified lines, its market penetration and profitability improved.

What are the best positions to take in order to enter a segment? There is no sure-fire formula. Two effective ways, though, are (1) over the top—or, as some many marketers call it, skimming the cream—and (2) under the rest—or, as I call it, Less R Us.

Skimming the Cream

This is my favorite entry point for a new business or product line, whether in the consumer or the industrial sector. My rationale stems from seven factors:

1. The price is high, which means you have more room for manufacturing cost inefficiencies as you ramp up production.
2. The margins are usually higher than in lower-priced segments of the same market.
3. The market size is often relatively small, which means you will have to contend with fewer, if any, major competitors.
4. There is something nice about claiming you are the highest-quality product or service.
5. The high-end market seems to have resilience even in recessionary times.
6. Demographic shifts due in part to the two-income household are helping the class market become a mass market.
7. The entire world is shifting to an emphasis on quality and reliability. It is an absolute requirement, for example, if you want to penetrate the Japanese market.

To visualize possible service offerings at the high end, describe the ideal product and service (refer back to Chapters 3 and 4) for the segment of your targeted market that needs the highest possible quality. How could standard products and services be enhanced to appeal to a highly discriminating customer? What additional features could be included? Assume price to be of no importance. I call this the "if you have to ask the price you can't afford it" category. One consumer product category that exploded in the 1980s is the super-premium ice cream segment. While the ice cream category as a whole has been relatively flat, this upper stratosphere segment has been charging ahead at 20% annual growth. Haagen-Dazs was the company that fueled the growth of the segment, and the company exploded in size from a small, regional producer to a national force. Kraft's Frusen Gladje brand was another successful entry. Its advertised positioning sums up this category: "Enjoy the guilt."

Mrs. Fields did the same for chocolate chip cookies. It offers the ideal cookie—fresh baked, all natural ingredients, and warm. Cookies over two hours old, and cold, are given to the Red Cross. Starting in 1977 the company has grown to six hundred stores worldwide in 1987, all company-owned. Interestingly, the "soft cookie" segment at retail, created by packaged goods companies in response to the explosion in cookie shops, is not doing as well. Packaged soft cookies are just not the same as a fresh baked, ultra-high-quality cookie that warms the mouth as it tingles the palate.

The trend to gourmet foods is another example of companies taking the high road. But there is no simple recipe for transforming a mass brand into a class brand. Brand images become so ingrained that it is nearly impossible to change people's perceptions. Usually an established brand leader has to come out with a whole new brand in order to attack the high-end segment.

A similar approach can generate profits in industrial markets, although price is more of a factor here. But corporations are certainly willing to pay for top quality as long as it adds value to their own operations or products. Which classes of your industrial customers demand quality more than the others? How do they define quality? What ideal products and services can be provided to them? In aluminum extrusions, for example, electronics manufacturers have very tight tolerances on heat sinks (the parts that dissipate heat) and therefore are willing to pay a premium. Specialty steel is another example. Stainless, tool, and superalloys account for less than 2% of industry volume, but 10% of industry sales dollars. When the carbon steel industry was hemorrhaging in the mid-1980s, many specialty steel companies were still profitable.

Tandem Computers, Inc. provides another example of how an ideal product can be designed for a market segment requiring "perfect" quality. In 1974 Jim Treybig realized that certain industries, such as airlines and banks, could not tolerate downtime in their computer systems. Tandem's solution was fault-tolerant computers. They avoid downtime by linking two or more central processing units so if there is a failure in one, the work is automatically transferred to the other, while the faulty parts are repaired. Tandem's revenues in 1987 increased 35% to slightly over $1 billion, yielding a bottom line of $105 million.

Less R Us

Entering a market via the low road is another favored way to attack an industry. But just coming in with a low price with the hope of later raising it to make a profit is not the answer to anything but a way to go into Chapter 13. You have to redesign the business totally, stripping out substantial costs of manufacturing, marketing, and/or distribution. Only by doing this can you be reasonably assured of a profit when you have penetrated the market. Remember, industry leaders generally have the staying power to match your low price if you attack them in one of their high-priority markets. Assume that you will have to drop your price yet another 20% below your entry position to maintain your edge. If you can still make money at that level, you may have a genuine opportunity. Survival can depend on knowing when not to pick a fight.

The other major caution is not to eliminate quality while you are reducing costs. Some reasonable level of product or service performance has to be delivered no matter how low the price. Beware that a "cheap" positioning can kill a product in the 1980s and 1990s. The market is looking for reasonable quality at a low price, and superb quality at higher prices. The poor quality and service/low price market segment is nonexistent.

People Express attests to this point. Its redesign of the traditional airline was elegant: use low-cost, nonunion labor and pilots who wear many hats; employ a simplistic reservation system; fly older, depreciated aircraft; and offer a no-frills service. Its incredibly low prices initially attracted a lot of passengers. But it also attracted selective price cutting by the majors, nullifying some of its competitive advantage. This, combined with horrible service (and overexpansion), did it in. Travelers just wouldn't put up with the overbooked flights, frequent cancellations, and the airline's ability to instill new meaning into the term "no-frills."

With the downfall of People, a gap opened in the market: a low-priced airline that offers reasonable service. America West, with its hub in Phoenix, is attempting to fill it. Like other low-cost airlines, its employees are nonunion and wear many hats, and it uses fuel-stingy airplanes that require two pilots instead of three. But its passengers do not get bare-bones treatment. America West offers cocktails and free newspapers on every flight.

There are many examples of companies that have successfully stripped out costs and delivered a viable product or service. When the SEC deregulated stock transactions and eliminated the fixed rated system in 1974 in favor of negotiated fees, Charles Schwab repositioned his three-year-old brokerage firm. His market (and cost) positioning of no research, no advice, and no hand-holding has since revolutionized a venerable industry steeped in tradition. Yet the stripped-down personal service the company does provide is top quality: prompt, courteous, efficient, and accurate. What Schwab eliminated was the sales pressure, a prevalent pet peeve and a brilliant insight.

Crown Books is another example. "If you paid full price, you didn't buy it at Crown Books" is its position, and a clear one at that. Or take the residential real estate industry. Help-U-Sell is now the fifth largest real estate company in the United States, according to *Entrepreneur* magazine. Help-U handles all the technical details, advertises the home, and provides sales tools and advice. The owner shows the property and, upon closing, pays roughly half the normal 6% commission.

Some low-roaders have incredible staying power. One of the classics is Hormel's Spam, which turned fifty in 1987. Four billion cans of this legendary mystery meat have been sold since 1937, and sales are still growing at 3% a year. More than 100 million cans are sold each year, yet hardly anyone admits to eating it. Incredible, for a product that GIs called "the meat that failed its physical."[9]

The key to the Less R Us strategy, then, is to redesign the business to reduce costs dramatically but still preserve an acceptable, if not a high, level of quality.

EXPANDING SHARE

Once you have achieved an enviable position, increasing market share requires the same two principles that were successfully used to enter it: niche hunting and innovation. Why? Because if you don't, your competitors will. General Foods' strategy in the coffee market illustrates how to expand share. As the market leader, it entrenches itself by segmenting and resegmenting. GF offers a much wider variety of coffee brands and types than its competitors. Each brand is positioned for a different usage situation, so they aren't competing: Maxwell House for morning consumption, decaffeinated Sanka for the home, decaffeinated Brim for the office, and International Coffees for special occasions.

Finding new applications for existing brands is another approach. With overall coffee consumption down, Coca-Cola is trying to establish itself as an eye-opening alternative with its "Coke in the Morning" radio and billboard campaign. Coca-Cola's initial focus is on the south, where soft drinks are already somewhat accepted as a morning beverage. Coke reports that 12% of the soft drinks consumed in 1987 were in the morning, versus 9% ten years ago.

Avoiding a commodity status where customers distinguish competing products merely on a price basis is the challenge in mature markets. In the $2.5 billion consumer battery market, for example, Duracell, with a 30% share in 1987, added "freshness dates" to its packaging. Ralston Purina's Eveready division, with 50% of the market, came out with "The Conductor," a full line of premium-price, high-output alkaline batteries designed specifically for the audio equipment market.

New brands are created so that the positioning of the mother brand can remain in tact. This is particularly important when trying to reach out to new segments. Not long ago General Motors' Cadillacs were status symbols. However, in an attempt to respond to the energy crisis and the resultant cry for fuel efficiency, and to introduce production economies, it downsized the cars and gave them the same "platform" as some of GM's other models, its so-called E/K cars. Besides trying to squeeze traditional customers into the smaller cars, they hoped to convert affluent young buyers who were favoring expensive, sportier imports. Sales of GM's luxury cars, which carry the highest profit margins, plummeted in 1986 and 1987. Instead of simultaneously penetrating two market segments, its line of luxury cars did not fit well into any niche. So select your target markets carefully and use a singular strategy for each. With this in mind, your next challenge is to structure your marketing organization.

CREATIVE SELLING

Selling is not usually considered a job requiring a lot of imagination. However, developing a strategy for a particular account can require just as much ingenuity as conceiving a plan of attack for an entire class of customer. All of the concepts I have discussed thus far apply, only on a smaller scale.

Sales strategy has to do with identifying all the decision makers and influencers, developing a winning positioning versus the competition, and cementing a long-term relationship. Sales tactics—that which is done when a salesperson is face to face with a customer, such as making the presentation, overcoming objections, and employing various closes—kick in later.

Program Selling

I first came across the term "program selling" when I was doing strategic planning in the aerospace industry in the late 1970s. This approach was used by the most successful companies selling either to the military or to Boeing and other mainframe manufacturers. The first step with each account is to identify who the key decision makers are as well as anyone else who could influence the decision. A separate positioning should then be developed for each person in terms of his or her viewpoint and personal stake in the buying process. Certainly the prospect's chief engineer, design engineer, systems integrator, maintenance engineer, purchasing agent, and top management all have separate motivations.

Sometimes a single sales person can cover all these people, and at other times a team selling approach is better. Intel used this full coverage strategy in winning a major contract at Ford Motor Company for the microprocessor used in electronic carburetion systems. In the face of fierce competition, Intel's management got to know all key managers at Ford. In addition to superior design, Intel's management commitment to Ford was a deciding intangible factor.[10]

The Sales Sequence

Understanding the specific steps prospects go through in making a purchase can give you a substantial edge. I performed a market survey for a major manufacturer of earthquake detection systems and found out, among other things, that the general steps customers follow in selecting a supplier are

1. Develop a preliminary design for the system.
2. Specify minimum requirements that have to be met.
3. Talk to vendors of instrumentation to see what is available.
4. Call industry experts, a limited number in this industry, for their recommendations of which vendors have the best equipment, service, and maintenance.
5. Ask preferred vendors to quote on the system.
6. Evaluate the proposals and make a selection.

We brainstormed how to help the customer lean toward my client's instrumentation at each step in the process. For example, this company dramatically stepped up its direct marketing, personal contact, and engineering support to industry experts in order to capitalize on word-of-mouth influence.

ROI Selling

Quality and reliability are essential selling points. But what frequently is left out of the sales presentation is how the product or service can increase a customer's return on investment. Texas Instruments has been advertising its "total cost of ownership" positioning to OEMs for good reason. TI's quality and service can be translated into cost or asset reductions for its customers in incoming inspection, inventory, system manufacturing, OEM warranty, and end-user maintenance. The true cost of integrated circuits, TI claims, is five times the initial purchase price.

Another example is how Safety Systems, a leading manufacturer of airplane fire protection systems, positions its product with the Air Force. It has proved that its patented continuous-length thermal detectors are incapable of giving a false alarm of a fire or overheat situation. Competitor units are good, but not as reliable. Since a false alarm leads to an aborted mission, which is unacceptable and extremely expensive, Safety Systems gets its price, which is more than double what competitors charge.

Trojan Horse Strategy

Attacking major new accounts through the back door can be far more productive than frontal assaults, which can be repelled by entrenched competitors. The strategy is to gain a foothold through serving a small niche in potentially large accounts and later going after the big orders. Art Gensler, whom I mentioned earlier in this chapter, says, "I don't mind doing small jobs for big people." He calls it his "nibble away strategy." Gensler and Associates will take a small order (which most of his major competitors will ignore) from a large prospect as a way to prove the company's skill and service. For example, Gensler is expert in building design consultation, in which it evaluates another architect's work. This can lead eventually to the point where the client says, "Why don't you do it all?" Art Gensler says that his company once designed an elevator in an executive's house.

Apple Computer used the back door into the corporate market. Its direct assault failed in 1984, but it won big with a more subtle entry via desktop publishing. In 1987, Macintoshes and other computers and peripherals to businesses more than doubled to 45% of revenues and accounted for more than half of its profits. Interestingly, the sales were not generally to computer managers, the classic entry point, but to individual department managers who wanted to print fancy reports, brochures, and other documents. With both feet in the door, Apple is now selling more powerful Macs for spreadsheet and engineering workstation applications.

Everyone Sells

Many companies think that only salespeople sell. But the most progressive companies involve as many people as possible. The greater the contact with the customer, the more the company can creatively recognize and respond to customer needs. At IBM for example, job descriptions for all people, whether they are line or staff, describe the position's "customer connection," spelling out how the person fits into the sales and support system. IBM executives all have key customers assigned to them, albeit in conjunction with the local company sales rep.[11]

Serv-A-Portion, the country's largest manufacturer of portioned packaged condiments—those little packets of ketchup and mustard you find at McDonald's and elsewhere—uses the same concept. CEO Ron Kunkel had all senior executives manage one or more house accounts. So the company is in tune with customer needs, and highly innovative as a result.

KEEPING CUSTOMERS THROUGH SERVICE

Innovative approaches to closing sales will not keep your company growing profitably if you do not have repeat customers. Consider the cost of obtaining new customers at your company versus the cost of maintaining satisfied existing ones. The final aspect in the marketing equation is service. Just as with sales, I am speaking here not of the tactical but of the overall strategy for it. Management often focuses on the individual tasks—product reliability, delivery, support engineering, and customer relations—without regard to an integrated positioning (there's that word again) that can give the company a competitive edge. Here is the way to create a strategy for profitably delivering product support.

Defining Service Needs

Your first step is to determine what types and levels of service customers expect, and the costs to them if they do not get it. This is best done with a customer survey. It should not be conducted by your sales force or customer service department. Salespeople have a natural bias to overservicing, and customer service people may lack objectivity regarding their current performance.

It is crucial to distinguish between market segments in doing your survey, because different types of customers need various levels and types of service. In fact, this may help you segment your markets in a new way, or creatively uncover new niches. What you cannot afford to do is over-service some segments and underservice others.

While doing the survey, determine how you compare with your competition in each segment on each customer criterion. Defining your competitors' service positionings shows you what you are up against. For example, in the drug distribution market, McKesson Corporation, the industry leader, claims to fulfill totally 97% of its retailers' orders within forty-eight hours.

The second step is to assess the effectiveness of current service programs from the perspective of the providers. Cover with operating management such topics as

- The performance standards now in place and management's perception of how the company measures up
- The major types of customer complaints your company receives and how they are handled
- Areas where improvement should be made, and how it might be done
- The bottlenecks to providing perfect service, and possible ideal solutions
- How the company at present caters to the different needs of various market segments, if at all.

Choosing a Strategy

Compare the results of the two surveys. It can be highly enlightening. Soft points as well as company strengths will emerge. All possible strategy ideas for customer support should be collected. Then each one should be evaluated in light of (1) customer needs by segment, with the segments prioritized by level of attractiveness to the company, (2) the cost of providing the service level, (3) competitors' service levels, with an eye to both the minimal level needed to match them and the level needed to provide your company with an edge that will be perceived by customers, and (4) your company's total quality program, to be discussed in Chapter 14. Synthesizing an overall service strategy in the above manner can result in your company's adding a significant weapon to the corporate arsenal.

THREE THINGS TO REMEMBER

There were three recurring themes in this chapter. First, you cannot treat all customers alike, nor will they treat you and your competitors alike. You need to search out and focus on one or more specific niches in your total possible market. Second, in order to stand out from the competition, you need to position your company and its products in your market uniquely. You have to do the same in each niche you have targeted. Third, all aspects of your marketing strategy—distribution channels, organization, advertising, sales, and customer service—flow out of the first two.

How one views the market determines one's competition. We will now turn from customers to competitors.

12

Creating the Competitive Difference

TO stay one or more steps ahead of the competition, you need to know who they are and what they are up to. You also have to know yourself. In the words of philosopher Tsutomu Oshima:

> If you don't understand yourself, you will lose one hundred percent of the time. If you understand yourself, you will win fifty percent of the time. If you understand yourself and your opponent, you will win one hundred percent of the time.

The purpose of this chapter is to give you a framework for understanding your competitors so that you can develop a competitive advantage in the eyes of the people who count: customers. Understanding your competition is a fundamental aspect of strategy development and should be a component of every decision—whether it is to enter a new market, release a new product or service, construct a plant, or modify your existing strategy or tactics. Competitors can also be the ultimate smug control device.

WHO ARE YOUR COMPETITORS?

No self-respecting executive will admit to not knowing his competition. But many a company has more competitors than management thinks. Here are the five classes of competition you need to understand.

1. *Direct Competitors.* These are the easy ones to identify. They compete with you in the product and service areas where you are strongest. For example, Pepsi competes with Coke in the branded cola segment, along with other lesser-known brands. Semidirect competitors are the supermarket private label brands, which sell for considerably less.

2. *Peripheral Competitors.* Peripheral competitors sell products that are closely related to and can be directly substituted for yours. In Pepsi's case, this would include 7-Up, A&W Root Beer, and other brand name manufacturers of sodas. Again, we have to include the supermarket private label brands as well. Each company is trying for a bigger share of the stomach, trying to get consumers to drink more of one type of beverage and less of another.

3. *Indirect Competitors.* These competitors are not as obvious. They sell products to your customers that are in totally different categories but could be substituted for yours. Milk, juice, coffee, wine, and other beverages are Pepsi's indirect competitors. In some cases, indirect competitors can hurt you more than direct ones. Look at what fish and chicken did to suppliers of beef. And sometimes targeting an indirect competitor can be more rewarding than going after direct ones. Coca-Cola's campaign to attack the breakfast segment, the stronghold of coffee and juice, is an example.

4. *Emerging Competitors.* These companies are attempting to enter your product/market segment or a crucial peripheral one. They usually come in three basic forms. The first is the large company that is entering your industry segment via startup or acquisition, the latter being the most common now. The second is an indirect competitor that is broadening its product line and market segment focus, as Coca-Cola did with Sprite. The third is the startup that is entering your market. As will be covered in the next chapter on technology planning, this kind can be the biggest threat. It can also be a great source of ideas and acquisitions.

5. *Potential New Competitors.* These are companies that may enter your business. Some are logical candidates. If you were their CEO, you wouldn't hesitate to come after your company's market. Others you hear about through intelligence sources. They are either doing market research

in your industry or making an acquisition search. Knowing how to deal with them if they were to enter would put you way ahead. At the very least, they should be included in your contingency planning.

"We Have No Competitors"

Some organizations enjoy such a lock on their market segments that they appear to have no competitors, much as the Catholic Church controlled the dispensing of the Christian Sacraments in the Western world for centuries, and still does in some countries. (However, it is losing "market share" in South America, one of its biggest strongholds.) The *Wall Street Journal* is an example. In recent years it has seen indirect but strong competition from *Financial Times, Investor's Daily,* the *New York Times,* and even *USA Today.* The *Journal* has seen its circulation level out at 2 million while ad lineage has fallen, partly in response to rate hikes. The stock market crash didn't help. Staff shakeups have occurred at the Dow Jones unit, and cost-cutting is the order of the day.[1]

Unions have classically battled with management, but now it's union versus union in many regions. Interunion clashes are occurring more often as memberships shrink and they go after "new business." In Pittsburgh in 1984, for example, the United Steelworkers and the United Food & Commercial Workers battled over supermarket clerks and meatcutters who were members of the USW. District 15 director Andrew Palm said, "We're not backing down. We are going to take the food workers on, and let the best union win."[2]

WHAT YOU NEED TO KNOW

Expecting to know everything about your competition is unrealistic. So the first thing you need to do after identifying it is to glean two types of information: (1) what is readily available, largely from secondary sources, and (2) what could lead to changing your business strategies or tactics—critical competitive intelligence. Exhibit 12–1 presents the most important kinds for most businesses. Yes, this information can be gathered legally and ethically. You just need to know where to look and how to piece it together.

EXHIBIT 12–1

Critical Competitive Intelligence

At a minimum, you need to know the following about each of your competitors:

- Size—products and market share
- Emphasis—products and markets
- Strategies—past, present, and future
- Results—profitability and strategic
- Ownership—public, corporate, management—and its viewpoint
- Management—who, and its philosophies
- SWOT—strengths, weaknesses, opportunies, and threats
- Resources—their war chest, as well as that of investors
- Technologies—present ones and what's coming
- Operations—methods of manufacture, and costs and assets
- Market positioning—how customers view them
- New product plans—what they will release next
- Service—customer relations and guarantees

SOURCES OF COMPETITIVE INTELLIGENCE

Develop competitive profiles by piecing together many bits of information. Sometimes this is easy. In the 1960s and 1970s teams of Japanese executives and engineers toured American manufacturing plants, cameras in hand. Their information-gathering system was straightforward and effective. They used what they learned from us to beat us at our own game. You don't see many American companies conducting plant tours like that any more, so Japanese companies have found more subtle, but still highly effective, ways to collect competitive information. Most successful American firms use similar techniques. Here are a variety of them.

Easy Sources First

Quite a lot of information is available just for the asking. This is where you should start.

- *Information from the Competitor Itself.* If it is a public company, order annual reports, 10Ks, press packages, and any financial reports. (If it is a private company, get a Dun & Bradstreet report.) Other standard pieces of information include company catalogs, sales promotion sheets, advertisements, and newsletters.

- *Published Documents.* Industry surveys by market research and stockbrokerage firms may be available. Industry magazines frequently feature companies and their strategies. A subscription to the home town (or regional) newspaper (and a check with the local library) can yield in-depth articles on firms that would not show up in the trade press. A database search can also turn up articles.
- *Indirect Information Sources from Competitors.* These include speeches by their executives at association meetings, Rotary Clubs, and other nonindustry organizations. Articles in professional magazines by engineers, marketing managers, and other middle-level management can be quite revealing. And always gather as much information as possible at trade shows.
- *Government Sources.* Zoning, the Universal Commercial Code, environmental bureaus, and tax assessment offices have extensive information on local plants, sometimes including blueprints and lists of machinery. Federal patent filings can help you discern their technological direction. Aerial photographs of plants may be available from highway administrations or public works departments.

Ask Anyone Who Might Know

Getting primary information from people in the industry who are knowledgeable is highly effective.

- *Customers.* Superb sources, they can be asked to rate competitors against your company on key buying factors, reputation, positioning, and other strategic points. Depending on what you are after, it is sometimes better not to divulge your company affiliation so as not to bias them. (A consultant can be of great help here.)
- *Suppliers.* They are an excellent source of information on raw material trends and volumes, emerging technologies, financial strength of companies (from any receivables problems the suppliers have), company reputations, and other items.
- *Competitors Themselves.* Calling executives and managers of your competitors can often be an excellent way to get information. But this is best left to consultants. I am constantly amazed at what people will reveal if they are asked in the right manner.

Strategic Sleuthing

Sometimes, mild cloak-and-dagger techniques are called for. Here are three examples.

- *Plant Site Observations*. Simply watching a manufacturing or other type of facility can give you rough ideas of the number of employees, capacity utilization (from the percentage of parking spots used), number of shifts, and size of the plant (from pacing off the building). The number of trucks in and out over a period of time can yield raw material consumption and sales volume.
- *Product Serial Numbers*. Friendly customers, distributors, and dealers can give them to you on a regular basis. Often done in some sort of sequence, they can give you sales volume by period.
- *Corrugated Boxes*. The name of the box manufacturer is shown on the container. If contacted, its personnel may tell you how many boxes (and what types) they sell to a competitor, giving you a volume estimate.

Analytical Assessments

Truly understanding the competition involves going beyond just collecting information.

1. *Reverse Engineering*. In many industries, the first unit of every new product is purchased by a competitor. Some companies do benchmarking, as it is called. Xerox, like many other companies, disassembles rival products and reverse engineers them. General Motors has a 90,000-square-foot shop devoted specifically to tearing down and analyzing competitors' automobiles.
2. *Cost Reconstruction*. A competitor's cost structure can be built up from many of the above sources. Raw materials and parts can be costed out by your purchasing department. People and volume estimates give you a sense of productivity. And your knowledge of their equipment indicates production rates.
3. *Organizational Analysis*. Knowing the style of your competitor's top management can help predict strategic moves. Understanding a company's culture and values is also useful. Some firms always interview employees of competitors who are considering leaving or who have already done so. Others use executive recruiters to do this for them. At the very least, track your competitor's want ads, taking particular note of new types of employees.

The real value of these approaches comes when they are employed systematically.

ORGANIZING FOR COMPETITIVE ANALYSIS

Individuals contribute competitive information, but it takes a team to distill the essence and develop strategies to capitalize on it. What's needed first is a commitment from the CEO and top management to the idea that gathering competitive intelligence is important. Next, the type of information must be specified. Without direction, the effort can collect abundant detail yet miss the crucial points.

In my experience, it is astounding how much information on competitors is available right inside your company. Marketing managers, sales people, engineers, purchasing agents, plant managers, and others all have something to contribute. The challenge is collecting fragmented information and putting it into a big-picture evaluation.

Competitive Role-Playing

One of the best ways to gain insight into what your competitors may do next is to conduct corporate war games. Have your management team act as if it is the management of one or more competitors. This can give you (1) a deeper understanding of your competitor's viewpoint, (2) an appreciation for its strengths and weaknesses, (3) a list of its strategic options, and (4) a feeling for what it might do next. It can also be fun. I used competitive role-playing with the top management of an electronic products manufacturer, after reviewing information culled from many of the above sources. We formed three- and four-person teams, each with an engineering, marketing, and operations person. Each team was asked to spend two hours developing a "short form" strategic plan for a particular competitor. They threw themselves into the task, achieved a level of involvement impossible with conventional competitive analysis, and increased their own camaraderie as well. When we reconvened, the leader of each team presented a competitor's plan, including objectives, strategies, new product concepts and release dates, investment priorities, and other particulars. What was eye-opening was that some executives had earlier said these same competitors had little or no new strategies or products planned. The competitor strategies proved highly useful in developing my client's own strategies and contingency plans.

You say you have a near monopoly on your market, or you manage a nonprofit organization that has no competitors. Then create a phantom one, says Peter T. Johnson, former administrator of the Bonneville Power Administration. "Engage in some constructive imagery," he says in *Harvard Business Review,* and "you can combat complacency."[3] Role-playing the phantom competitor, and making believe you are bidding against one with every customer contact, can put entrepreneurial energy into your organization.

MAXIMIZING YOUR COMPETITIVE ADVANTAGE

Back in the late 1970s a very large diversified company in the United States would say it was looking for an "unfair advantage" in each of its businesses. Management dropped this terminology, perhaps in fear of creating problems with the SEC. But the company's philosophy still holds. And it is a leader in most industries in which it competes.

The law of comparative advantage was developed by David Ricardo in the early nineteenth century. It says that people and organizations should specialize in what they do best relative to everyone else. I put it this way: You have to do everything well, but something extraordinary.

Let's take a look at a few competitive advantages. The Unix operating system is quickly gaining popularity because of one huge advantage: It has been available on many operating systems, unlike the systems of IBM, Apple, and DEC. The fact that it has been a bit hard to use is overridden by its ability to be used on machines from PCs to supercomputers. Even Apple has a Unix system for its Macintosh.

Apple has been able to stake out unique ground in the PC industry. It has superior graphics and computing capabilities in many applications, and its defensive strategy of aggressively suing clone manufacturers eliminates all direct competitors. As a result, it has gross margins that range up into the 70 percentiles on each Macintosh it sells, margins usually found only in such industries as pharmaceuticals.

One of Federal Express's advantages in overnight letter and small package delivery is that it created the industry. (Consider 3M's FIDO philosophy—First In Defeats Others.) But then there were two, three, four, and more competitors. Fred Smith says the main difference now between

Fed Ex and its competitors is that "they do not have the tremendous capability that we have in the electronics field to track, trace, and control the various items that are put through the system. We also deliver earlier, and more on time, than our competition."[4]

Offensive Strategies

An insightful evaluation of your competitors' profile should enable you to answer the following questions:

- On their strengths: What can we learn from them? Can we develop the same ones, only better? Can we avoid their strength in competing with them? Can we blunt it, or even use it to our advantage?
- On their weaknesses: Can we exploit them? How do we prevent ourselves from acquiring the same ones? Should we target that company specifically and go after its customers?

Many companies have copied the winners in their industries in order to develop the same strengths. What takes more ingenuity is converting a competitor's strength into a liability. For example, does your largest competitor's size make it less flexible in the market? Speed in implementing even small strategy improvements can be to your advantage.

Capitalizing on a competitor's weakness, if even a temporary one, is also effective. The confusion created when two companies are merging, for example, may provide an opening with certain customers that you never had before. Targeting a specific competitor is common. When 7-Eleven went into the money order business, its radio commercials asked: "Is the Post Office your idea of greased lightning?"

Hewlett-Packard made DEC its choice of enemies in the business systems market with a program called "Top Gun" after the movie. William Murphy, head of business systems marketing, praised fifteen salespeople who made five or more "confirmed kills"—closed sales against Digital— in 1987. In 1988 he targeted IBM as well and sent out "killer kits" of marketing data to support the effort.

One competitive strategy, if your opponent is undefined, is to define him. This applies to politics as well as business. Back in the 1988 presidential election, George Bush defined Michael Dukakis before Dukakis defined Bush. Dukakis failed to respond to Bush's bare-knuckle attacks fast enough. Bush was clever, moved quickly, and won.

Ways to turn your own company's weaknesses into strengths should also be considered. Heinz turned what should have been a marketing nightmare—a ketchup that had to be shaken to coax it out of the bottle—into a winner by emphasizing in television commercials how thick it was. It didn't matter that competing brands like Hunt-Wesson might be tastier. Heinz changed the standard of quality in this $500-million food segment and gained market leadership.

Defensive Strategies

Drawing first blood can give a sizable advantage. But be ready to defend your strategy against competitive reaction. Patents, trademarks, copyrights, technology trade secrets, and business know-how are some of the most common defensive tactics. They can be used in conventional ways and in innovative ones as well. Kawasaki Heavy Industries was being sued in a product liability suit on its Jet Skis. To prevent disclosure of design drawings and other proprietary information, the company came up with what *Forbes* calls "the litigation ploy of the year." It had its law firm copyright the documents. The plaintiffs could not reproduce them and communicate them to other plaintiffs' attorneys, making everyone's case much more difficult to litigate.[5]

On a more conventional level, Abbott Laboratories keeps competitors from selling test kits for one of its leading analytical test instruments through, as a planning executive at one competitor called it, "software in a 'black box' and reagent coding." The executive says Abbott will change the software to defend its lock on the test kits for its instruments, even if it has to suboptimize its costs. Perhaps the best defense, however, is constantly giving your customers more quality and service than they expect.

The Complete Competitor

The complete boxer is good in all aspects of the game. He can jab and run, get inside and cause damage, stand toe to toe and trade punches, and, when the opening appears, deliver the knockout punch. Sugar Ray Leonard is an example, with showmanship thrown in for good measure.

The complete company is much the same. It is strong in all the success factors of its industry. For example, on a business trip to Holland, I met the marketing manager of Philips's medical systems division and found out the reasons his company leads the market: (1) Its equipment is at least equal to the best, (2) its manufacturing methods are constantly being improved,

(3) its marketing adds value by supplying free consulting services to hospitals on how to organize and operate their departments, and counsels them on getting government funding and approvals, and (4) Philips is headquartered there. This is a hard competitive profile to beat.

A tough, complete competitor on a smaller scale is Diagnostic Products Corporation in Los Angeles. It is the leading independent manufacturer of diagnostic test kits in the world. Recently listed on the New York Stock Exchange, it has averaged over the last ten years annual gains in revenue and net income of 29% and 32%, respectively. In 1987 it reached $36.9 million in sales and $9.2 million in net income, for a 19.9% return on equity. And the company is debt-free.

Sigi Ziering, chairman and CEO, described to me the manner in which Diagnostic Products competes with its fifty competitors, including divisions of Abbott Laboratories, Becton-Dickinson, and Baxter Travenol:

> We entered the business of immunodiagnostics in 1971 by penetrating a number of smaller niches, with less competition, and in which we could make a quality contribution at a lower price. Now we are priced competitively and entering larger niche segments of the health care diagnostics market such as allergy testing.
>
> There are five key competitive factors in our business: quality, service, research, marketing, and low-cost manufacturing. We watch every detail and try to be excellent in all five. Our biggest edge is in quality, because of our unsparing efforts to control and maintain month-to-month consistency in constituents derived from blood, et cetera. Related to quality, we have a significant effort in ongoing quality control efforts throughout the product life as well.
>
> Our second most important edge is, I definitely believe, we are the low-cost manufacturer in our area of specialty. We have increased productivity at a compounded rate of 11% annually for the last four years through automation and volume increases.[6]

Supporting the above two competitive advantages are Diagnostic Products' research and development capability, which recently is emphasizing biotechnology (12% to 15% of revenue goes into R&D), and a dramatically expanded marketing, sales, and service organization. All the success factors work together to form a complete competitor. Top management's goals are to reach $100 million in revenue by 1991 while maintaining profitability.

IT'S WAR

Taking your competitors seriously is essential to winning in business. Domino's Pizza CEO Thomas Monaghan in 1988 said he was rolling up his sleeves for a marketing battle with Pizza Hut and Little Caesar Enterprises for dominance of the $13 billion pizza market. With Domino's currently in second place, Monaghan stated: "I want people here in the company to think of it as war, because somebody's got to emerge on top in two or three years." Domino's biggest advantage over competitors is its guarantee of delivering in thirty minutes or they refund $3.00. He adds, "We have to have the best pizza and the best delivery service. That's what I'll go to the brink on."[7]

If there is going to be only one winner in your industry, you certainly want to be it. One of your strategic weapons is technology, the subject of the next chapter.

13

Technology Mapping

SCIENTISTS are learning from slugs. The nervous system of the garden slug operates at 150 MIPS (150 million instructions per second). The fastest computers currently operate around 20 MIPS. Not that we feel mandated to close the slug gap, but such simple facts lead us to believe there is potential for technological progress.*

TECHNOLOGY SUCCESS FACTORS

Technology can be your company's biggest source of opportunity—or biggest threat. The purpose of this chapter is to show how to turn it into a competitive weapon. One way is to emulate winners. In the 1980s successful companies changed the way they plan and execute technology strategy. Some of the principal things they now do differently or better:

* Garden slugs, in fact, are studied in research programs at the famed Bell Laboratories. Scientists believe they can learn from slugs in developing neural network computers that are truly artificially intelligent—which through intuition could solve certain complicated problems almost instantly.

- Define the role of technology in the company and, most importantly, link it to overall corporate strategy
- Determine which technologies to pursue by defining the life cycles of present ones, and identify and develop the upcoming winners
- Increase the creative productivity of their scientists and engineers
- Dramatically speed up the process of developing new products and technologies from idea conception through full-scale manufacturing
- Experiment with new ways to organize the R&D effort, and integrate it with other departments in the company
- Capitalize on outside resources through strategic alliances with many types of organizations

The underlying concept, however, is that technology and strategy are inseparable. So even if you are not directly involved with the R&D function of your business, you must at least understand how it relates to your function.

The concepts presented below come from my consulting with dozens of high- and medium-technology firms, from interviewing executives in both large corporations and startups, and from research on firms that have used technology to their advantage. In addition, I have direct experience in various engineering positions for Becton-Dickinson and Co. in the early 1970s, including product and process design, manufacturing engineering, and new product manufacturing startup.

HAUTE TECHNOLOGY FOR ALL INDUSTRIES

You say your company is not in a technology-driven industry? Technology development is the main means to competitive superiority in more industries than people think.

- Food companies spend millions on the research and development of new products. Nabisco Brands, for example, laid out $40 million for a new research center in 1986. And if NutraSweet Co.'s Simplesse all-natural fat substitute makes it to the market as planned, this "fake fat" will revolutionize low-calorie cooking.
- Money managers at Wall Street firms are using information technology (IT) to win competitive advantage. Bear Stearns's edge in mortgage securities rests largely on the company's advanced computer-based information systems.
- Specialty Equipment Corp. in Worcester, Massachusetts, received a patent on a machine that makes corrugated boxes that eliminate the need

for taping and stapling. The bottom of the knocked-down box locks into place when it is opened, and shippers can collapse it for reuse. Says president Fred Dowd, "It's a high-tech innovation in a low-tech market."[1]

· The toy industry's Worlds of Wonder took off with LaserTag (and later crashed). Nintendo, the leader in computer games for kids of all ages, invented the "no-stick joy stick," in which a console senses your movements so you can box with Mike Tyson. Even Lego is going high tech by linking its construction toys with a software program designed by a learning theorist at MIT.

· Procter & Gamble's Ultra Pampers grabbed 15% of the disposable diaper market in 1987. A super-absorbing, polyacrylate polymer that turns into a gel when wet keeps it from leaking. P&G locked up the supply of the scarce material by financing the Japanese vendor's plant construction.

· Who is National Semiconductor's largest chip customer? IBM or another high-tech company? No, General Motors. And GM led the list of the largest R&D spenders in 1987 with $4.1 billion, as against IBM's $3.9 billion. Ford was third, ahead of such technology-based companies such as AT&T, GE, Du Pont, Eastman Kodak, and Hewlett-Packard.

Technology should not be considered a panacea, however. Albert Lee, a former speechwriter for Roger Smith and author of *Call Me Roger*, faults the chairman of General Motors for "insisting on technology as the corporate cure-all. It hasn't proved to be yet." In all fairness to Smith, the payback from GM's technology may be down the road. Rarely does a major technology push result in short-term returns. GM's results in the early 1990s will tell all. Let's now turn to a process for technology planning.

CREATIVE TECHNOLOGY PLANNING PROCESS

The approach to developing and implementing a technology strategy is the same as in overall business planning, except that the content of the steps is different:

1. Understand and map the industry's technologies—Analysis
2. Identify business and technology opportunities—Creativity
3. Evaluate and select technology strategies—Judgment
4. Allocate resources to technologies and programs—Planning
5. Implement the programs and monitor results—Action

Teamwork and communication permeate the process, but the key point is that technology must be planned, not managed. What can make this difficult is that many technology-based industries are cyclical. The classic statement confirming this was the first sentence in Andy Grove's President's Letter in Intel's 1986 annual report: "We are pleased to announce that 1986 is over."

UNDERSTANDING TECHNOLOGY

Information is at the core of all innovation. So obtaining a deep understanding of the technological underpinnings of your company and industry is crucial when developing a technology strategy. Assuming you have performed strategic analyses of your markets and competition, your next step is to take a technology inventory. Identify all distinct technologies that are used in your company, no matter how obvious they seem, and categorize them in each of the following four frameworks:

1. *Levels of Technology:* Corporate, division, business unit, product segment, market segment
2. *Areas of Technology:* Product, manufacturing, applications, systems, marketing, et cetera
3. *State of Technology:* Basic research, applied research, development (product and process concepts), engineering (products and process designs)
4. *Importance of Technology:* Supportive (necessary but widely available in industry), critical (currently of highest impact), strategic (the next key technology), and emerging (for use in the long term)

Using a matrix for each of the above, assess your strengths and weaknesses in each. Do the same for every one of your competitors, both current and possible new entries. As was discussed in Chapter 12, the latter can be the most devastating, because they are not married to a current technology or manufacturing process.

Technology Life Cycles

Technologies have life cycles, just like products and businesses. Knowing where your technologies are in their life cycles—emerging, growing, maturing, or declining—is important. Exhibit 13–1 demonstrates the path. As a new technology emerges, it has a slow start in impacting product performance (and company financial performance) relative to the R&D investment needed to bring it to market. Then something happens. As its basic science and engineering principles become well understood, technological progress speeds up. Engineering refinements increase the product's benefits to customers, decrease the cost to give it wider appeal, and accelerate growth in both performance and revenue. The length of this period of rapid progress varies by technology.

Then something else happens. Technological achievement slows down. R&D deadlines are missed. Creativity dries up. Engineering morale sinks. No matter how much R&D is thrown at the technology, returns diminish. The reason is that only so much product performance can be achieved. As Richard Foster explains in his excellent book, *Innovation: The Attacker's Advantage:*

> Technology even variously defined always has a limit—either the limit of a particular technology, for example, the ultimate density of devices we can get onto a silicon chip, or a succession of limits of several technologies that together make up the larger technology or product or way of doing business.[2]

It is imperative to understand the limits of each of your company's technologies and those of your competitors. Pay most attention to strategic and critical technologies (as defined above).

EXHIBIT 13–1
Technology Life Cycles

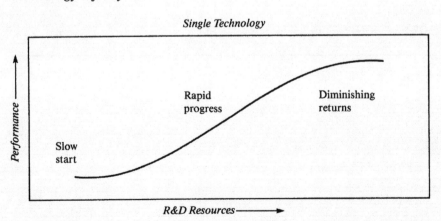

Single Technology

Technology Mapping

When the primary technology of an industry is peaking, invariably ones to replace it are being explored by companies either inside or outside of the industry. When these new technologies are reduced to practice (patent terminology for the first working prototype), a leap in performance occurs. Then it goes through the same growth-to-maturity pattern as the first one. Exhibit 13–2 shows computer printer technologies in their three basic stages of performance. Biotechnology has gone through three phases as well: protein chemistry, monoclonal antibodies, and now, recombinant DNA.

Tracing back the historical performance of technologies in your industry and plotting them on a graph as in Exhibit 13–2 can be enlightening. Then creativity kicks in. Complete the technology map for your industry by speculating on emerging and future technologies, plotting them as well.

IDENTIFYING TECHNOLOGY OPPORTUNITIES

Winning companies push the limits of existing technologies while identifying and developing new ones. Lew Branscomb, chief scientist at IBM, explains how his company goes about it: "Our corporate research organization identifies all the major technologies on which our business depends—electronic logic technology, for example—and always has two major projects in place for each technology. One is aimed at determining

EXHIBIT 13–2

Technology Leaps in Computer Printers

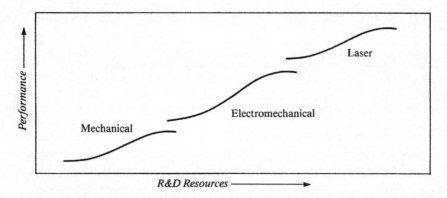

what limits nature sets to the improvement of current mainstream technology. The second project is aimed at the single most promising radical alternative."[3] For example, IBM is researching a new material for semiconductors, gallium arsenide, because it is much faster than those made of silicon (but difficult to work with). Simultaneously, in March 1988 IBM made and tested the world's fastest silicon circuits, which had a switching time of 13 picoseconds (trillionths of a second), ten times faster than any commercially available chip.

Two advancements were needed in the silicon experiment. One was for the electrons to travel a shorter distance, which IBM accomplished by reducing the size of the transistor parts to one-tenth of a micron (versus one micron for one-megabit chips). Second, it cooled the chips down to 321 degrees below zero so that the voltage would not burn up the one-tenth-micron transistors.[4] Interestingly, in May 1988 IBM announced it had produced the first commercially available chips measuring a half-micron across.

Technological leaps are often achieved by trying to develop a deeper understanding of the science involved. Merck & Co., considered by many financial analysts to be "the class act in pharmaceutical research," jumps beyond attempting to identify new drug compounds. It spends research dollars on trying to understand how diseases work.

Combine Technologies

Combinations of technologies can result in leaps. The ink-jet printer required advances in a wide range of them: ink chemistry, nozzle fluidics, semiconductor technology to make the nozzles from silicon, ultrasonics to convert the stream into droplets, charged particle dynamics to guide the droplets, and electronics for the logic of the system.

On simpler scale, Cooper Lasersonics in 1985 introduced the first mouse-operated ophthalmic laser. A mouse similar to that used with personal computers provides eye surgeons with exceptional ease, speed, and safety in directing and focusing the laser beam.

Combine New with Old

New technology joined with old can bring about the resurgence of the latter. The optical microscope became obsolete in the 1950s when the electron microscope, with its far greater power, leaped to the front. But the electron microscope can be used only on dead and dehydrated tissue. Shinya Inoue, a biologist-inventor at the Marine Biological Laboratory at Woods Hole, Massachusetts, married the outdated light microscope with new video technology. The result is nothing less than a revolution in microscopy. Video microscopy gives greater magnification and makes it possible to manipulate images, create stunning three-dimensional depth, and add color. And in combination with a third technology—fluorescence—cells can be injected with proteins that glow so researchers can see where these building blocks of nature end up in the cell's architecture.[5]

The oldest "technology" to be revived, so far as I've heard, was featured in "Return of the Leeches," an article in the *San Francisco Chronicle* in January, 1989. Sounding like a horror movie, it was, rather, a new medical treatment. Thanks to leeches, available from Leeches U.S.A. Ltd. in Westbury, New York, for $6.00 each, certain skin-graph operations are successful that previously were derailed by blood-clots. Besides devouring excess blood, the leeches introduce chemicals through their saliva glands to prevent blood-clotting. Medieval medicine at its best.[6]

Talk to Customers

What do the gas chromatograph, transmission electron microscope, ultraviolet spectrometer, and NMR spectrometer have in common? They were initially developed by customers. Your R&D department is certainly not the only source of new technology and product ideas. Studies of their sources have shown that customers play a large role. The few exceptions are in process industries such as pharmaceuticals and chemicals. But even in these, many breakthroughs occur first outside the company in university and government laboratories.

Eric Von Hippel, professor at MIT's Sloane School of Management, reports that customers are the primary source of innovations in many industries, the two most prominent being scientific instruments and semiconductor/printed circuit boards. There, he found that customers supplied 77% of them and 67%, respectively.[7]

On the surface, your sales force would logically be the best conduit for customer ideas. They are in constant contact with customers. However, it is a rare salesperson or rep that can look to the future. This is not to fault them. Their job is short-term-oriented—to overcome objections and to get the order. Unfortunately, those objections, which can lead to pet peeve insights, do not get back to the engineering labs in usable form.

The four best groups of people to tap customers for product and technology ideas are management, marketers, engineers, and consultants. One of the programs I frequently set up with clients starts with putting their management and engineers onto the customer's premises. With some training, they can learn to ask open-ended, insightful, and leap-type questions to gather tremendous food for thought. A side benefit I've heard from marketing and sales people is that their customers like to speak with their management and engineers, one on one. In the case of engineers, the customers see this as service, because the engineers can answer questions a salesperson couldn't begin to address.

Customer service reps can also be a source of ideas. WordPerfect, the software company, is impressively responsive. First, its telephone support service is superb, for which I can speak first-hand. Second, when I, as a customer, proposed a program enhancement during one call, my customer service rep immediately typed it into his computer, along with my name and phone number. The immediacy made me feel that I was heard.

Other External Sources

Competitors can also be a source of technology ideas. Some techniques for researching them were presented in Chapter 12. The masters at this are Japanese companies. "Much of [Japan's] success has been built on bought, borrowed or stolen technology," stated *Fortune,* on December 21, 1987. "Now U.S. companies are striking back—but a two-way street is still far-off."

Government agencies can be suppliers of technology. The patent office should be regularly contacted for the latest development in your industry. Universities can provide a tremendous source of technology and research help. And who do you think is one of the largest funders of university research in the United States today? Japanese companies. One prominent engineering university is getting so much money from Japan that it has set up a liaison office in Tokyo.

CHOOSING TECHNOLOGIES

The heart of the process is the allocation of resources to technologies. As Richard Foster says in *Innovation: The Attacker's Advantage*:

> The key to both attack and defense is picking the right technology. The best strategy may be to pick the adolescent technology with the highest limit because it is never clear when a new technology is really going to emerge.

The biggest mistake companies make is sticking with a technology too long. The motivations not to change are strong. It is comfortable, your engineers understand it, your manufacturing is in place, it is low-risk. Converting to a new technology means the entire organization is upset. It has to go through a learning curve; new types of engineers will be needed; major capital investments could be required; and the risk in change appears high. Recall, however, the leaps in product performance and cost effectiveness that new technologies can make in an industry. Whole industries are redefined when the right new technology comes along. For example, the mushrooming use of FAX machines is transforming Federal Express's market. Fed Ex is no longer in just the overnight delivery business but is in the information industry.

Many a company has held onto its old technology in the face of competitive entries, which should have caused a rethinking of strategy. A high-level executive of a medical instrument company described to me how his organization reacted in the classical NIH-way to Abbott's new fluorescence polarization technology in the early 1980s. The initial reaction was "the instrument wouldn't work." When it did, they changed to "it's not a threat because it can only perform a few blood tests." As Abbott's machine gathered customer acceptance, the response became, "We are one of the industry leaders and don't have to worry." Within two years Abbott Labs had a full line of tests for their one-button, automated machine and was the leader in the market segment.

Competitive technology threats can come from distant industries. Cetus Corporation, a genetic engineering firm, received a patent in 1986 for a new industrial lubricant. Pixar Company, born from special effect technology to produce movies on the order of *Star Wars,* introduced in 1988 a computer with stunning animation capability for three-dimension X-ray videos of human bones, at almost half the price of competing customers.

The best protection is to use the strategy Lew Branscomb of IBM described: expand the limits of your current technologies while simultaneously investigating new ones on the leading edge. Many firms use technology shootouts. Emerging competing technologies are developed in parallel by separate teams. When one proves superior, the members of the losing teams are transferred to other projects. While this concurrent development initially can be more expensive, it spreads risk. It also speeds up development.

FAST NEW PRODUCT DEVELOPMENT

Superior companies have been doing everything possible to accelerate the product development/manufacturing startup cycle. This has received more press in the last few years than any other technology issue, and for good reason. Compaq Computer, for instance, must come out with new models to replace old ones about every nine months. Rod Canion, Compaq's CEO, states: "Your last successful product doesn't mean olive oil. One success is gone almost before it even happened. We never even consider slacking off. You've got to keep running."[8]

Fast new product development (NPD) not only enables you to beat your competitors to the market, it is cheaper, too. Aggressive managements are not looking for a 10% or 20% decrease in the time of the development cycle. They are clamoring for cutting it in half, or even by two-thirds. Why? Because our competitors in the Far East can do it that quickly and are continuously trying to get faster. Honda, for example, has a four-year product cycle from new car concept through market introduction. The big three in the United States usually take six years.

Turbocharging the New Product Process

There are four overriding principles for dramatically compressing the cycle time between idea conception and product delivery to customers.

1. *Be prepared to change radically* the way your organization engineers products, introduces them to manufacturing, and pushes them through the distribution system.
2. *Map your present system* steps and timing, and brainstorm at many levels of your organization on how to cut the overall cycle-time in half or less by (a) reducing the time of individual steps, (b) eliminating or condensing steps, (c) removing all bottlenecks and slack time, and (d) running steps in parallel rather than in sequence. The last item has been called the rugby approach to NPD.
3. *Form interdepartmental teams* that work together from concept design through initial manufacturing. (Honeywell calls theirs Tiger Teams.) Set target dates, give them a budget, let them manage themselves, and get out of their way.
4. *Continue to pursue improvements* to the system even after you have made great strides.

Given these four essentials, employ some or all of the thirty techniques presented in Exhibit 13–3. I've used combinations of them with clients in a variety of industries to help them achieve major improvements. For example, a process instrumentation manufacturer reduced its concept-to-manufacturing cycle from two years to seven months.

STRATEGIC TECHNOLOGY ALLIANCES

One way to reduce cycle time is to tap outside resources. These strategic partnerships include R&D subcontracting, technology licensing, joint ven-

EXHIBIT 13–3

Rapid New Product Development Techniques

- Communicate the corporate vision to all employees.
- Make speed a fundamental company philosophy.
- Plan two to four product generations in advance.
- Map your present NPD process and time spent on steps.
- Totally redesign the process assuming perfect communication.
- Combine or eliminate steps in the process.
- Identify all bottlenecks and eliminate them from the system.
- Parallel process new products (rather than sequentially).
- Use autonomous, interdisciplinary, flexible teams.
- Put marketing, manufacturing, and quality people on them.
- Streamline the product approval process.
- Involve suppliers early in the design process.
- Break down department and divisional walls.
- Sharpen the engineering department's focus.
- Test-market product ideas quickly.
- Get consensus on action plans.
- Establish key indicators on timing.
- Make deadlines sacred.
- Incorporate rapid feedback loops on results.
- Design for manufacturability.
- Designers spend time in manufacturing, and vice versa.
- Develop manufacturing tooling during product design.
- Let design engineers buy their own parts.
- Insist on complete and perfect specifications.
- Get it right the first time.
- Use CAD, CAE, CAM.
- Set quality standards early in product design.
- Train everyone in teambuilding, running meetings, speed.
- Give first article high priority in manufacturing.
- Assign best manufacturing personnel to production start-up.
- Seek continuous improvements in cycle time.

tures, acquisitions, and sales. IBM, for instance, shared the development of its PC. It purchased its microprocessors from Intel, floppy disks from Tandon, printers from Epson, monitors from Matsushita, and its operating system from Microsoft. Sun Microsystems has technology agreements with AT&T and Technology Instruments, to name two. The Netherlands' Philips has made its high-tech strategy, "If you can't beat 'em, join 'em." In the mid-1980s, *Business Week* reported, Philips was joining 'em at a one-per-month clip.[9] Cannon provides photocopiers to Kodak. General Motors and Toyota share manufacturing technologies. Hewlett-Packard and Toshiba have been exchanging engineers and sharing semiconductor technology for seven years. Even the research powerhouse Merck & Co. occasionally licenses new pharmaceuticals and contracts out R&D.

As we know, many corporations are entering into joint ventures and alliances with companies in Japan. Technology sharing and market penetration are the two major reasons. Results have been mixed, however. It appears that our Far Eastern friends are far better at extracting technology benefits from such relationships. A survey by A. T. Kearny found that three out of four Japanese executives felt that alliances were effective, while only 17% of American CEOs felt positive about them.[10]

Sometimes companies give too much away even here at home. Andrew Grove admitted in Intel's 1986 annual report that management had poorly handled the 1983 boom in semiconductor demand. It licensed other chip manufacturers to produce Intel microprocessors. Grove wrote: "We met our customers' needs and helped expand the total market for our products, but we also lost control over a generation of our products and created our own competition."

The safest, yet often untapped, place for technology alliances is within the corporation—between divisions and subsidiaries. It is amazing how many companies don't leverage what they already have. A classic case of lack of cooperation was when NCR clung to its electromechanical cash registers in the early 1970s when competitors were coming out with computerized versions. Ironically, another division of NCR was developing computers at the time. So tap interdivisional technology opportunities. How to do it was covered in Chapter 9.

PUTTING TECHNOLOGY INTO STRATEGY

Technology strategy is important. But it must emanate from corporate strategy. When research and development targets are focused on corporate targets, the entire organization can deliver results.

One fundamental question that has to be answered is whether your company wants to be a technology leader or follower. Being second does have quite a few advantages. The technology is proven, the market is verified, and you can learn from your competitor's mistakes. IBM follows this strategy in emerging markets, as it did with the PC. Many smaller firms have to take this route because of limited resources. Success depends on the ability to come out quickly with a second generation product that leapfrogs competitive offerings in performance and/or price. But beware of competitive retaliation. One top executive from a major computer company advised: "Never play leapfrog with a unicorn."

14

Reinventing Operations

OVER the last ten years, America has relinquished to other countries the lead in the production of items that were formerly our strength: automobiles, steel, semiconductors, television sets, shoes, clothes, and many others. If we are not going to become a land of "hollow corporations," as *Business Week* calls them, we need to reinvent our manufacturing base.

Creativity and innovation are at the heart of manufacturing revitalization. A totally new approach has to be created and managed in order to deliver the quantum increase in improvement needed to catch up with, and then surpass, our Asian and European competitors. In the mid-1980s many companies recognized the need for an effective operations strategy. Not so many have an idea of how to develop and implement one. This chapter will explain how.

MODERNIZED MANUFACTURING

The path to major increases in manufacturing performance is not the same for every company. A custom approach must always be undertaken. However, I find winning companies share a common philosophy.

183

- *Corporate Strategy Drives Operations.* Production is a competitive weapon not just on the basis of low cost, but as the delivery system of the market position of the company.
- *Continuous Productivity Improvement.* It's needed because competitors, especially foreign ones, are not standing still.
- *Flexibility.* The production system must be able to handle a wide variety of the same product family with little or no penalty for switching between items on very short notice.
- *Speed.* Products must be designed and introduced into manufacturing fast and, once in, produced on very short cycle times.
- *Quality.* Catching up with the Japanese is a long journey in most industries, and nothing short of a flawless factory will put us ahead.
- *Careful Use of Technology.* Automation, computer integrated manufacturing, and new assembly technologies have to be pursued, but not considered a cure-all.
- *Participation by All.* People—their ideas, enthusiasm, skills—from all levels of the company must work together creatively to better the firm.

Clearly, companies will have to excel at all seven of these essentials in order to compete successfully in global markets.

CORPORATE MANUFACTURING STRATEGY

Broadly speaking, everything a company does is related to everything else. Yet there is a tendency for management to view manufacturing through a microscope as a cost center and nothing more. Some top managers go so far as to see it as a necessary evil of doing business—where people get their hands dirty.

Manufacturing must be viewed as part of an integrated system that delivers to customers the value promised by marketing and sales. Process design, plant configuration, human resources, information and control systems, degree of automation, relationships with suppliers, and just about every other variable in manufacturing is dependent on corporate marketing strategy. For example, the design of the ideal company for a high-end furniture manufacturer would be totally different from one at the low, commodity end of the market. The expensive furniture company would have specialized distribution through exclusive retailers, lead time in making the furniture (most probably to order), and would operate as a job shop. Management's challenge would be to oversee a large variety of styles and models, short production runs, expensive materials, rigorous quality standards, and technically trained craftsmen.

In contrast, the low-priced furniture manufacturer would probably make and distribute a limited line of models and sell them through a large number of volume-oriented retailers. Production lot sizes would be large, finished goods storage necessary, and the work force largely semiskilled and unskilled. Management's challenge would be to manufacture goods of adequate quality at rock-bottom costs.

Manufacturing needs a strategic plan to state its mission, vision, prioritized objectives, strategies, values, and action plans. Only then can it be aligned with the company's overall strategy.

CONSTANT, QUANTUM IMPROVEMENT

Chipping away at waste and inefficiency is one way to improve productivity. But it is not nearly enough, particularly if the competition includes companies in the Far East. Successful companies look for quantum increases in productivity in order to get or maintain their leads. The philosophy in Japan is continuous, never-ending improvement. Honda's chief executive, Soichiro Honda, said in 1988 he wanted a 300% increase in productivity in the coming years. Honda already is a low-cost producer and the world's fastest developer of new automobiles.

Threatened by low-cost Korean imports, New Japan Steel Corporation invested millions of dollars in artificial intelligence systems for its blast furnaces. Management claims this will lower silicon impurities and result in the purest steel in the world.[1] Toshiba has also been under attack from newly industrialized countries (NICs). Its Total Productivity program and other cost-cutting measures saved the company an estimated total of $800 million from April to September 1987. Toshiba uses cardboard statues in place of workers at its Fukaya video cassette plant to illustrate how much the company has cut back on labor through automation.[2]

Winning companies in the United States also follow the continuous improvement philosophy. AMP Inc. in Harrisburg, Pennsylvania, controls 15% of the world market for electrical connectors. This $2.3 billion company has factories in seventeen countries and ten thousand patents worldwide. To maintain a grip on the business, AMP's two thousand R&D personnel work with customers at every stage of product development, creating new connectors and new auto-assembly equipment for them. But what keeps AMP's edge is constant improvement. CEO Walter Raab's ambitious goal in 1984 was to improve by a factor of 10 on fifty different measures, from shortening product development to cutting scrap and rejects. By 1988 it had made major gains on most of those goals. ROE was 18.5%.[3]

FLEXIBLE MANUFACTURING SYSTEMS

Leading-edge firms have discovered that flexibility and volume are not at odds with each other. Nor are quality and cost. Exhibit 14–1 shows the difference in philosophy between unenlightened and enlightened companies. The key elements of flexible manufacturing systems (FMS) are teams of multiskilled workers, focused plants, computer aided design (CAD) and

EXHIBIT 14–1
Flexibility, Quality, Cost

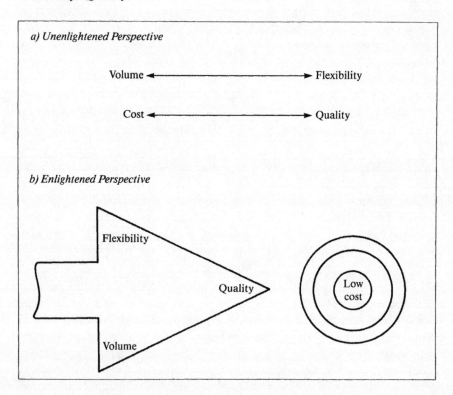

manufacturing (CAM), quick setup procedures, common parts, and just-in-time throughput.

Flexible Work Force

The ideal is that everyone learns everyone else's job. This way they can cover for one another and rotate positions to relieve monotony. America's unions are slowly coming around to this. They have to be convinced to move away from a dedication to narrow job classifications and toward an endorsement of multiskilled workers. This, combined with the team concept, is a powerful, flexible force. Self-managing teams are self-motivating. In addition, they provide an elegant solution to balancing the production line, because tasks can be reassigned quickly within teams. This is invaluable when manufacturing a variety of models or where there are unexpected changes in product flow.

Focused Factories

Hewlett-Packard, Control Data, Kodak, Westinghouse, and GE are just some of the companies that are busting up functionalized plants and reorganizing them by product group or market segment. This "factory within a factory" concept adds not only flexibility but quality as well. In a total overhaul of its approach to television set manufacturing, General Electric compressed management layers at its plants from nine to six and cross-trained workers. It is now turning out a wide variety of sets in small lots for market niches. GE is doing the same with dishwashers, adjusting production to regional preferences. Californians like machines with a wider selection of cycles than people in the Midwest, for example.[4]

Multiple facilities is another approach. Not only are they more flexible, they are less risky. Medco Containment Services, described in Chapter 10, could have chosen to operate out of one huge, cost-efficient mail order pharmaceutical facility. But it chooses to have eight automated phamacies throughout the United States. Chief financial officer James Manning gives the reasons for this.

1. We don't like all of our eggs in one basket. Acts of God—fire, flood, etc.—are not a terminal threat to us.
2. There isn't a sufficient supply of registered pharmacists in any one area. Each pharmacy employs 50 to 200 of them. We couldn't attract

    many more pharmacists than that in one area without increasing the
salary structure or compromising on standards.

3. Our clients want a Medco facility reasonably close to them, even if
only for reasons of perception.

4. We only locate in states with favorable generic drug substitution
laws.[5]

CAD/CAM

Computer-aided design and manufacturing systems can reduce costs. But
their most significant contribution is in flexibility. Moore Industries International (MII), a small but rapidly growing manufacturer of instrumentation for the process industries, is an excellent example of what can be
achieved with CAD/CAM. Located in Sepulveda, California, MII can
manufacture 17 trillion different variations of its eight product groups—
without engineering support. Its resistance bulb transmitter, for example,
can be ordered with one of eight electrical inputs, five outputs, eight
electrical options, ten housings, and five power inputs. This yields 16,000
combinations. When the thousands of specials that have been ordered and
designed over the years (and now do not require engineering) are thrown
in, the number of resistance bulb transmitter configurations totals 34
million. When an order is taken and entered into MII's computer, it
instantly produces parts lists, drawings, and manufacturing lineups. "All
of the software was custom written over the last twenty years," says Len
Moore, CEO. "We started writing it when there were twenty people in the
company. My secretary and I took turns keying in the data from our
engineering 'blue books.' I would read to her, and vice versa."[6]

    Simplifying setup procedures, having all of the tools to adjust machinery
at the worker's fingertips and organized on pegboards, reducing the number
of parts needed in models, and using modules are other methods to increase
flexibility. One additional way deserves special attention: speed.

RAPID MANUFACTURE
AND DELIVERY

Producing more faster is the order of the day. Emphasizing the importance
of time is one key. Like football players on Monday mornings, Domino's
Pizza employees periodically watch "game films" of the fastest pizza
people in the chain. One shows a delivery person wearing athletic shoes

running from the truck to the building, taking stairs two at a time (elevators in low-rise buildings are avoided), and carrying the pizza like a halfback going for a touchdown. The result is on-time delivery and hot pizza.[7]

Merck & Co. races its new drugs into production by using multipurpose modular facilities consisting of flexible units that can be rapidly altered to meet changing requirements. The ingredient requirements for one of its antibiotics, Primaxin, were met by a production network spanning three plants and numerous outside suppliers. Yields from the process reached in two years a level that was expected only after five. In addition, Merck's new products are much more potent than the ones the company introduced in the 1960s, hence they require production quantities much smaller than in the past. Management had foreseen this in its strategic planning and had designed its facilities accordingly.[8]

Just-in-time (JIT), invented by the Japanese, not only speeds things up, but reduces inventories and increases machine utilization. In contrast, many companies in the United States still use the JIC (just-in-case) approach of having inventory buffers at all machine interfaces, which has the opposite effect. The whole organization can be speeded up by improving methods, removing bottlenecks, and using JIT. Output rises, increasing productivity and pumping up profit. In operations, time *is* money.

TOTAL QUALITY

"Get better or get beaten" was the message in a June 8, 1987, article in *Business Week* entitled "The Push for Quality." To compete, companies need what I call flawless factories—ones that produce products customers consider perfect, at the lowest cost in the industry. This is the aim of Japanese companies in their *hinshitsu* (quality) programs.

Quality and cost need not be at odds. "HP has learned that a focus on quality is actually one of the best ways to control costs," says John Young, president and CEO of Hewlett-Packard. The company's Cupertino printed circuit board site in just eighteen months reduced defects of auto-insertion of parts from 30,000 parts per million (ppm) to 5,600 ppm. Defects from the wave soldering process went from 5,000 ppm to 6 ppm. "Yet the result of those improvements was an investment savings of $900,000," Young reports.[9]

There are a dozen fundamentals for achieving top quality/bottom cost.

1. *Develop a Quality Strategy.* Joseph M. Juran, W. Edward Deming's counterpart in Japan in the 1950s, contends that quality must be a formal

part of the overall business plan and of each manager's annual performance review. Quality plans typically include a definition of present quality levels and costs, a statement of quality objectives, an overall strategy on how to organize for improvement, and a list of specific action programs and responsibilities. Some examples of quality objectives:

- Attain world class quality by 1991, with "world class' meaning equal to or better than all competitors from all countries.
- Reduce product returns during the one-year warranty period from 0.5% of sales to 0.1% by 1991.
- Reduce the cost of quality from 28% of sales to 25% in 1991, 20% in 1992, and 15% in 1993.

2. *Entire Company Must Improve.* Quality improvement doesn't apply just to products, but encompasses all aspects of the organization. As stated in the 1988 book *Juran on Planning for Quality*:

> The purpose of quality planning is to provide the operating forces with the means of producing products that can meet customers' needs, products such as invoices, polyethylene film, sales contracts, service calls, and new designs for goods.[10]

Research and development can improve product design, speed up cycle time, and release correct documentation to the factory. Marketing and sales can increase order accuracy, customer service satisfaction, and forecasting accuracy. Administration can increase timeliness and accuracy of reports and paperwork (invoices, etc.), and can improve service and other functions in the company.

In fact, view it as a total system. As shown in Exhibit 14–2, total quality starts with your suppliers (and their suppliers), includes what your company does, and ends only when the customer (or your customer's customer) has used or consumed it. If there is a breakdown anywhere in the system, such as customers who are using your product incorrectly, it reflects on your company's quality and must be addressed.

3. *Top Management Involvement.* At the beginning of this book, I emphasized that imagination starts at the top. Quality does as well. Management's role is to dramatize the importance of quality to everyone, take overt steps in solving quality problems, and personally monitor quality levels. Every Monday morning at 7:30 A.M., for example, the CEO and thirty or so top executives at Kellogg have breakfast together. Each person samples three cereals from one of the company's five U.S. plants. Then they discuss quality factors—flavor, appearance, texture, "snap, crackle,

EXHIBIT 14–2

Total Quality

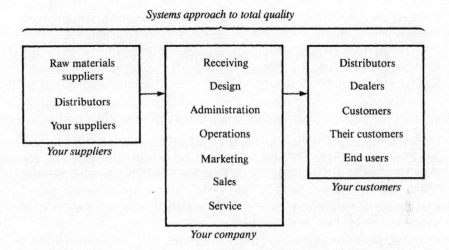

Systems approach to total quality

Raw materials suppliers	Receiving	Distributors
Distributors	Design	Dealers
Your suppliers	Administration	Customers
	Operations	Their customers
Your suppliers	Marketing	End users
	Sales	*Your customers*
	Service	

Your company

and pop,'' mouth feel, and bowl life—and grade each sample. These top executives are tough judges, since only about 15% of the cereals receive the top rating. They have been doing this since 1979.[11]

4. *Management Circles.* Top management sets the tone, but execution is by middle and lower management (down to supervisors), and front-line labor. Cross-functional, multilevel task forces, what I call Management Circles, have to meet on a regular basis to identify quality improvement opportunities, brainstorm solutions, and implement them. Laborers must do the same on Quality Improvement Teams. Chapter 9 explains how to organize and facilitate teamwork of all kinds.

5. *Customer-Based Values.* True definitions of quality can come only from customers, both external and internal. Recognize that everyone in an organization is both a customer and a supplier. Inside the company, the key questions to ask are: (1) What are the most important characteristics of the products and services each person receives and "sells" in the manufacturing, paperwork, and communication chains? (2) What value added does each person provide? (3) How can the system be changed to increase dramatically both quality and value added? The same applies to external customers.

Go for the biggest items first. In the early days of Chrysler's turnaround, Richard Dauch, executive vice president of manufacturing, applied resources where customers would see the most results. He automated the operations necessary to eliminate rattles and squeaks that drove customers crazy. Another high-customer-visibility area he overhauled was the paint shops. They used to be infernos of heat and dust, yielding "orange peel" finish (something that belongs only on citrus). The paint shops are now as clean as surgical theaters, are decorated with fountains and greenery, and produce an excellent finish. Furthermore, Chrysler was the first of the big three to apply a final layer of clear coat, now an industry standard.[12]

6. *Set Radical Goals.* Small increases in quality are not what is sought. They aren't good enough. Worse, trying for small increases doesn't force your people fundamentally to change the way they think and function. HP's Young says he set the "stretch objective" on improving product failure rates by a factor of 10 during the decade of the 1980s. "The same old way would not have done the job," he says. "Expectations needed to be changed about what was possible." Radical goals lead to creative leaps, which in turn lead to leaps in profit.

7. *Monitor Cost of Quality.* The cost of quality (COQ) is made up of two components: necessary costs and avoidable ones. Necessary costs include preventive maintenance and inspection. Avoidable costs consist of scrap, rework, redesign, warranty service—basically all corrective actions—plus inspection that can be eliminated.

Using the language of money when talking about quality will get management's attention. Most companies find COQ ranges from 20% to 30% of revenue. (Exhibit 14–3 presents the COQ for a manufacturer of instrumentation before it undertook a quality program.) Determine your COQ by asking all managers in your organization: "What if everyone in the company—from the president on down—did everything right the first time, thereby eliminating the need for inspection, rework, and quality control. How much would you save?" The objective then becomes to remove as much COQ as possible. Huge returns can be realized if it is approached properly.

8. *Design Quality In.* Japanese executives look at mistakes in a positive light. As Deming explains, roughly 80% of all quality problems are due to the system, not people. Also, most of that 80% is chronic and can be eliminated, while only a small amount is sporadic. Given this, the strategy is to redesign products so they can be manufactured perfectly under poor conditions. This will assure top quality if the plant is operated intelligently. Redesign the plant, equipment, setup procedures, information systems, roles of workers, inspection procedures, and management style, and you may achieve "zero defects," to use Phil Crosby's term. And involve

EXHIBIT 14–3

Cost of Quality for an Instrument Manufacturer

DEPARTMENT	DOLLAR VALUE	DESCRIPTION
Engineering		
Mfg. support eng.	$ 2,150,000	75% of effort finding & correcting errors
Line support eng.	350,000	20% overall (80% customer-generated)
New product eng.	4,200,000	60% overall—general error detection & correction
	400,000	50% of all prototype parts
Subtotal:	$ 7,100,000	
Manufacturing		
Document control	$ 600,000	50% of all time overall spent on clerical
Production control	450,000	25% overall—general error detection
Production	700,000	100% of 30 rework people
Production test	3,500,000	100% of department direct labor
	350,000	Inventory shrinkage
Machine shop	90,000	25% of 10 people
Stores	203,000	Calculated average
Scrap	247,000	Per records
Purchasing	500,000	40% of time overall
	880,000	20% of inventory overstocked
	100,000	5% of POs are change orders
Subtotal:	$ 7,620,000	
Sales Department	$ 2,000,000	25% of time overall
	250,000	50% FAXs, 30% phone calls
Subtotal:	$ 2,250,000	
Advertising	$ 240,000	10% overall for correction
	700,000	25% of department budget
	100,000	30% of first time costs
Subtotal:	$ 1,040,000	

continued

DEPARTMENT	DOLLAR VALUE	DESCRIPTION
Finance	$ 360,000	33% of 20 people
	20,000	20% of paperwork
Subtotal:	$ 380,000	
Marketing	$ 30,000	10% of management's time
	120,000	30% of time spent fixing problems
	50,000	Corrections to manuals
Subtotal:	$ 200,000	
Personnel	$ 120,000	30% of 10 people—error detection
EDP	$ 600,000	10% of time for error detection & systems problems
	120,000	50% of paper wasted
Subtotal:	$ 720,000	
QA Department	$ 5,000,000	100% of department
IC Test Dept.	$ 35,000	Yield loss on ICs
	210,000	Cost of equip. calibration
Service Dept.	360,000	45% of department
Training	120,000	Approx. 1 day/year of each worker, inspector, etc.
Subtotal:	$ 5,725,000	
Corp. Staff	$ 600,000	20% of 40 people
Total Cost of Quality	$ 25,755,000	
Revenue of Company	$117,000,000	
Cost of Quality as % of Revenue	22%	

suppliers to make them part of the solution. Drastically trimming the number of suppliers you use and certifying them makes this feasible. The same goes for white-collar ''factories'' as found in the insurance, banking, airline, and other service industries.

9. *The Quality Improvement Process.* One of the major causes of lack of quality improvement in a company is the absence of a structured process

that can be used at all levels. Once the COQ in an organization has been determined by department, management circles and quality improvement teams can be unleashed on the largest cost areas. Each group should employ the following five steps:

  I. *Identify problems and opportunities.* Flow chart internal and external customers, suppliers, products, services, steps, and cost elements. Find out what's being done right and wrong. Rank them in terms of their impact on defect rates and COQ, and root out their causes.

 II. *Create possible solutions.* Describe the flawless factory making your products. Brainstorm ways to eliminate causes of problems entirely, and how to get the rest of the organization to do what is being done correctly.

III. *Evaluate alternatives.* Turn wild ideas into feasible solutions and then evaluate them in terms of positive impact, cost to implement, chance of success, etc.

 IV. *Develop action plan.* Define what has to be done and, if necessary, prepare a proposal to management.

  V. *Implement.* Put the plan into action, monitor results, and make further improvements.

This process offers employees the opportunity to come up with ideas for improvement, make more decisions, and fix flaws in the system.

10. *Statistical Support.* Statistical process control (SPC) is both profound and simple. Aside from statistics, you need only: (a) track key process variables (such as dimensions on a piece of steel) and plot them on control charts next to each machine or work station; (b) set limits on tolerances; (c) if operating outside limits, find causes and remove them; (d) if operating inside limits, improve consistency by reducing complexity of methods, setup procedures, and tooling; and (e) ideally, make all of this the responsibility of the machine operator. Quality control personnel become trainers and facilitators. Crosby, for example, recommends removing inspectors and eliminating rework areas so that the system will not allow any mistakes. If workers know this, they will have a new view of what is the minimum acceptable quality level—perfect.

11. *Train the Troops.* To get the most out of employees, they need to be trained on the job in the other eleven keys to quality. Japanese and Korean companies, for example, make tremendous training investments in each individual and continue to train them annually. As new technologies are implemented, additional intensive training is required. More on this will be covered in the next chapter.

12. *Constant Improvements*. To get results quickly, start first with the largest cost of quality areas. But don't stop after a few major successes. On the contrary, use your first ones to show everyone what can be accomplished with an improvement program that draws on their creativity. Quality is a never ending process.

Quality can even drive your advertising. Kaufman & Broad, a major California homebuilder, invites the public in its advertisements to "walk through our homes naked." The accompanying photo is hardly seductive, however—a picture of exposed beams, studs, and dirt. The point they are making is that the company has nothing to hide and is proud of its construction quality.

USE TECHNOLOGY CAREFULLY

America continues lag behind Japan in automation and plant investment. The U.S. Department of Commerce reported in January 1988 that there were 40,000 robots in Japan and 10,000 here. Private investment in plant and equipment as a share of GNP was 17% in Japan and only 10.2% in the United States. But U.S. companies are making progress. Many firms have or are installing nearly fully automated facilities. Allen Bradley Co., for example, as far back as in 1985 threw the switch on a fifty-machine assembly line for 143 varieties of starters of electrical motors—all untouched by human hands. President J. Tracy O'Rourke asserts that the ability to make just one copy is crucial. "If you don't believe that," he declares, "you'll lose." He has chosen automation as his vehicle.[13]

Factory automation, of course, is not new. Manufacturers have been automating high-labor processes for decades. In 1971, as an engineer at Becton-Dickinson, I helped design and was given full responsibility to start up a fully automated production line in the plant. It assembled, labeled, and packaged 15,000 blood sampling devices per hour and replaced a crew of twenty laborers working two shifts manually assembling the products. We quickly learned that perfect quality was needed when no inspectors or laborers were present. To accomplish this we had to add automatic inspection stations that discarded unacceptable parts.

Certain processes are easier to automate than others. Richard Dauch, executive vice president of manufacturing, has increased the robot population at Chrysler from 300 in 1982 to more than 1,200 in 1987. They are used for welding and assembly operations. But he knew they could not be used on older-model trucks, because doing so was too complicated. So he stuck with manual welding.

Manufacturing technology doesn't consist just of robots. Nestlé Foods

Corporation, for instance, uses differential scanning calorimetry (DSC) and nuclear magnetic resonance (NMR) to analyze the fat in its chocolate at some facilities. And the most important piece of technology at many plants is the computer workstation armed with manufacturing resource planning (MRP), software that automates parts ordering, inventory control, and manufacturing scheduling.

One of the biggest blocks to justifying automated systems is traditional cost accounting. According to it, the savings from most automation do not justify the cost. A new math for manufacturing is needed that views manufacturing technology from the perspective of all of the benefits it can bring: increased flexibility, better quality, shortened production cycles, and greater customer satisfaction. Instead of automating to cut costs, it should be thought of as a way to get new customers and hold on to existing ones. Your business's very survival may depend on it.

IMPROVEMENT THROUGH PEOPLE

Capital and labor no longer are opposing inputs in the production equation. Whereas in the past one replaced the other, today the two must work in unison. In fact, all of the above strategies can happen only when people are motivated, organized, skilled, and focused. How to make this happen is covered in the next chapter.

15

Leveraging the Organization

"BACK when they called it the personnel department, we didn't have these problems," a top executive complained, referring to his company's human resource function. The CEO countered, "That's because we never considered who was going to implement our strategy. If you recall, it rarely ever got executed." Walt Disney said it best: "You can dream, build, and create the most wonderful place in the world, but it takes people to make the dream come true."

STRATEGIC ORGANIZATIONAL PERFORMANCE

The senior managements of progressive companies know that the most well-conceived strategy is useless if the organization can't, or doesn't want to, execute. But the extent to which these corporations assess and monitor their people resources varies considerably. A survey of Fortune 500 firms in 1984 found that while 54% of the companies prepare strategic human resource plans, only 15% had comprehensive systems.[1] Exhibit 15–1

EXHIBIT 15–1

People Planning Process

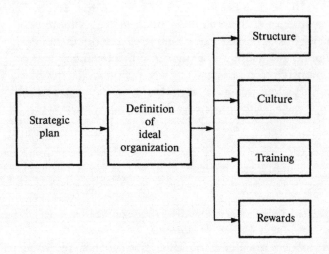

presents the process for strategic human resource planning. While there are many elements involved, the four essentials are structure, culture, training, and performance.

Citicorp in the mid-1970s ranked last out of thirty banks in a survey of customer service satisfaction. Management decided it no longer wanted to be a bank; it wanted to become a financial services company. Not only did its strategy and identity have to be changed, the customer service issue had to be resolved. Management analyzed the back office operations and developed a totally new human resources plan. Departments were reorganized, jobs redesigned, computer workstations added, salaries upgraded, and individuals focused on a small number of clients. Customer service improved dramatically, and the workforce was substantially reduced. Citicorp today is the premier financial services company in the nation.[2]

STRATEGIC ORGANIZATIONAL STRUCTURE

"Can This Elephant Dance?" was the title of a February 1988 *Time* magazine article. It described IBM's liberation of its divisions.[3] As CEO John Akers stated, "We are making IBM more open, more flexible, and more agile." Akers's vision contrasts highly with the centralized company he inherited. In a fundamental change, the Armonk, New York, headquarters no longer calls the shots on products, markets, and manufacturing. Instead, thousands of IBM headquarters employees were transferred to business units responsible for each arena: PCs, mainframes, communications, and components.[4] IBM is just one example of the organizational restructurings sweeping the nation. The moves are intended to make companies more responsive to customers, increase white-collar productivity, and, in general, match organization design to strategy. The most effective approach is a decentralized network, organized by market.

Decentralized Networks

It's easy to decentralize, but a proper balance must be struck. "In my mind it's like parenting," says Robert Waterman. "Too many rules and the kids rebel. Not enough rules and the kids rebel."[5] For decentralization to work, crucial values must be ingrained in division management. Furthermore, it must have a clear vision of what corporate is after. Broad resource allocation, unit performance measurements, and strategic planning for new and related businesses still have to be kept central. And in the case of a single-industry business, operating systems are best done by headquarters for the purpose of speed of execution and economy of scale.

Italy's Benetton Group, for instance, has achieved the ideal balance between capitalizing on the advantages of small-scale flexibility and large-scale systems. Its 4,500 franchised clothing shops in seventy countries totaled $2.5 billion in sales in 1987. While these retail outlets act autonomously in order to cater to local styles and needs, a worldwide computer network links each shop with the corporate office, which in turn is linked with its nine factories and subcontractors. The centralized system offers management exceptional responsiveness to changes in fashion trends. To increase flexibility, the plants do not dye the fabrics until the garments are finished. Sales per square foot in the stores run several times the retail industry average.

Many multinationals are adopting this innovative network-type organization structure. Everyone is connected to everyone else in terms of both strategy development and execution. The relational database technology offered by Oracle Corporation and others is helping this trend along. This technology can make virtually all the company's information available to front-line decision makers.

Market-Driven Organizations

Beyond networks, or within them, the four most common ways to organize are by function, product, geographical area, and market segment. As companies grow, they usually end up serving more than one market with more than one product line through more than one channel of distribution. Given today's need to be "close to the customer," to borrow a phrase from Tom Peters, all companies should give some thought to reorganizing at least some of their people—at a minimum their marketing and sales departments—by market segment.

Many successful firms are structured in this manner. IBM's mainframe and minicomputer marketing operations have been organized in this way since the 1970s. Customers are segmented by industry such as financial institutions, hospitals, airlines, retail, and others. This enables IBM's salespeople calling on these accounts to be experts at solving each customer's specific types of problems. Any company selling systems would benefit from this structure, rather than selling individual products through many uncoordinated salespeople. National Semiconductor is another example. In 1987 it reorganized its marketing departments to focus on chip applications. Before, salespeople had been assigned to the company's various chip technologies.

One of the key moves DG Mouldings made in the early 1980s was to assign a different marketing manager to each of its three markets: home centers, mobile homes, and industrial accounts (picture frame manufacturers, door manufacturers, et cetera). While the product in essence was the same—lineal mouldings—each segment required different distributors, product development, and customer support. Manufacturing operations within DG Mouldings' factories were also segregated by market in many respects. Recall the factory within the factory concept discussed in the previous chapter.

If dropping your present orientation sounds too disruptive or risky, try a transition move. Assign marketing, engineering, and operations specialists to a few of your key market segments, or to one or more of your high-priority new segments. These specialists can work with your existing sales and operations people to provide them with the detailed training and strategies they need to customize their ways.

Packaged goods companies in the past were less inclined to organize by market segment because of the homogeneous nature of supermarkets. As a result, food manufacturers generally used a product-oriented organization structure commonly known as "brand management." But now even this industry is focusing through an approach called "regional marketing." In a relatively new trend for national consumer goods companies, General Foods, Campbell Soup, Procter & Gamble, Frito-Lay, and others have decentralized their marketing departments so that they can tailor their strategies to each region. This gives them the flexibility to take advantage of local differences in demographics, seasons, media, and competitive situations. Advertising and promotion are customized, and in some cases so are the products as well. For example, Campbell introduced a spicy version of its nacho cheese soup and Ranchero beans in the Southwest, where the Hispanic population is a major factor.

Customizing the organization can lead to complexity, however, which can increase costs. Borden backed into regional marketing through acquisitions of regional food companies, some forty during 1986 and 1987. The regionals create new products as well as borrow them from one another, which keeps Borden's national competitors confused as to what product is coming out next. In 1987 Borden grew 30% to $6.5 billion and increased profits by 20% to $265 million. So the next time you want to take a fresh look at how to organize your marketing and sales departments, start with your market segmentation scheme and work backwards. This way your markets become the focal point for your entire business. It is a great way to keep existing customers happy and to acquire new ones while you are at it.

Creating new divisions for new product/market segments is almost mandatory in those cases where you do not want customers to associate your new product or service with the old. This dissociation strategy was used by Disney with its Touchstone Pictures and by Honda with its Acura. Disney needed to preserve the family positioning of its base business. Honda needed to create snob appeal for its pricy new sports car. Both strategies worked. Creating a new division can allow a new culture to take hold in your company. But what if the culture of your entire organization needs adaptation to the competitive environment of the 1990s?

CHANGING THE CORPORATE CULTURE

The origin of organizational culture dates back to ancient Greece. It was invented by Pericles, the father of Athens's Golden Age. In a funeral oration for Athenian soldiers in 431 B.C., he described the ideal organization to his troops: democratic government, individual dignity, promotion based on merit, fun ("When work is over we are in a position to enjoy all kinds of recreation for our spirits."), and innovation ("Athens does not copy the institutions of our neighbors. It is more a case of our being a model to others than our imitating anyone else.''). Developing a strong culture was important to Pericles, because he needed a unified team. Athens was at war with Sparta.[6]

Alan Kennedy, co-author of the 1982 book *Corporate Cultures,* is one of the key revivers of the culture concept. In 1975, as a consultant for McKinsey & Co., he was dismayed that a client in implementing the results of a major cost reduction study after six months actually increased costs by a few million dollars. The client's approach to implementation of the McKinsey recommendations was to hire cost reduction specialists in each department. His team realized it was the company's culture at fault. It had been a growth company for so long, it implemented cost reduction in the same way. ''The mentality of management had to be changed,'' Kennedy states.[7]

Two Automobile Company Cultures

Ford Motors undertook a radical and highly successful shift in corporate culture in the mid-1980s. It left an era of acrimony behind to embrace a new one of teamwork and, as CEO Donald Peterson calls it, ''getting along.'' To win skeptics over to the new way, Peterson and his senior executive used every opportunity to show that, first, they got along, and second, group efforts such as the Team Taurus was the way of the future. But old ways die hard. Middle management was the biggest block. To convert them, numerous small group meetings were needed to help them find ways to work together better.

The Stuttgart headquarters of West Germany's largest corporation was reeling from a top management restructuring in July 1987. The dispute was over whether Daimler-Benz, maker of Mercedes cars, should continue its aggressive diversification program. Chairman Werner Breitschwerdt, who was against the strategy, quit. Germany's most powerful banker, Alfred Herrhaulsen, whose bank owns 28% of Daimler-Benz, and who was chairman of Daimler-Benz's supervisory board since 1985, won. ''I want to lead the company into a new and promising future,'' he said. ''Before 1985, Daimler-Benz was a car manufacturer. Now it is a complex, diversified company. We need to achieve a new corporate culture, a new mentality.''[8]

Ford needed a cultural change in the middle and bottom of the organization. Daimler-Benz underwent one at the top.

Assessing and Modifying
Your Company's Culture

To understand your organization, you need to know its values, philosophies, beliefs, and practices. You also need to be aware of the origin and strength of them. Sources of information for a values clarification include (1) the type of offices and manufacturing facilities, (2) the size and nature of the organization structure, (3) published information for internal and external consumption, (4) interviews with employees at all levels, and (5) interviews with customers, competitors, and anyone else knowledgeable about the business and its people. Also, the type of people who get promoted and demoted (or fired) will provide excellent insight. An analysis of the above information contrasted with the ideal culture for a specific company and its strategy will yield one of four outcomes:

1. A strong culture that is matched to the company's strategy
2. A strong culture that is mismatched to the strategy
3. A mix of cultures in different divisions or departments
4. A lack of a clear-cut culture

Those companies that fall into the first category need only continue what they are doing to reinforce their existing values. Firms in the second category need cultural overhauls in order to successfully put their strategies into action. Companies in the third category have to develop a unifying theme, while preserving the individualistic points that may be needed to operate successfully in each division. Firms in the fourth category have to reshape and add vitality to their value systems.

Changing a culture is a challenging and slow process. Communicating to all employees the vision and strategy of the company, along with the ideal values needed to implement it, is a first step. This should be done through written documents and repetitive oral explanation in a cascading manner: CEO to vice presidents, VPs to middle managers, middle management to supervisors, and supervisors to the front lines. Beyond that, use the change process outlined in Chapter 8.

How Apple Evolved Its Culture

Earlier in the book I talked about Apple Computer's outstanding success in the late 1980s. The company underwent a dramatic strategic shift. Says John Sculley, ''We totally repositioned Apple out of the home computer market and into the business market, while continuing in the educational market."[9] To accomplish this, a shift in corporate culture was needed. Cheryl Wicks, Apple's Performance Management Strategy expert, described it to me as follows:

> You can't change a culture until you understand what it is now—the good and the bad. The blue jeans and t-shirts, for example, are artifacts. They are not our total culture. Apple is about trusting people's judgment and trying to transform their creative talents into success. [Exhibit 15–2 presents the picture Wicks uses to describe this.] This belief system could be any organization's—that of the Girl Scouts, the Presbyterian Church, whatever. Apple is different because of our objectives. Beliefs plus objectives equals behavior, and behavior leads to action which leads to success.
>
> What our company has to change is the core of the apple. The first major cultural change was accepting the notion of creating great systems. Our original people were "one person–one computer" types who would insist, "I don't do systems." In 1986, John Sculley at a worldwide conference spoke of connectivity, but added, "My saying this is

EXHIBIT 15–2

What Is the Apple Magic?

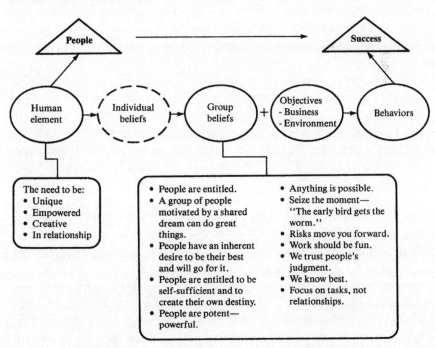

a network/systems company will not make it so.'' Many Apple people said "no way.'' They had the entitlement to say "no'' because at Apple people are encouraged to speak their mind.

Over time, John Sculley spoke about it in many speeches he made in the company, all the while acknowledging he could not edict it. In addition, our marketing people began saying the outside world was changing, and that the business market, a target, used more systems than the education market. We want to be in both markets. People came to accept the broader vision of the company. Other tools for making the culture change were hiring some systems people and modifying some of our reward systems.

The second major cultural change Apple made was to make it easier for people to do business with us. Some customers would say, "We love your products, we love your image, and we hate dealing with you. It's difficult.'' We have since reorganized and formed a Customer Satisfaction Group, which handles distribution, customer service, and customer support.[10]

The statement on the cover of Apple's 1987 Annual Report says it all: "Human creativity—not machine efficiency—is the true measure of our progress.''

STRATEGIC TRAINING AND DEVELOPMENT (STD)

There is no better way to unlock employee potential than through strategic training and development (STD). It is a continuous process. If your company is in a stable situation, new employees have to be brought up to speed and existing ones developed for future roles at higher levels. If your company is changing its culture or strategy or both, it needs to assimilate new skills and values. Training (short-term focus) and development (long-term impact) are both needed.

Training should not only provide knowledge but enable employees to apply the new knowledge on the job. In the best STD programs, employees learn by doing. Take quality. Many programs offered to companies by training firms are all theory and technique. A few theoretical examples are included in the seminars, but the client's actual problems go untouched. In the programs that I endorse, employees receive a bit of theory, have techniques shown to them, and then use the techniques on real-life problems and opportunities in their companies. The result is that the training "sticks with them'' and the company gets to implement programs for increased profit. General Electric does a form of this in its Action Learning approach to executive development. Once a year in its Business Management Course, consulting teams of attendees are formed to go to a GE operation where they research, analyze, create solutions to, and make recommendations on an existing business problem.[11]

Motorola spends about 2.5% of sales on training. Much of it has been in plant and office automation, quality, and statistical process control. The results have been dramatic. "We've documented the savings from the SPC and problem-solving methods we've trained our people in," Bill Wiggenhorn, training director at Motorola, reports. "We're running at the rate of return of about 30 times the dollars invested—which is why we've gotten pretty good support from senior management."[12] Return on training (ROT) can be immediate and substantial.

Even nonprofit organizations have to run themselves like a business nowadays. So STD is essential for them as well. "The cemetery operation of the Catholic Archdiocese of Los Angeles has a $40 million budget, two hundred employees, unions, ten operations spread across two states, and the support staff functions of a medium-sized business," says Doyle Young, president of On-Site Plus in Concord, California, a training firm working with the Archdiocese. "It plans several years out and provides management training to its multicultural workforce." On-Site distinguishes itself by the variety of training it offers from its network of four hundred experts who work on a contract basis. Training many times is the missing link in strategy implementation. Make sure it is not one in yours.

ORGANIZATIONAL PERFORMANCE

Training is an enabling function. Performance pay is a motivating one. In the battle for the hearts and minds of your employees, the multiplier effect comes from your reward system. Setting up a performance-based plan requires a mixture of seven elements: base pay, merit pay, short-term incentives, long-term incentives, benefit perks, autonomy, and working environment.

Automatic across-the-board pay raises are no longer the rule in most companies. Performance—individual, team, department, division, and total corporation—is being tied to compensation. Even companies that had avoided any kind of performance-pay system in the past are seeing the light. There are two major advantages to employers. First, the programs are motivating. Second, corporations can keep a lid on fixed costs and increase rewards only when overall financial performance produces the funds to do so.

Some firms give unilateral rewards to everyone in appreciation of teamwork. Wells Fargo, for example, gave each of its 22,000 employees an early Christmas present in 1987—a $100 check to thank them for their hard work during the Wells–Crocker merger. Each person also was told he or she could take a day off of his or her choice. Len Moore, CEO of Moore Industries, in 1988 gave all production workers the week between Christmas and New Year's off with full pay because the company achieved a targeted production level in each of the months during the latter half of the year.

In the implementation of strategy, ROI stands for return on the individual.

PART

FOUR

Corporate Restructuring

16

Creative Corporate Planning

IN December 1986, T. Boone Pickens was quoted as saying, "The main event—the restructuring of corporate America—will go on." It has. The wave of restructurings in the eighties was aimed at undoing the diversification efforts of the seventies. Organizations streamlined themselves to stand up to global competitors and to defend against takeovers. They also altered corporate structure to serve customers better and for other reasons discussed in this chapter.

Resources are being shifted at blinding speed in and out of industries and businesses by companies large and small. Top managements are stripping expenses and assets out of their operations to become more cost competitive. And a wide variety of mechanisms are being employed to finance the movements of capital.

Some companies, no doubt, undertook wrenching cutbacks and selloffs in a knee-jerk response to a major earnings shortfall or takeover attempt. However, many top managements have well thought out game plans behind their moves to increase shareholder value. I shall concentrate primarily on the latter.

Everyone Is Doing It

Major corporations by no means have a corner on the market. For example, the Soviet Union is going through a change at the time of this writing. Its *perestroika* (restructuring) at one point looked as if it were going to turn into a *peretryaska* (shakeup) as a result of opposition to Mikhail S. Gorbachev's reforms. But in early 1989 things again look back on track. Interestingly, Gorbachev is calling for a competitive economy very similar to capitalism.

In May 1987 a headline in a major metropolitan newspaper read "The Restructuring of the U.S. Beef Business." The industry was staggered in the late 1970s when consumers became alarmed over high fat and cholesterol levels in beef. Annual per capita demand fell from 94.4 pounds in 1976 to 76.5 pounds five years later. In addition, foreign competitors— mainly from New Zealand, Canada, and Ireland—have captured 10% of the U.S. market with their less fatty cattle. Hundreds of cattle producers here have streamlined, sold out, or gone bankrupt. In trying to cater to market needs, they are developing new, leaner cattle. Also, "boutique" producers are springing up, with "designer cattle" that are fed organically or raised on beer, believed to produce leaner, tastier meat. One day there may even be robotic roundups. Today, however, the cowboy and his horse's jobs are still secure.[1]

REASONS FOR RESTRUCTURING

Restructuring is pervasive, and it doesn't appear to be a temporary phenomenon. This is in part because there are so many reasons to do do. I found that out when I organized and chaired a conference in 1985 entitled "Corporate Restructuring: How Five San Francisco Companies Are Doing It" for the San Francisco chapter of the Association for Corporate Growth. Each of the companies—McKesson, Transamerica, Levi Strauss, Crown Zellerbach, and Castle & Cooke—had a different story. Here are the nine most prevalent reasons to restructure:

1. *Sustain Growth and Financial Performance.* This is the healthiest reason to restructure a company—to maintain a track record of high returns to stockholders. To the top managements of some companies, restructuring is not an event but a continuing process of response to shifting economic and competitive forces. The epitome of this is General Electric. Since John

Welch became chairman in 1981, GE has sold more than 250 businesses or product lines and bought 350 others. Those that went did not fit in with the company's strategy of global leadership. John Welch requires a business unit to be either number one or number two in an industry, or not to be part of GE.

Deal-making is not GE's only restructuring strategy. Productivity improvement was a high priority between 1981 and 1988. The company reduced its workforce by 100,000 workers, 25% of the total, while increasing revenues nearly 50%. In doing so, Welch completely transformed the culture of the organization from a large bureaucratic organization into a lean, mean one that is totally focused on performance. John Trani, chief of GE Medical Systems, calls the company's managers "win-aholics."

John Welch's vision is of a GE that is worth more than any other U.S. company in terms of market capitalization. Since 1981 it has gone from tenth to third. To do so required a move out of commodity businesses such as televisions and appliances, and into high-tech manufacturing, broadcasting, and investment banking. It has been tough on a lot of people. But, as *Business Week* reported in December 1987, "Like it or not, the management styles of more and more U.S. companies are going to look a lot more like GE's."[2]

2. *Back to the Core.* The most common restructuring move is deconglomeration, the undoing of past corporate diversification programs. Many companies found that diversifying added at least as much risk as it was supposed to hedge against. They have gone back to focusing on their original core business, where their strength has always been. Borden is one example. The company was once what CEO Romeo Ventres calls a "smorgasbord of companies—we had women's clothing, fertilizer, a phosphate rock mine, perfume, a fast-foot chain."[3] Most of those have been divested, although Borden still remains a multibusiness corporation. It now focuses on six groups: dairy products, pasta (seventeen regional brands), snacks, niche grocery products, nonfood consumer brands, and chemical specialties. In 1987 Borden grew 30% to $6.5 billion and increased its return on equity to 17.2%.

Another example of reverting to one's roots is Household International. Formerly called Household Finance Corporation, it got caught up in the diversification fad in 1961. Over the next twenty years it bought a hardware chain, discount grocers, furniture retailers, an Alaskan airline, National Car Rental, banks, savings and loans, insurance companies, a dredging company, and numerous manufacturing firms. Revenue in 1984 was $8.3

billion, with earnings of $234 million. But then performance became erratic. "Now everyone looks for a common theme," says Donald Clark, chairman and CEO.[4] So investment bankers got rich again through the divestiture of most of its manufacturing divisions, the $5 billion retail group, National Car Rental, and others. The company slimmed down to $3.4 billion in revenue in 1987, with an ROE of 19.4%. Ironically, management considers its growth division to be its original business— Household Financial Services.

3. *Poor Prospects for the Core Business*. Sometimes a streamlining is called for, but not back to the original core business. Lagging sales or global competitive threats can cause a company to get completely out of the business for which it is best known. One restructuring in July 1988 touched everyone who spent time as a child in penny arcades. The pinball wizard, Bally Manufacturing Corporation, sold its coin-operated amusement games subsidiary to concentrate on divisions that dominate their markets: casinos, slot machines, and health clubs.

Firestone means tires, right? Not any more, at least not from the manufacturing standpoint. Firestone Tire & Rubber sold 75% of its tire business to the Japanese in early 1988. It had been third in market share, but management saw little potential for sales growth and profitability. It will concentrate on the retail automotive aftermarket business, where margins are better and capital-intensiveness is much lower. (In contrast, the market leader in tire manufacturing, Goodyear, restructured in 1986 by divesting its energy and aerospace businesses to concentrate on tires.)

The most notable corporate transformation is American Can's remake into Primerica. In 1980 its top management came to the conclusion that the future was grim for its capital-intensive heat process food can and packaging materials business. Even though it was number one in the industry, it faced overcapacity, low growth, and declining profits. American Can's strategic planning told management that both high growth and returns awaited in the distribution and service industries. They were also far less cyclical and capital-intensive. Management spent a year between the spring of 1980 and the spring of 1981 analyzing 120 different service businesses. It chose three: financial services (specifically insurance), specialty retailing, and direct marketing. Then came the transformation. Thirty divestitures and fifteen acquisitions later, the company changed its name. By 1986 all of Primerica's revenues came from the target industries. It did not own a single business it had been in ten years earlier.[5] Gerald Tsai, Jr., chairman and CEO, says: "Inside the company, it was clearly understood to be a radical break with the past. It was a visionary undertaking—a major leap into the future.''[6] In 1987 Primerica sold more individual life insurance than Prudential and Metropolitan combined, originated $2 billion in home mortgages, owned the largest direct mail company in the United States and sold more records and tapes than any other music retailer. Earnings per share in 1987 were $3.35 (for a ROE of 12.3%) versus a loss of $7.31 in 1982.

4. *Volume or Profit Shortfall.* Not all restructurings have to be as radical as Primerica's. The ones highlighted in the press most often involve a business downturn and require the sale of underperforming assets, the scaling back of operations, and layoffs. Most major American banks have restructured along these lines as a result of foreign loan losses. Bank of America is a notable example. To rebuild the capital structure and restore profitability, it sold numerous assets for financial gain: its world headquarters, FinanceAmerica, its Los Angeles head-quarters, Tokyo real estate, BancAmerica Acceptance Corp., Banca d'America d'Italia, Charles Schwab Corp., BankAmerica Finance Ltd., Consumer Trust Services, its West German retail bank, its East Asia bank card operations, and other smaller assets.[7] B of A made it back into the black by the third quarter of 1987 and recovered further in 1988.

Hospital Corporation of America, the nation's largest hospital chain, spun off 104 of its acute-care hospitals to its senior managers in 1987 for $1.8 billion in cash. This was a major change in HCA's operating philosophy, which had been to accumulate as much capacity as possible. But management needed to downsize to its core hospitals in order to try to maximize returns to stockholders. The transaction left HCA with only seventy-five hospitals, fifty psychiatric hospitals, and management service contracts for about 250 hospitals owned by others.

5. *Equity Carve-Outs.* How do you realize full value from a business that is only partially related to your core but is performing very well and has a recognizable name? One option is, of course, to sell it. The other is to sell part of it to the public, which is called an equity carve-out, or a spinout. W. R. Grace, for example, did this with its Herman's Sporting Goods division.

McKesson Corporation in 1987 spun out two of its highly successful subsidiaries, Armor All Products Corporation and PCS, Inc. Armor All enjoys an estimated 90% share of the automotive protectants market and now is owned 16.7% by the public. PCB is the leader in computer-based prescription claims, processing through a network of 90% of the drugstores in the United States and Canada. Investors own 13.8% of it.

Equity carve-outs are effective for achieving greater visibility and fuller appreciation of high-performing business units. They also can improve incentives to subsidiary management through stock options and the like. Management is also held more accountable, which is in itself motivating.

6. *Breakup Value.* In the mid-1980s, breakup value became the new buzzword on Wall Street. It is a measure of the value of the separate parts of a company, which often is greater than the market value of a company based on the price of its stock. I was introduced to this concept ten years before it became jargon, when I was a senior strategic planner for Kaiser Industries. Top management announced in 1975 it was going to liquidate the company with $4 billion in assets and 45,000 employees, because the parts were worth more than the whole. For the next twelve months I valued subsidiaries, prepared prospectuses, identified possible purchasers, and assisted in negotiations. Stockholders received proportionate shares from the spinoff of Kaiser Cement, Aluminum, and Steel, plus cash from the divestiture of Kaiser Engineers, Broadcasting, Sand & Gravel, Aerospace, its insurance division, corporate headquarters, and other miscellaneous assets. The total value received per share of Kaiser Industries stock was $17.00, as against a preatomization price of $9.00.

Breakups frequently occur after a takeover. Beatrice Co. was purchased in 1986, through a leveraged buyout, by Kohlberg Kravis Roberts (KKR), for $6.2 billion. At the time of this writing, more than $7 billion of assets has been sold. The remaining Beatrice Food Group (Hunt tomato products, Orville Redenbacher popcorn, La Choy Oriental foods, and Butterball turkeys) generated revenues of $4 billion in 1988. It is as though KKR were paid $800 million to take it, less the energy and expenses of disposing of the pieces. Not a bad profit.

7. *Leveraged Buyout.* The classic takeover mechanism is, of course, the leveraged buyout (LBO). Typically, 5% to 20% of the purchase price is in equity (many times even this is borrowed), and the rest is financed with a combination of bank debt and, in the larger deals, junk bonds. The ideal candidate is a company in a mature, noncyclical industry; one that generates heavy cash flow to service debt; has excess assets that can be sold off to repay the principal; and has expenses that can be streamlined to increase margins.

The leverage buyout king is KKR. In 1988 its holdings made it the second largest U.S. conglomerate, slightly behind General Electric in revenues. KKR owns a majority interest in such well-known companies as RJR Nabisco, Beatrice Foods, Duracell, Fred Meyer, Motel 6, Safeway, Owens-Illinois, Stop & Shop, and Jim Walter. And KKR's George Roberts and Henry Kravis have the financing lined up to buy $40 billion more of corporate America.[8]

Frequently the LBO is used as a way to fend off a takeover, or to prevent one. In 1985 Levi Strauss & Co. was taken private by President Robert Haas and the Haas family for $1.6 billion. Their purpose was to remove any takeover threat and to free themselves of criticism from Wall Street. Since then, the company has undergone a sweeping restructuring that included plant closings, sale of its less profitable divisions, and large staff cuts. Financial results in 1987 were the best since 1983 in terms of profit ($135 million), and the highest ever in revenue ($2.86 billion).[9] Employees report that Levi is a leaner, more aggressive company.

8. *After the LBO*. The bonanza in restructurings via the LBO has left many companies leaner, but more heavily in debt. The real question mark is what will happen in the next economic slowdown or recession. Not only will the operating profits of most of these companies decline, but cash flow to cover interest will become tight, and the value of asset sales will diminish. Numerous companies could be in deep trouble. An August 8, 1988 *Business Week* article was headed: "Live by the Junk Bond, Die by the Junk Bond."

The banks that loaned the LBOs money will also be in trouble. As of July 1988, the nation's twenty-one largest banks had lent some $17 billion for LBOs, nearly a quarter of what Third World countries had borrowed from them. Financial institutions seem to go through cycles of overlending—to Latin America, to real estate in Texas, to farmers, and now LBOs.[10]

Perhaps the situation will be remedied by the latest craze: round-tripping, or what's called the "reverse LBO." After selling parts of the companies to pay off debt, manager/owners are taking the companies public again. *Inc.* magazine reported in March 1987: "And who knows? It may be only a matter of time before a company makes its second round-trip. Perhaps the owners will collect frequent-flier coupons along the way."

THE RESTRUCTURING PROCESS

The objective of corporate restructuring—for that matter, of running the company—should be to maximize financial returns to stockholders. This is done in multidivisional companies by optimizing the value of the individual business units, thereby maximizing the value of the whole portfolio. Value is defined as the total long-term return to stockholders: the discounted cash flow of the combination of stock price appreciation plus the dividend stream. But both of these are difficult to forecast, at best. So most financial analysts use two more tangible figures: growth in net earnings and return on equity, particularly the latter. For example, when the retiring CEO of Westinghouse, Douglas E. Danforth, was asked what he considered to be his biggest success as a chief executive, his reply was: "Quantitatively, it's moving our return on equity—the final measure of your effective use of financial resources—from about 12%, which is mediocre, to over 20%, which we believe is sustainable and will put us in the top 5% of the performing industrial enterprises in the country."[11]

How should a multidivisional company go about restructuring itself to increase ROE and growth in earnings? The process involves those same generic five steps of Creative Planning, but with a different focus:

1. Define Your Business (analysis)
2. Develop a Vision (creativity)
3. Rank Your Divisions (judgment)
4. Determine Your Major Moves (planning)
5. Rejuvenate, Divest, and Acquire (action)

Let's take a close look at each of these.

Define Your Business

Your exact approach to this first step will depend on how much strategic planning your company has done in the past. First, you need to profile your divisions. Each may contain a number of product/market segments. If so, these may have to be analyzed separately. Summarize for each division and, perhaps, each product/market segment:

- Profitability—in earnings and return on investment
- Growth rate—historical and potential
- Cash flow—historical and expected future
- Types of customers—industry, size, etc.
- Competitive position—strong, medium, weak
- Cyclicality—with respect to the economy

- Excess assets—that can be stripped away
- Cost reduction potential—if streamlining is in order
- Technologies—both for products and for manufacturing
- Synergy potential—with your other divisions
- Potential for innovation—to increase your competitive edge

The above factors are general and apply to most businesses. Additional or different ones may be needed for your particular industry, as well as the overall nature of your business.

Once you have profiled your business units in detail, develop a set of corporate investment criteria. These will be used to compare your divisions against one another for the purpose of determining which to invest in and which to streamline or even divest. For instance, Exhibit 16–1 presents a list of criteria with their definitions for a large, diversified company with which I worked. A number of critical insights developed when they were applied to its twenty-plus divisions. Cyclicality, for example, was very important for two reasons: (1) The firm had hemorrhaged during the previous recession, and (2) another recession was imminent. In a three-day retreat, top management decided to sell off five then profitable but highly cyclical divisions as quickly as possible. All were sold at or above book value in three months. Within five months a recession occurred, and the markets of these divisions plummeted. The diversified company went through the recession with only a 10% drop in earnings, an outstanding performance considering what would have happened had not management immediately restructured.

Develop a Corporate Vision

Developing a vision was covered in Chapter 7 in the context of writing a strategic plan. With multiple businesses, your challenge is a bit different, and more complex. Review the profiles of your business units and select a business for your core that will be the foundation of your corporate strategy. Size is one criterion, but not the dominant one. Core businesses also should have strong profitability, be in an attractive industry, possess a competitive advantage, and be able to serve as a base from which to expand. Highly diversified companies can have two or even three core businesses, but I would not recommend having more than that. Otherwise your firm is really only a financial holding company. The huge NEC has two: "C&C," computers and communications.

Exhibit 16–1

Corporate Investment Criteria for a Large Diversified Company

WE WILL INVEST IN OUR DIVISIONS THAT:

1. *Capitalize on the Company's Strengths*
   • Management's expertise and past success are in two areas: distribution services and specialty building materials. We will stress these areas in the future.
   • Investments outside these areas must (a) offer very attractive financial returns, (b) possess minimum risk, and (c) not consume large amounts of cash.

2. *Present Attractive Financial Returns*
   • Each division's return on investment must be raised to a level exceeding its cost of capital.
   • A return less than the cost of capital is tolerable only when (a) near-term earnings growth is rapid and (b) returns will increase significantly when growth slows.

3. *Possess Growth Potential*
   • Give particular emphasis to divisions serving high-growth market niches.
   • Also invest in divisions that can increase their penetration of moderate growth markets.

4. *Offer Low Earnings Cyclicality*
   • Maintain low profile in businesses serving cyclical markets.
   • The exception is when a division (a) realizes very high returns in good times, (b) focuses on less cyclical segments of the overall market, (c) serves two or more acyclical markets, and (d) has flexibility due to a small fixed asset base.

5. *Represent Potential Critical Mass*
   • Invest heavily in divisions that have or can attain a dominant position in their market or niche, enabling them to (a) be the price leader, (b) have economies of scale, and (c) control distribution.
   • Favor those divisions that have synergies with others.

6. *Can Build Customer Franchise*
   • Invest in noncommodity products and services that are or can be enhanced through some unique value added.
   • Favor divisions and product lines in which we can develop (a) brand preference, (b) customer loyalty, and (c) premium pricing.

Next, identify existing interrelationships between your business units. Then go one step further: Create a list of potential interdivisional opportunities that could be exploited if the system and cooperation were in place. How to do this was covered in Chapter 9 on facilitating teamwork between divisions.

Now it's time to develop a vision of the ideal overall company. This should include which divisions will be expanded, which streamlined, and how they will all work together. Think of the long term, beyond the constraints of today's in-place management. If any part of your company could be moved or combined with another, which would it be? If two or more divisions could exploit emerging opportunities, how would they do it?

The CEO of one large conglomerate that needed to be restructured asked his top twelve people (most were operating executives) to prepare for a two-day off-site meeting as follows. Each had to write a two- to ten-page letter describing the ideal company five years hence: structure, divisions, philosophy, and even the size and function of the corporate office (they had fun with this last one). The letters were then reviewed at the retreat one by one. There were common thoughts on certain issues, and some excellent new ideas on others. After extensive discussion, a consensus was achieved on a corporate streamlining consisting of both expense reductions and the sale of four divisions. Nearly all the strategies were implemented within twelve months. Management didn't wait five years, the horizon of the exercise.

Rank Your Divisions

With your core business selected and your ideal company visualized, you are now ready to go back and reapply your corporate criteria a final time. Assess each division and business unit on a scale of 5 through 1 or "high, medium, and low," and give an overall rating to each. Then do a forced ranking of them against one another using one criterion: attractiveness for future investment. In other words, which divisions do you want to build more than the others during the planning horizon?

Overlay on your ranked list of divisions the following five categories, starting from the top and working down: (1) heavy investment businesses, (2) medium investment businesses, (3) low investment businesses, (4) turnaround businesses, and (5) divestment businesses. Exhibit 16–2 spells out the definitions of these categories as well as possible strategies for each.

How many of your divisions fall into each category will depend on two factors:

1. The amount of funds the company has for investment. This must be balanced by its need for cash to service debt, mount a takeover defense, buy back stock to increase return on equity, or meet other requirements.

Exhibit 16–2

Division Classifications

1. *Heavy Investment Businesses*
   - Draw on the corporate strengths
   - Meet all other corporate investment criteria
   - Are long-range growth areas for the company

2. *Medium Investment Businesses*
   - Draw on the corporate strengths
   - Offer an attractive financial return
   - Meet most of the other corporate criteria reasonably well; all of them at least acceptably

3. *Low Investment Businesses*
   - Draw on the corporate strengths
   - Recent marginal financial returns; have to prove themselves
   - Competitive positions only marginal

4. *Turnaround Businesses*
   - Draw on corporate strengths, or at least could, if positioned properly
   - Recent poor financial performance
   - Will be turned around financially within two years or divested

5. *Divestment Businesses*
   - Recent poor financial performance
   - Do not draw on corporate strengths
   - Serve cyclical markets

---

2. Your expectation of the cash to be generated or used by the divisions in each category. If you have one very large cash contributor (or cash cow) in the low investment business category, you obviously can afford to have a number of heavy and medium investment businesses.

Remember, that cows need to be fed in order to keep producing milk. Starving cash contributors over a long period can put them on the sick list (into the turnaround category). Periodically reinvest in them, moving them up into the medium or even heavy investment categories for a year or two. Otherwise, someday management will be asking: "Where's the milk?"

A red flag is not having any divestment businesses. Restructuring is a continuous process, not an event. At any given time, nearly all large companies should have something to dispose of. Selling low-performing assets or ones that do not fit with the corporate strategy will free resources that could be better deployed elsewhere. One place to look for divestment opportunities is in your turnaround category. These are businesses that are not necessarily losing money but are just not making their cost of capital.

Don't let them linger in the turnaround mode too long. Giving them a thousand days (roughly three years) is more than enough, and only if they fit with the core. As in poker, you have to "know when to hold 'em, and know when to fold 'em."

Prepare Your Plan and Implement It

It's now time to develop a time-phased corporate restructuring plan. It should present

· The mission, vision, objectives, and strategy for the overall corporation
· The objective, strategy, and financial forecast for each division
· How the portfolio of divisions will shift over time
· What you are going to do with each division, and when
· A summary of the financial implications of your divestitures and reinvestments, with particular attention to cash flow
· An overall financial forecast for the entire corporation

A number of pace-setting firms put in their corporate plans the value of each of their divisions if sold off as a separate business. If the value of a corporation's outstanding equity is less than the sum of its parts, management knows it ought to do something, or a raider may. Westinghouse, for example, continually measures how much each of its twenty-three business units is worth on the open market. Senior management allocates capital on the basis of what it will do for the value of Westinghouse overall, not for earnings per share. Emotional ties to businesses are not part of the company's strategy, as shown by its divestiture of its ninety-year-old lighting business.

Think like a raider. The best managements do exactly what raiders would do before they get a chance to do it.

THE RESHAPING OF McKESSON CORPORATION

In the late 1970s McKesson Corporation began a gradual restructuring process that was still going on in 1988. In an in-depth interview, John Weaton, executive vice president of administration and the company's chief planner for the last fifteen years, explained how the company has gone back to one of its earlier roots:

We began the process long before the word "restructuring" became a popular buzzword. In 1975 we looked at our five groups of businesses: dairy (and other foods), drug distribution, chemical distribution, wine and spirits distribution, and real estate. We found that a significant number of them had unsatisfactory profitability.

We spent the next four years trying to improve the performance of all of our businesses. The biggest improvement in performance came in drug distribution. We changed the rules in the industry by supplying independent drug retailers with our Economost computer system. This helped them bring costs down so they could be competitive with the large chains, and it helped make us the low-cost producer.

We classified our businesses into one of four categories: (1) high growth/high return, (2) high growth/low return, (3) low growth/high return, and (4) low growth/low return. In addition, we used three other criteria: cyclicality, fit with the company, and critical mass to become an industry leader.

In 1979 and 1980 we sold our commercial and residential real estate development operations. To be successful in this business, major decisions need to be made decentrally, which is not our style. Furthermore, the business is highly cyclical.

Next went our food businesses, in 1982 and 1983. This was a tough decision, given that the dairy business was one of our roots (the company's name was Foremost–McKesson prior to 1983). But we felt we could not achieve a high enough return on investment in our dairy operation, or become an industry leader in our other food areas. So we divested Foremost Dairies, Mueller Pasta, and our other food divisions.

We sold our chemical distribution business in 1985 for three reasons. It was cyclical, there was a higher risk of environmental problems than in our other businesses, and we were a small player. We had 4% of the wholesale segment, and the wholesale segment was only 20% of the market. Most chemicals are sold direct.

Our most recent divestiture was our wine and spirits distribution business, which we are just now selling. There's no growth in the industry, and the distributor has little clout with the supplier. The strength lies with distillers who control the franchise at any time.

Our story is not only of divestitures. The funds were redeployed in internal expansion and selected acquisitions of nondurable consumer goods distribution companies. We purchased three large drug distributors—one each in Florida, New York, and the Northeast. We also acquired three large service merchandisers, which serve supermarkets, a related business."[12]

Today, McKesson is the nation's largest wholesale distributor of pharmaceuticals, health and beauty aids, and general merchandise. Revenue in

1987 was $4.8 billion. Return on equity was 13% and had improved steadily over the previous four years.

THE RESTRUCTURING(S) OF GENERAL MILLS

General Mills was at one time in the electronics business. No, that is not a misprint. In the 1950s management thought the food industry was slowing and that it had to diversify. From a base of Gold Medal Flour and Wheaties, it went into specialty chemicals and, yes, electronics. In the 1960s management reevaluated the company and got out of electronics.

In the late 1960s management decided to diversify again, but this time with a bit more focus. It became a consumer conglomerate acquiring companies in the following industries: food (of course), toys, apparel, restaurants, retailing, luggage, coins, stamps, travel, direct marketing, furniture, and jewelry, while broadening its specialty chemicals business. Another round of divestitures was undertaken in the late 1970s and early 1980s to pare the list down.

Bruce Atwater, Jr., chairman and CEO of General Mills, described management's thought process in the 1980s in a speech to the Minneapolis chapter of the Association for Corporate Growth in December 1987. In 1983 General Mills' top management had analyzed its five remaining industries against three corporate criteria: (1) return on capital, (2) volatility, and (3) growth potential (see Exhibit 16–3). Toys and fashion were industries that were working-capital-intensive, had moderate returns on capital, and were highly volatile—unattractive compared with the other three groups.

In January 1985 management got board approval to explore getting out

Exhibit 16–3

General Mills Industry Characteristics in 1984

Industry	Return on Capital	Volatility	Growth Potential
Food	High	Low	Low
Restaurant	High	Moderate	High
Toys	Moderate	High	Moderate
Fashion	Moderate	High	Moderate
Retail	High	Moderate	High

EXHIBIT 16–4

General Mills' Business Categories in 1987

CATEGORY PLANNED	DIVISIONS	REAL GROWTH	PLANNED INVESTMENT (1989–91)
Core	Big G Cereals (Wheaties, Total, Kix, Cheerios), and Red Lobster Restaurants—45% of sales.	6%	$550 million
Established	Betty Crocker, Bisquick, Gold Medal, Dinner Mixes, International Food—32% of sales.	3%	$150 million
Growth	Yoplait, Snacks, Gorton's, Red Lobster International, The Olive Garden, and other new food categories—23% of sales.	15%	$500 million

of toys and fashion. In May 1985 it announced a disposition plan for twenty-five companies, totaling a quarter of General Mills' assets. Parker Brothers, Ship'n Shore, Izod Lacoste, and others were divested by August 1986. Atwater explained that the company's structure in 1988 consisted of businesses in three categories: core, established, and growth. Exhibit 16–4 shows which divisions fall into each category, and the expected growth rate and the investment planned over the next three years.

The results from General Mills' restructuring, to quote *Business Week* on August 8, 1988, "have been nothing short of astonishing." Return on equity leaped to 31% in 1986, and ten more points to 41% in 1987. Is top management done? No. Bruce Atwater in his speech said:

> Companies must constantly experiment with new ideas, not all of which will work. General Mills is by no means sitting still. We continue to restructure, planning to divest inappropriate holdings and planning to grow in our primary fields of interest.

Talbot's and Eddie Bauer were both highly profitable and on the list of probable long-term "keepers." However, they were sold in 1988. Japanese and German companies offered extremely high prices for the companies, yielding funds that could be used to buy back General Mills stock, trading at lower prices after the October 19 stock selloff, to boost earnings per share and return on equity.[13]

Divestitures should always be considered when the long-term value of of a division is much higher to another company than to your own. Which leads us to the topic of strategic acquisitions and divestitures.

17

Acquisition Bargains, Divestiture Coups

CORPORATE COURTINGS

Business Week came out with a startling statistic on January 12, 1987: "If mergers and acquisitions were to continue at 1986's rate, every public company could be turned over to new owners by the year 2001." Between 1982 and 1986, some 12,200 companies and corporate divisions, worth nearly $500 billion, changed hands—nearly a fifth of the market value of all traded corporate stocks.

Exhibit 17–1 presents the number of deals over $1 million in value that have occurred from 1980 to 1988, as tracked by W. T. Grimm. Alex Ladias, research director with the firm, states:

> The falloff in 1987 was due mostly to the change in the tax law that came into effect on January 1, 1987. The capital gains rate for corporations was increased from 24% to 28%, forcing buyers to offer more attractive bids, and thereby lowering their returns. There was a rush to close deals in fourth quarter 1986 that would have been done in 1987. By 1988, transaction growth was back to normal.[1]

EXHIBIT 17–1

Acquisitions in the 1980s

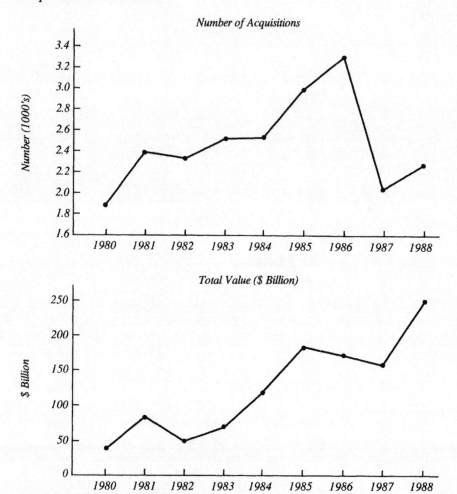

Source: W. T. Grimm, Chicago

THE GOOD, THE BAD,
AND THE TERRIBLE

With so many transactions done each year, one would expect to hear that acquirers are reaping large rewards. However, it has been said that mostly it is just the stockholders of the acquired firms who realize increased value. Many studies of the results of acquisitions come to the same conclusion:

- One-third of all acquisitions are profitable—their ROI to the acquirer is greater than the cost of capital.
- One-third are roughly break-even—they generate a marginal ROI (about equal to the cost of capital).
- One-third are unprofitable—they either have a return considerably less than the acquirer's cost of capital, or they outright lose money.

The first part of this chapter is devoted to the principles and approaches involving the top third—undertaking profitable purchases of companies. I call these "acquisition bargains," which is what they are, relative to the amounts paid for them. The chapter closes with how to sell a company for the highest price.

TWENTY-NINE TYPES OF BARGAINS

If some acquisitions work and many more don't, what differentiates the winners? A chief factor is that the acquirer going into the deal has a clear understanding of why a superior ROI will be achieved. A second is that the acquirer has more than one reason, which lets the buyer hedge its bets. Rarely does everything go exactly according to plan in an acquisition.

A key tenet of creativity is to generate as many options as possible. Here in six categories are numerous ways an acquisition can be a bargain for your company. Strive for as many as you can in each deal, and you will maximize your chances of success.

Strategic Synergy

This is the most talked about reason for making acquisitions—the one plus one equals three rationale. Many times, unfortunately, the synergy turns out to be a mirage. But often enough, it is real. Companies can have chemistry. Maybe even physics.

1. *Marketing Synergy*. Two companies join forces in attacking shared market segments with benefits accruing to both. Metropolitan Life Insurance acquired Century 21 in 1985 for $251 million. Richard Loughlin, president and CEO of Century 21, described in 1988 the legitimate marketing synergy achieved: "When a home is sold, an independent Metropolitan franchisee sells the new owner a homeowner insurance policy, with the real estate agent sharing in the commission." Century 21 is by far the largest residential real estate broker in the country, handling 11% of all home sales, totaling $2.2 billion in commissions in 1987.[2]

2. *Geographical Synergy.* Sometimes the easiest way to move into a new geographical territory is to buy your way in. This is what led Wells Fargo to purchase Crocker Bank. Wells Fargo was strong in Northern California and Crocker was strong in the southern half of the state. The combination was a natural. It also allowed management to streamline redundant systems, consolidate branches, centralize automation operations, and combine the two ATM systems. It was one of the most successful bank mergers in history. In 1988 Wells Fargo grew substantially, but more importantly, it had an outstanding return on equity of 24%.

3. *Technological Synergy.* A pivotal technology can often be acquired easier than developed internally. This is the reason for many high- and medium-technology acquisitions. At times this combination helps the acquiree more than the acquirer. Monolithic Memories was sold to Advanced Micro Devices in 1987 for this reason. Irwin Federman, formerly CEO of Monolithic Memories and now vice chairman of the board of AMD, explains:

> We were number one in bipolar semiconductors but out of manufacturing capacity in a growing market. Also, we had no position in C-mos, which we needed and which was growing rapidly. AMD had both. Using the paradigm of the trees, the two companies had very few overlapping branches, but nearly totally overlapping trunks.[3]

4. *Operational Synergy.* An acquiree may have facilities that could manufacture some of the parent firm's products, or vice versa. Or a large firm can offer a small technology company the distribution capability it lacks. Maintaining a sales force is expensive. Furthermore, small firms many times can't sell enough to recoup research and development expenses, which are proportionately lower at larger companies.

5. *Raw Material Synergy.* To maintain operational flexibility, companies are careful not to overcommit resources to raw material production. But sometimes backward integration is necessary. Texaco's acquisition of Getty Oil was largely for this reason. It ended Texaco's potentially disastrous decline in oil and gas reserves. And the price of Getty, $9.9 billion, was relatively inexpensive compared with the cost of finding new oil and gas reserves, plus the other operations of the company.

Strategy Moves

Here are five strategic reasons for purchasing a company that involve synergies between the acquirer and acquiree, but have broader rationales behind them.

1. *Industry Dominance*. Highly fragmented industries are often ripe for a strong acquiring player who can then gain industry dominance.

- McKesson Corporation strengthened its position as the largest pharmaceutical wholesaler in the country by acquiring three large distributors in strategic geographic locations.
- Computer Associates leapfrogged Lotus Development and Microsoft in 1988 to become the largest software house in the country. CA acquired sixteen software companies between 1982 and 1988 and reached $710 million in sales with a 20% ROE.
- The largest and broadest-based trucking service company was assembled the same way. In just six years, Ryder grew through pivotal acquisitions to $4.6 billion in revenue with $187 million of net earnings for a 14.8% ROE.

Many other companies leveraged their strengths via acquisitions to become industry leaders.

2. *Startup More Expensive*. Many times, starting up a new plant or developing a new consumer brand is far more expensive than acquiring one. Most major food companies are constantly looking to get somewhere else on the supermarket shelf. But it takes $80 to $120 million to launch a major new product nationally. Purchasing one is far less risky. Food brands with strong franchises are largely immune from foreign competition, have staying power due to their consumer franchise, and usually are quite profitable.

3. *Get a Toehold*. Quaker Oats Co.'s strategy is to acquire small and think big. Its corporate plan is to buy small, independent companies and build their brands by taking them national. Quaker Oats offers bigger marketing budgets and wider distribution. It did this, for example, with its 1983 purchase of Stokely–Van Camp (pork & beans, Gatorade, and other brands).

Kraft buys well-established regional brands and finds that taking them national can generate substantial income. All-American Gourmet (Budget Gourmet frozen entrées), Knudsen, Frusen Gladje and Celestial Seasonings are four examples.

4. *Acquire Up*. This is when a company swallows a much bigger one. Usually a LBO is involved, whereby the larger company's debt capacity is used to acquire itself. An example is Britain's Blue Arrow PLC purchase of Manpower. Manpower's revenues were 2.5 times the $480 million of Blue Arrow when the takeover was made. And Manpower's stock was selling for twenty times earnings. Regardless, the consistent

growth and cash generation qualities of the temporary office help industry provided the leverage power Blue Arrow needed. Another example is the way NV Homes purchased Ryan Homes, three times its size, and nailed down the number one spot in homebuilding in 1988. After buying Ryan, headquartered in Pittsburgh, Dwight Schar closed unprofitable operations in Houston and Atlanta, and broadened Ryan's market focus from strictly entry-level homes to include medium-priced ones for trade-up buyers.[4]

5. *Strategic Flexibility*. Sometimes the purchase of a smaller company can give the parent flexibility either in the marketplace or in operations that would be difficult to achieve on its own. Domaine Chandon, the company mentioned earlier as the first joint venture of a premium European champagne company and an American firm, purchased the Shadow Creek sparkling wine brand from Corbett Canyon in 1988. Shadow Creek, at 23,000 cases a year, is tiny compared with Domaine Chandon's 400,000 cases. What it offered was flexibility. Domaine Chandon's growth is limited due to its insistence on using Napa Valley grapes exclusively. With Shadow Creek, Domaine Chandon can import grapes from anywhere in California and produce wine at its parent's modern winery in Yountville.[5]

Portfolio Purchases

Many companies have a stock market valuation well below the sum of their parts. In the case of privately held companies, they can be undervalued in the mind of the owner for a variety of reasons.

1. *Excess Divisions*. Any company that is in so many businesses that the overall organization is hard to understand represents an opportunity to be stripped down to its core. If you analyze these companies, as covered in the previous chapter, many turn out to be genuine bargains. Classify a candidate's divisions into four types: core businesses, related divisions, unsuccessful diversifications, and nonoperating assets. Then develop a valuation based on building or renewing the core and related divisions (particularly those that are synergistic with your own company), as well as divesting the rest to pay down debt.

2. *Excess Assets*. Selling off or reducing assets of a purchased company is not an unusual way for an acquirer to reduce its up-front investment, improve ROI, and pay down debt. Be sure to look for the less obvious, those hidden or excess assets that can be dollarized quickly. For example,

is there a plant located on real estate that is worth more as a commercial development? Perhaps the production from this plant can be consolidated into another one of the candidate's facilities, or one of your company's. Also, study inventory and receivables levels. Sometimes you can find a company that carries far more than necessary.

3. *Undervalued Assets*. As opposed to stripping a company of its assets, some have assets on the books at values far less than they are worth. One example is hundreds of acres of land that contain vast resources such as timber, oil, natural gas, or minerals. Crown Zellerbach's timber resources were a superb opportunity for gain for Sir James Goldsmith when he took over the company. Retail chains with numerous outlets report the cost of their holdings at book values substantially less than market value. In other cases, the assets are not even on the books, such as a real estate lease costing well below the going rate per square foot.

Bottom Fishing

Are you tired of paying premiums for companies? How about industrial scavenging—buying companies that are out of favor for a variety of reasons. It can be lucrative. But bottom fishing is done best by buyers who thoroughly understand the industries of their targets. Here is what to look for:

1. *Turnaround Opportunity*. There are opportunities in businesses left for dead by others. Companies in trouble usually can be purchased at substantial discounts from book value. However, you have to be able to breathe new life into them, or the seller's problems become yours. Silicon Valley analysts lauded National Semiconductor's 1987 acquisition of Fairchild from Schlumberger Ltd. National paid about twenty cents on the dollar for a company that lost $1.5 billion over the previous eight years. The centerpiece of the deal for National was Fairchild's logic chip division. The combination of companies is a major supplier in transistor-to-transistor logic. National also gained a much stronger position with the military.[6]

2. *Turnaround in Progress*. Sometimes a major corporation has a poor performing division to unload. It is willing to sell the division for book value or less. But in its impatience, it doesn't realize that a turnaround is just around the corner. Another situation where a turnaround is in progress but unrecognized is when a public corporation takes a mighty writeoff. The worst is behind the company, but sometimes the stock market doesn't recognize the fact. A savvy buyer who spots this early can acquire a

company that will emerge as quite a value and at a price well below its worth.

3. *Expense Reduction.* Some companies are noted for operating successfully with a tight control on expenses. Gannett built a chain of more than ninety newspapers, mostly in smaller markets, by buying up family-owned dailies and instituting operating systems and controls that are reowned for turning profits. The cash flow from those properties provides the capital Gannett uses to acquire still more companies and for expanding *USA Today* which it started up in 1982.

4. *Undermanaged.* The ideal ingredients of a turnaround opportunity are good products, a good market, and bad management. In 1980 Joseph Welch bought Bachman, a leading East Coast manufacturer of pretzels since 1884. He says he did so because "the company was losing about $10 million a year on sales of $43 million. But the pretzels and the brand name were still great." He fired the management team, moved the corporate office from New York to Reading, Pennsylvania, slashed costs, and instituted a sales commission structure tied strictly to performance. By 1986 Bachman's operating profits were $4.3 million on sales of $66 million, and the privately held company had market shares in Boston and New York of 45% and 27%.[7]

5. *Need Capital for Expansion.* As will be discussed in the next chapter, a major cause of turnarounds is a company growing beyond its means and running out of cash. These can be great acquisition opportunities for low-growth companies with cash to invest. Alternatively, some companies in embryonic industries reach a stage in their development when a major influx of capital is needed to capitalize on, for instance, a technological discovery. Biotech companies classically raise money for research and development, and if they turn up a promising development, enter into a joint venture for funding or are acquired outright.

6. *LBO Castoffs.* "One Man's Trash Is Another's Treasure" was the heading of a 1986 article in *Forbes.*[8] It was about two Miami accountants, Arthur Hertz and Michael Brown, who "found treasure qua junk in the unwanted parts of Wometco Enterprises." KKR was the seller. It had bought Wometco for its broadcasting and cable TV divisions amidst a variety of odds and ends ranging from Coca-Cola bottlers, vending and food service operators, and even a wax museum in Japan. To "help" KKR divest the operations within one year of purchase to qualify for preferred tax treatment, Hertz and Brown did a bulk purchase for a 10% discount. They in turn sold off most of the pieces, keeping only the heavy cash generators, primarily vending machines operations and movie theatres.[8]

Financial Fits

Strategic reasons could be involved in the following transactions, but the primary motivation is a financial opportunity.

1. *Underleveraged*. Many buyers have used the excess cash and borrowing capacity of the acquired company to purchase it. Leveraged buyouts are based on this concept, plus the selloff of assets and the reduction of costs to service debt. LBOs were covered in the last chapter.

2. *Expensive Debt*. Smaller firms do not have the banking relationships large profitable companies can have. One way to value an acquisition is based on a multiple of after-tax (and after-interest) earnings. A few percentage points in interest rate can make a big difference in net earnings for a highly leveraged smaller firm. Multiplied by a factor of six to twenty, the differential in cost of debt can yield sizable savings in value.

3. *NOLCF*. Acquiring a company with a net operating loss carry forward (NOLCF) is a tax-sheltering move. While this was sought after more in the 1970s and early 1980s before the tax reform act, it is still a viable strategy. Fuqua Industries, the Atlanta conglomerateur, used this approach repeatedly. In 1985, for example, it purchased Triton Group, with $200 million in tax-loss carry-forwards. Fuqua in 1987 had $772 million in revenue and an ROE of 26%.

4. *Coming Cash Flow*. Some companies are wrapping up an investment spending period of a year or more. Cash flow is negative and earnings temporarily depressed. This is the time to buy. For example, public utilities became attractive takeover targets in the mid-1980s when their construction programs were winding down. In addition, noncash earnings imputed to the funds invested in the construction of plant and equipment are replaced with cash earnings produced by the facilities.

5. *Earnouts*. This final financial fit occurs in the structuring of the deal. If you cannot reach agreement on price, make an offer contingent on the future performance of the company. The down payment could be what you think the company is worth (or lower). Additional payments over a period of years can be based on earnings in excess of some amount, such as this past year's level. If the acquired management team delivers on its forecast, its members individually stand to be paid what they think the company is worth. This way they share in the risk of the future earnings or cash flow and are highly motivated to perform. But there are some cautions in using earnouts. Be sure to spell out in the acquisition agreement exactly how the earnings will be measured. Tie ROI to the calculation (or put controls on the amount to be invested) so assets are not thrown at the business to stimulate profit. And don't expect to integrate the acquired company too

much, for it performs best when acting relatively independently during the earnout period.

Cyclical Plays

Timing is everything, the saying goes. It certainly can be for acquisitions, as the following demonstrate.

1. *Recession Prices Low*. An economic or industry recession (they need not be coincidental) can provide superb opportunities to purchase companies below their true values. Stone Container embarked on a strategy to buy capacity of liner-board at deep discount when the market for it bottomed out in the mid-1980s. Stone purchased Brown Fiber System of the Continental Group in 1983, the packaging businesses of Champion International in 1986, 49% of the Seminole Kraft Corporation also in 1986, and Southwest Forest Industries in 1987. Roger W. Stone, chairman of the board and CEO of Stone Container, reports, "We bought Southwest Forest industries on a mill adjusted basis of 23 cents on the dollar, and this was clearly in line with our other recent major acquisitions. There is, however, no replacement value for lost opportunity." He goes on to say, "Few business people are willing to take that kind of risk in an industry with pricing practices that remind me of Dolly Parton, who said, 'You would be surprised how much it costs to look so cheap.' "[9]

2. *Stock Market Soft*. The same concept applies to all industries when the stock market is in a slump. Cash-rich companies can pick up bargains by purchasing public firms, even at sizable premiums. In a recession, privately held companies also come cheaper for two reasons: (1) Their earnings are usually depressed, and (2) comparative values of public companies are lower.

3. *Strong Currency*. Foreign investment in the United States via acquisitions of domestic companies increased when the dollar was at a low in 1987. British corporations, in particular, were jumping on the opportunity to make great buys because of currency differentials. Alternatively, as the dollar strengthens, U.S. companies should consider foreign acquisitions and joint ventures, if it makes sense strategically.

4. *Less or Acyclical Additions*. Highly cyclical or seasonal businesses often look for acquisitions that smooth their cycles. These can come in the form of a business that has more steady revenues and earnings or, better yet, a cycle opposite that of the purchaser. A residential aluminum window manufacturing company I worked with purchased a small storefront (com-

mercial window) manufacturer as a means of entering the commercial segment. The commercial building market usually lags behind the residential by a year or more. The combination is far less cyclical than either one separately. Smoother revenue streams make for a much more profitable company on a year-to-year basis.

5. *The Window Is Closing.* Merger mania is sometimes caused by a situation in an industry that makes companies in it highly attractive. Buying one early, before prices skyrocket and all the best ones are taken, is imperative. In other instances, the closing of the window is driven by government regulations. Take Europe 1992 for example. It is anticipated that after the twelve Economic Community nations become the United States of Europe in terms of their reduction of internal trade barriers, protectionist measures will be instituted for outsiders. The time to buy one or more companies in Europe is well before January 1, 1993.

A PROCESS FOR ACQUIRING BARGAINS

Companies that acquire in haste repent at leisure. It is easy, because of enthusiasm, to move rapidly on a particular deal. But the key to an effective acquisition program is to follow a well-defined process. It will maximize your opportunities, minimize your mistakes, and enable you to pay the lowest price. The five steps to making acquisition bargains are shown in Exhibit 17–2. They are: (1) develop an acquisition strategy and selection criteria, (2) identify attractive candidates, (3) evaluate target companies, (4) negotiate the best deal, and (5) integrate the acquired firm.

Your Acquisition Strategy

Chances of making a successful acquisition are much higher if your strategy is sound. If you do not have a clear overall vision of where your company is going, and how it is going to get there, an acquisition will accelerate your journey into confusion. So start with an assessment of your current business. Be in a position of knowing not only what you want to purchase, but why. Acquisition, remember, is only one alternative among several possible growth strategies, including internal development, joint venture, licensing, subcontracting, and distribution arrangements. The CEO of one multidivisional company I worked with insisted that division managers

238

EXHIBIT 17–2
The Acquisition Process

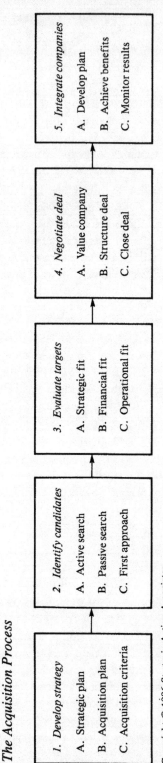

1. *Develop strategy*
   A. Strategic plan
   B. Acquisition plan
   C. Acquisition criteria

2. *Identify candidates*
   A. Active search
   B. Passive search
   C. First approach

3. *Evaluate targets*
   A. Strategic fit
   B. Financial fit
   C. Operational fit

4. *Negotiate deal*
   A. Value company
   B. Structure deal
   C. Close deal

5. *Integrate companies*
   A. Develop plan
   B. Achieve benefits
   C. Monitor results

have an up-to-date strategic plan before they could seriously propose an acquisition.

Next, develop an overall acquisition strategy. You should be able to summarize it in a few words. For example, General Foods' strategy in the mid-1980s was to acquire food processing companies that could benefit from GF's product research and development, raw materials and procurement systems, and massive distribution capability.

Beyond the overall statement, you need a more detailed plan, which should spell out the following:

· The objectives of making an acquisition, and the rationale or strategy for it
· The financial resources available and their form
· The expected timetable, which can take three months to a year or more to closing
· Who will do the searching, evaluating, negotiating, and integrating
· The expected use (and expenses) of outside resources: consultants, investment bankers, business brokers, lawyers, accountants, et cetera
· The way the search will be undertaken
· The criteria for selecting candidates

Willard F. Rockwell, past chairman of Rockwell International, said: "Conducting an acquisition is like playing chess. You don't just plan your next move, you plot out the whole game." Let's take a close look at acquisition criteria, because they are an area requiring both strategic thinking and creativity.

What Is It You Want to Buy?

There are many detailed checklists available for evaluating acquisition opportunities. The problem is that they are generic. They have no value in screening *in* acquisition bargains. You need to make your own list of criteria. Start by defining the ideal company to purchase. (Refer to Chapter 3 on creative leaps.) Describe it in detail. If there are different types of companies, or ones serving alternative market segments, rank them. A forced ranking will crystallize your thinking and prove invaluable later in the process when comparing opportunities.

Exhibit 17–3 presents the acquisition criteria of the conglomerate discussed in Chapter 16. They are tied to the resource allocation scheme of five business classifications for the company's existing businesses. Acquisitions were desired only for heavy and medium investment businesses.

EXHIBIT 17–3

Acquisition Criteria of a Large Conglomerate

Strategic Criteria

1. *Fit with the Company*. Acquisitions will only be considered for heavy and medium investment divisions (see Exhibit 16–2). Candidate companies must integrate with our divisions on both a marketing and an operational level.

2. *Unique Product or Service*. The acquired company must have a competitive edge which allows it to generate margins higher than average in its industry.

3. *High-Quality Image*. The company must be perceived by customers as a quality firm, even if its price positioning is at the low end of the market.

4. *Low Capital-Intensiveness*. The present and future investment in manufacturing and distribution facilities must be moderate, relative to sales volume.

5. *Strong Management Team*. The top management team must be highly capable and must intend to stay on for at least three years. (Management resources are important in all acquisitions, but crucial in high-technology companies.)

6. *Corporate Fit*. The candidate must meet all of the corporate criteria for strategic investment (see Exhibit 16–1).

Financial Criteria

A. *Acceptable Size:* The ideal purchase price is $5 million to $25 million, with a maximum of $50 million. The higher amounts are reserved for heavy investment divisions.

B. *Financial Return*. Pretax return on net assets should be at least 15% by the end of year one, 20% by year two, 25% by year three, and 30% by year four.

C. *Favorable Cash Return*. The discounted cash flow rate of return should be at least 15% for heavy investment businesses and 18% for medium investment businesses.

D. *Minimal Dilution*. Allowable dilution of earnings per share is 5 cents in year one and 3 cents in year two for companies acquired by heavy investment divisions, and 3 cents and 1 cent, respectively, for medium investment divisions.

To make your search effective, basic criteria must be gathered at three levels. Visualize three screens with different meshes: coarse (for searching), medium (for qualifying), and fine (for evaluating). In fragmented industries, perhaps one hundred to one thousand or more will be dropped on the coarse screen. Most will not pass through it. Those that will, maybe twenty to a hundred, will then be screened with the medium mesh. Perhaps five to twenty will emerge as companies to investigate. Using the fine mesh will narrow the list to two to five with which to negotiate.

Data that are easily and inexpensively obtained on companies are good for the coarse screen. More detailed intelligence is needed for the medium screen and can include product/market breakdowns, financial statements, information from telephone interviews with the candidates, and perhaps knowledge from personal visits. Last, very detailed information is, of course, needed to fine-screen the targets for acceptability. Only after your acquisition strategy and criteria are written down and agreed to by your top management team should you start looking for candidates.

Finding Good Acquisition Candidates

There are two basic ways to search for attractive companies to buy: passively and actively. Depending on your situation, you can use either or both.

In a passive search, send your criteria to some or all of the two hundred-plus acquisition brokers in the country, and wait to see what they present. Expect initially to be deluged with listings and prospectuses. After three months or so, the deal flow will settle down to a manageable amount. The problem with passive searches is that brokers do only minimal screening for you. Yet if you pursue and purchase one of their proposed deals, you (or the seller) have to pay them a full finder's fee. It is most likely to be the standard Lehman formula (developed initially by Lehman Brothers), which is 5% of the first million in price, 4% of the second million, 3% of the third, 2% of the fourth, and 1% of the fifth or more. For example, a $5 million acquisition would yield the broker a $150,000 finders fee on the deal. (Some intermediaries charge up to twice the Lehman formula.) Needless to say, a purchaser should not place a great amount of trust in their judgment. With commissions this size, a saint would have trouble telling a buyer the candidate was not right for it.

The active search is the best route to finding bargains. You target a segment of an industry, put all companies in it through your screens, and see what falls out. While this takes considerably more work, the benefits are big:

- It forces you to determine exactly what you want. Boiling down the large number of possibilities really makes you think of and use your prioritized criteria.
- You learn a tremendous amount about the industry segment, which will be valuable not only in making a selection but after you make an acquisition.
- Many times, the best companies are "not for sale." A legitimate buyer has to approach them first. It may as well be you. Excellent candidates

can be identified other than the "for sale" companies that probably have been shopped by your competitors.

- Frequently you identify companies for joint ventures and licensing agreements. In fact, a joint venture is a great trial marriage. I have recommended this to numerous clients. The joint venture period ratifies or disproves the potential synergy. Nippon Mining purchased Gould Electronics for $1.1 billion in 1988 after being engaged in three joint ventures. The purchase was the fourth largest acquisition of a U.S. company by a Japanese firm.[10]

How you undertake an active search is important. First, use all the industry information sources and directories you can find to narrow the possibilities. Dun & Bradstreet reports and other databases are also helpful. Then call the heads of marketing or the presidents of the prospects and tell them you are exploring cooperative distribution, joint venture, or "other" possibilities. A mutual contact such as a banker or lawyer may smooth the entry. The key is not to come on strong at this point. Tully Friedman of the investment banking firm Hellman & Friedman in San Francisco, which handled the Federated Department Stores auction, put it this way: "What started it all was Donald Trump purchasing 5% of the stock, stating his desire for another 20%, and saying 'I want a relationship.' " Fortunately, Robert Campeau and Macy's were waiting in the wings.[11]

With an exchange of information, employ your coarse screen. I have done this for many clients, including Japanese companies looking for U.S. acquisitions. Frequently I have kept the purchaser's name confidential during this stage.

Next, recontact the attractive companies, state that you see a potential fit, and indicate that you want to open discussions on cooperative opportunities. It is best to visit with the CEO at this point. Get into specifics of how the two companies could work together for mutual benefit. You have not yet specifically stated that you want to acquire the prospect. This is a first date, so move slowly. First, see if there is a fit. In fact, if there are no synergies, the candidate is not attractive. Once a strategic fit has been identified, the CEO of the candidate sometimes (in my experience, about a third of the time) is the first one to bring up the subject of an acquisition. If he or she doesn't, ease into the subject by asking "would you consider . . . ? "

Buyer Beware

Keep in mind these two important words when evaluating acquisition targets, particularly those that are for sale. As in marriage, the promise is "in sickness and in health." James Mahoney, an acquisition intermediary and editor of *The National Review of Corporate Acquisitions* (published weekly by Tweed Publications in Tiburon, California), says, "Many dicey deals result from underdone due diligence. And the price of careless acquisitions is very high."[12] Here are some ways to prevent mistakes.

· *Make sure you understand why they want to sell.* It may not be for the reason they are telling you. Confirm everything. An executive who had an excellent track record of successful acquisitions told me, "You need the following attitude: If your mother tells you she loves you, check it out."

· *Be sure the synergy is real.* We often get caught up in the excitement of the apparent strategic fit, and the operational strategy to implement it doesn't exist. I once worked with a company that had recently bought a wood products manufacturer and found out after the closing that the parent firm's commodity materials "were not quite right" for the acquired company's manufacturing process.

· *Look for hidden problem areas.* A technique I like to use with the upper and middle management is to interview each separately and say: "My client has a lot of money to invest in your company. If you could fix anything, what would you spend it on?" It is amazing how the problems come out, such as leaky roofs, worn out equipment, and major customer dilemmas. What you don't see is also what you get.

· *Compare the company with your ideal.* Be sure to go back and apply your criteria to the candidate. Beyond that, use the following investigative technique. Again, under the premise of preparing an investment and development plan (actually you are) ask each manager of the candidate to describe the ideal company. You may find that the ideal is tremendously different from reality. I did this during an evaluation of a major food wholesaler and found out the company's new automated warehouse was located in the wrong state. It should have been 150 miles south in the adjacent one.

· *Talk with customers, suppliers and others.* Anyone who does business with the target can be interviewed to help determine reputation, strengths and weaknesses, and business practices. This can be done confidentially if you use a consultant. Also, competitors are great for giving you the negative side of the company. Just be sure you filter out their biased perspective.

The final level of evaluation is the detailed one done by accountants, lawyers, and other diligent parties. Make sure you don't rush into these, skipping the strategic and operational evaluations.

Exhibit 17–4

Acquisition Valuation Methods

	Business Attractiveness		
	Fair	Good	Great
Capitalization Methods			
1. Multiple of pretax earnings	3–5	6–7	8–9+
2. Multiple of pretax cash flow	3–4	5–6	7–8+
3. After-tax discounted cash flow	18%	15%	12%
4. Book value plus multiple of excess earnings	2	3	4

Asset-Based Methods
1. Book value (as shown in financial statements)
2. Adjusted net worth (for real estate, intangibles, etc.)
3. Replacement cost (of assets, organization, customers, etc.)
4. Liquidation value (of tangible assets)

Comparable Methods
1. Prices and multiples from sales of similar companies
2. Price to earnings ratios of companies in industry

Other Methods
1. Value that can be financed (when undertaking an LBO)
2. Industry rules of thumb (use only when they are favorable to your perspective)

The next step in making an acquisition involves valuing the candidate, negotiating the price, and structuring the transaction. Exhibit 17–4 presents the most often used valuation methods. I recommend, whether you are buying or selling a company, that you use all of the methods listed. Buyers should then stress in negotiations the ones that yield the lowest values, and sellers the highest ones.

Agreeing on the multiplier of earnings, cash flow, et cetera, often is at the heart of valuation discussions. The range can be substantial. Ed McGrath, chairman of CAMA, Inc., a nationwide chain of acquisition brokers headquartered in San Francisco, uses pretax cash flow as the basis, with the following general multipliers:

• 3 to 4 for mundane businesses with low growth prospects, low customer loyalty, et cetera
• 4 to 5 for proprietary businesses with a brand name that is differentiated from the competition

- 5 to 6 for strongly proprietary businesses with high growth prospects, such as branded food companies and pharmaceutical manufacturers
- 7 to 8 (and even more) for hot industries such as biotech and companies with exceptional track records and/or earnings growth prospects.[13]

The above multiples can be applied to the financials of the present year, the average of the past few years, or the average of future years. If you are a seller, spend most of the time talking future potential. Buyers should take the posture of "buying what is" and negotiate based on the past, unless the future looks worse. The nuances of negotiating the detailed acquisition agreement (covenants and conditions, and representations and warranties) are beyond the scope of this book. Just be sure to use a lawyer and an accountant experienced in acquisition transactions.

Integration, or the Morning After

It remains to be seen how effective the marriage will turn out to be. This is the moment of truth. Actually, the time to have started thinking about integration was during the evaluation step of the process. After the funds have been transferred is a heck of a time to find out the body rejects the organ, or vice versa.

The objectives of integration are twofold: to preserve what you bought, and to build on it by realizing the potential synergies. What is needed is a detailed integration plan covering the following four areas:

1. Systems: accounting, purchasing, et cetera
2. Assets: product lines, technologies, facilities
3. Markets: customers, distribution channels, and salespeople
4. Personnel: management and operating employees

The amount of integration depends on the number and types of synergies you want to realize. The above ones are listed in order of easiest to hardest to achieve. Here are some suggestions for smoothing the transition:

- *Sell All Constituents*. Employees, managers, customers, suppliers, and all other parties from both companies should be provided with an explanation of the strategy and objectives of the merger. Many vehicles (meetings, memos, newsletters) will be needed for the message to sink in.

- *Integration Coordinator.* In any merger of significant size, a specific high-level executive should be assigned for marrying the two organizations. Kenneth Derr had this responsibility in Chevron's purchase of Gulf Oil in June 1984 for $13.3 billion. On January 1, 1989, he became CEO of Chevron.
- *Integration Task Force.* When both firms have to change to realize the common opportunities sought, form a team of people made up of executives from both companies. Unisys's W. Michael Blumenthal created an integration task force when he merged Sperry and Burroughs. Fortunately, the two companies' different mainframe architectures didn't clash. Sperry made computers for number-crunching and Burroughs for database management, each going to different sets of customers.
- *Promote Executives Across Both Companies.* Interchanging managers between the two firms can greatly accelerate integration and cooperation. But do not move armies. Senior executives of Sperry and Burroughs were distributed about 50–50 in top positions at Unisys.
- *Be Careful Competitors Don't Attack.* If they sense confusion, competitors will try to capitalize on it. For example, when Black & Decker spent $300 million for General Electric's small appliance business, competitors moved quickly. Sunbeam, Hamilton Beach, Norelco, and others all stepped up their advertising budgets and released a slew of new products
- *Don't Move Too Quickly.* It can create all kinds of problems, the worst being for customers. When Greyhound and Trailways were acquired and merged by Fred G. Currey of Dallas, he created the largest intercity bus system in the country. Almost immediately, fares were slashed and a huge advertising blitz was unleashed. Management got what it wanted: Ridership surged. But terminals became packed, ticket lines long, luggage lost, and buses delayed—all irritating to customers.

Perhaps the best way to begin the integration is to borrow from Chapter 9 on creative teams and hold a multiday joint meeting of the managements of the two companies. Define the objectives, strategies, and tactics to be pursued. Identify shared and unshared values. Discuss system and procedural likenesses and differences. Then develop a shared plan for closing the gaps and exploiting the common ground. This meeting will open constricted lines of communication, mitigate the ''we versus they'' attitude, and introduce a win–win culture. More than one of these conferences may be needed. Intimacy takes time. But it's worth it when it comes to acquisitions.

DIVESTITURE COUPS

In many companies acquisitions go through an entire life cycle—including divestment. As discussed in the previous chapter on corporate restructuring, dollarizing a division is a common and important strategy. There are two primary objectives in selling a company. The first is to obtain the highest price. The second is to find a good home for the operation and its employees. I define a divestiture coup as one that accomplishes both. The process of selling a company is similar to buying one. It's the same five steps, only from the opposite perspective:

1. *Develop a strategy.* Given the amount of money involved, it is essential to have an overall strategy for selling the company. It starts with a self-analysis and ends with a detailed action plan. Prepare a one-page summary on your firm to be sold. Focus on your strengths, but also mention your weaknesses—in terms of a potential buyer's strengths, that is. Then develop a detailed prospectus that describes your company in depth.

2. *Identify candidates.* Think strategically. What type of company would most benefit from acquiring yours? Do an analysis of industry segments, profiling all the best candidates. Also think in terms of which types of companies are likely to pay the highest price. Well-financed major corporations are good prospects. International firms looking to enter the United States are another high-paying category. The British, Canadians, and Japanese, in that order, were the most acquisitive nations in the United States in 1988. LBO groups are another potential, if your company is leveragable.

3. *Contact and evaluate targets.* The real art is contacting possible buyers and then playing hard to get. Screen them against criteria, just as if you were on the buying side of the table. A detailed evaluation is imperative if you are going to receive stock of the buyer as payment, and/or you intend on staying on after the sale. Make sure you will be happy with the style of the company.

4. *Negotiate the deal.* As on the buying side, negotiate with more than one potential purchaser at a time. If your company is highly attractive, hold a formal auction. Otherwise, do it informally. As for price, when I asked a client wishing to sell his business how much he wanted for it, he replied: "All I can get." "Dumb question," I said to myself. But you need to do some homework. Go through the multiple valuation process mentioned earlier. Be sure to normalize your financial statements by adding back expenses (particularly those of the top executives) that will not remain

under the aegis of the new owners. This will increase earnings and cash flow, and therefore the value of your company. And remember, terms are at least as important as price.

5. *Integrate the company.* Presidents who join other firms via the acquisition route often find that a month or two after the closing, the love boat springs a leak. Expect some integration difficulties, and be flexible. One day you may be on the other side of the acquisition integration table.

Whether you are the owner of a business or president of a multidivisional corporation, you have to realize that everything is ultimately for sale. It just takes the right time and the right price. J. B. Fuqua, the CEO of Fuqua Industries, described in 1983 how his company sold its radio stations despite their strong financial performance. The price was twenty-seven times earnings. He said, ''In a conglomerate, there is no way you can justify owning something that valuable to someone else.''

Another reason companies are sold is that corporate management has given up on a poor-performing division. Before doing so, try the resuscitation approach described in the next chapter.

18

From Turnaround to Takeoff

I started this book by saying that Creative Planning is for all levels of management. Similarly, turnaround techniques are not just for CEOs. They can be used by functional officers, product managers, department managers, supervisors, and even a team of first-line employees. Indeed, anyone with a problem area can invoke the principles covered in this chapter. Turning areas of poor results into high-performing ones is the responsibility of every employee in the company.

Also, turnaround management is not just for financially desperate companies. Pacific Telesis in San Francisco was considered the weakest sister by far of Ma Bell's family when AT&T was split up in early 1984. Even though the company's ROE was a reasonable 13.7% at the time of divestiture, Donald E. Guinn treated it like a turnaround situation. He reduced the workforce by 11%, slashed debt, revamped the old bureaucratic culture, automated its phone-switching network, and diversified into related products and markets. Guinn proudly calls his company the "Chrysler of Telecommunications."[1]

TURNING LOSERS INTO WINNERS

Just as healing a sick person and keeping one healthy to begin with require different approaches, turnaround management demands a distinctly different approach from growth management. Four aspects of handling the situation stand out.

1. *Bold Action.* Reversing the results of a company in a free fall can not be done by working harder. Managements in dire situations are usually working eighteen hours a day as it is. Dramatic change is needed. Most turnaround attempts that failed were undercut by halfway measures.

2. *Short Time Frame.* A company teetering on the precipice of death cannot afford the luxury of long-range planning, at least not as a first priority. Weekly, maybe even daily, strategy sessions and review meetings are initially needed. Nothing less will do in a time of crisis.

3. *Cash Flow, Not Profit.* With the exception of divisions of financially healthy public firms, with which quarterly earnings per share is important, the focus must be on cash flow. Most turnaround situations I've been involved with were running on fumes when I arrived. All areas of the company have to be prioritized according to their ability to generate cash to keep the wolves (banks and major creditors, usually suppliers) from the door.

4. *Big Rewards.* Every cloud has some kind of lining. In turnarounds, the silver is the reward to stockholders. Frequently the value of a company jumps threefold to tenfold when rebirth is achieved. Jack Tramiel bought the floundering Atari from Warner Communications in 1984 for no money down and $240 million in promissory notes. In two years he reversed the company's performance from a loss of $14 million in 1985 to a net profit of $57 million in 1987.

REVIVAL OF THE FITTEST

The rescue of a company headed toward bankruptcy and getting it back on the growth track usually require the following four stages.

Phase One: Recognition

A company can need a turnaround without management's even realizing it. The mere fact that a firm is not losing money doesn't mean it is not headed south. If a company consistently generates after-tax ROEs significantly less than its cost of capital (13% to 18%), eventually it will not be able to finance its growth. The odds of a turnaround are significantly better if action is taken before the company settles into a zombie state—the living dead.

Phase Two: Streamlining

Once the turnaround situation is recognized and the problems are analyzed, bold actions are needed. Usually, one has to deal with creditors to restructure debt, strip the company to its core business, reduce most or all asset categories, prune product lines and services, and cut back on the number of personnel. Rarely are organizations expanded out of a slump.

Phase Three: Stabilization

When light is seen at the end of the tunnel, hope that it is not an oncoming train. Cash flow is now at break-even or even somewhat positive, profits begin to appear, creditors are calm, and the organization is remotivated. You feel that you are turning the corner, but you are still not sure what's around it.

Phase Four: Rejuvenation

The company is back in the black in terms of both profit and cash flow. Debt is reduced on a steady schedule. In fact, you are confident enough to begin to invest in the future. It may even be time for external financing. The key to success, however, is to maintain the tight discipline. This should be a crucial part of your philosophy. Many a company has turned the corner only to slip back into financial jeopardy. Financiers, creditors, and boards of directors rarely give a second chance. This leads me to the most important point of this chapter:

> *If companies followed the principles of turnaround management in good times, there would be a lot less need for turnaround management in the first place.*

THOSE WEREN'T THE DAYS

Without writing a "How Not to Book of Business," it helps to understand what went wrong in companies in order to discover how to revive them.

Donald Bibeault did an extensive study of turnaround management and published his findings in the first, and I believe still the best, book on the subject, *Corporate Turnaround: How Managers Turn Losers into Winners.*[2] As shown in Exhibit 18–1, top managements usually bring the problems on themselves. Most often they are due to a combination of factors, with one overriding one, either internal or external.

Internal Causes

The seeds of destruction can be sown by management in a variety of ways.

1. *Overgrowth.* As discussed in Chapter 10, growing rapidly without strong profit margins and operational cash flow can put even a healthy company into bankruptcy. Fast growth also puts stress on operational systems. The top management of U.S. Sprint succeeded in making the company the fastest-growing national telecommunications carrier in the mid-1980s. Sprint added almost 3 million new customers in nine months. But it failed to equip the company with the necessary systems to handle the explosive growth. Tens of thousands of customers were billed incorrectly. Many didn't get billed at all. And cutthroat pricing in the industry squeezed profit margins and cash flow. In 1988 Sprint is still scurrying to survive.[3]

2. *Executive Ego.* This problem is related to overgrowth, and one of the causes of it: Ego gets in the way of common sense. Worlds of Wonder (WOW) is the classic example. *Forbes* reports that after achieving $93 million in first-year sales in 1986, Donald Kingsborough, CEO, set as his personal and corporate goal the surpassing of Compaq Computer's $329 million second-year sales figure so WOW could become the fastest-growing company in history (Compaq's first-year sales were $111 million).

EXHIBIT 18–1

The Principal Reasons for Corporate Decline

Internally generated problems within management's control	52%
Internal problems triggered by external factors	15
Real balance of external and internal factors	24
External factors beyond management's control	8
Sheer bad luck (Dun & Bradstreet 1977)	1
Total	100%

Source: Survey of eighty-one turnaround company CEOs undertaken by Don Bibeault in 1978 and published in *Corporate Turnaround* (New York: McGraw-Hill, 1982), p. 25.

To do this, he offered "dating" on $52 million of fourth-quarter sales in 1987, meaning retailers didn't have to pay until December. Unfortunately, sales of Teddy Ruxpin and Lazer Tag plummeted after Christmas, and retailers sent back much of the inventory. WOW crashed into Chapter 11. Ironically, Kingsborough missed Compaq's second-year sales record by a few million, anyway.[4]

3. *Betting the Ranch.* Another toy company lived far beyond its means in trying to develop new products when sales of its primary product, the Cabbage Patch Kids, were plunging. The top management of Coleco, the corporate equivalent of riverboat gamblers, "believed they had the magic touch," reports one financial analyst. According to the *San Jose Mercury News*, the downfall came from building up the company's product development and manufacturing efforts in the face of falling sales in order to save the firm. The opposite happened. In 1988, Coleco filed for Chapter 11 with debts of $540 million. If management had scaled back in 1986, when the first signs of a slowdown occurred, it could have managed the boom–bust cycle characteristic of the toy industry and kept its jobs.[5]

4. *Infighting.* Warring factions at the top affect the whole organization. A case in point is Gucci. In 1986 profits fell 57% to $5 million on $175 million in sales. The cause was a decade of family feuding and lawsuits between father and son, and cousin and cousin. In August 1987 the board replaced chief executive Maurizio Gucci with Maria Martellini, a professor from Italy's top business school. She has started to restructure the company and is trying to restore the exclusivity of the Gucci name, which has been tarnished with a drift into mass marketing.[6]

5. *Poor Controls.* Letting inventories and receivables get out of hand is a classic reason for business failure. Not understanding one's costs and poor financial forecasting are other reasons. Even in the most entrepreneurial of companies, controls are important to provide a balance to the high levels of enthusiasm.

6. *Bad Major Decision.* A single strategic decision can kill or maim a firm. Symbolics, the Cambridge, Massachusetts, pioneer in artificial intelligence computers and software, opted to pour money into its own costly hardware rather than cater to the market's growing preference for the general purpose machines supplied by Sun Microsystems and IBM. In fiscal 1987, sales softened to $103 million from $114 million, generating a loss of $25 million. The expectation of industry experts is that 1988 will be even worse while the company plays catchup with its software.

7. *Poor Quality.* Braniff International self-destructed as a consequence of a massive overexpansion and, more importantly, poor service. Long ticket lines, canceled flights, uncaring agents, and, if you were lucky

enough to make the flight, lost bags were all part of the company's downfall.

8. *Lack of Ethics*. A congressional study revealed that most of the thirty-five California thrifts that failed in the 1985–87 period fell victim to "serious insider misconduct." This included embezzlements, kickbacks, fraudulent property appraisals, improper loans to friends of insiders (or themselves), and, of course, padded expense accounts. The Federal Home Loan Bank of San Francisco had to act like the CIA with a special surveillance staff to uncover this atrocious behavior.[7]

The root cause of all of the above reasons is bad management. In most of the above cases, too, it snatched defeat from the jaws of victory.

External Causes

Tough times sometimes are caused by outside forces. But as you will see, the degree of damage is largely a function of how management dealt with the situation.

1. *Recession*. A single industry could be hit, or the entire national or world economy. Regardless, the severity of the effect on your company is, at least partially, under management's control. The two key questions are (1) Did they plan for the possibility of a recession during boom times to minimize its effect? (2) How quick and decisive were they to scale back once they had that first sinking feeling?

2. *Takeover Attempts*. In 1982 Brunswick, the oldest independent leisure company in the United States, was threatened by Whittaker Corporation. Brunswick's defense was to sell its crown jewel, its medical division, the part of the company Whittaker was after. Brunswick survived, but it was weakened. Many other firms have taken similar actions, combined with massive debt restructuring, and put themselves into the turnaround mode as a result.

3. *Technological Discontinuities*. In the fast-changing world of high-tech, you have to race just to stay even. On the other hand, it is dangerous to get too far ahead. When Amdahl released a new line of IBM-compatible mainframes in 1982, it guessed wrong. A few months later IBM unveiled a new operating system that was 10% different from Amdahl's. But as anyone who has worked with a computer knows, 90% compatibility is not enough. Predictably, sales stalled and margins plummeted. Not to make the same mistake twice, when IBM came out with its Sierra mainframes in 1985, Amdahl was waiting. Watch, wait, and then pounce was its

strategy.[8] It worked. By 1987 Amdahl's revenues increased 56% over 1986, and ROE was 18.5%.

4. *Competitor Moves.* Strategies by competitors can sometimes throw your company into a tailspin. These can include a highly successful new product introduction, a drastic cut in price to build volume, and a unique and effective new marketing strategy. As was discussed in Chapter 12, either beat them to it or, at least, anticipate and plan for it.

5. *Changing Markets.* Customer needs and buying motives can shift rapidly in consumer as well as industrial markets. Also, market volume can suddenly fluctuate downward, causing a drop in sales of the market share leaders. In 1988 this happened to both Storage Technology in disk drives and Wyse Technology in personal computers, two companies that had previously been outstanding performers.

Keep in mind, however, that turnaround experts unanimously claim that the primary cause of poor corporate health is overgrowth. Smart executives avoid it. When Steven Jobs was criticized for initially targeting only educational institutions with his first Next, Inc., computer system, he responded: "More companies tend to die of indigestion than starvation."[9]

THE CORPORATE RESCUE PROCESS

The following suggestions assume that you are brought in to replace the top manager and to breathe life into an operation. They, of course, would help the incumbent leader turn his or her own operation around as well. The process has five steps. In actuality, because of shortness of time, you may have to undertake some of the steps simultaneously. Regardless, at least start at the beginning.

Step One: Diagnose the Seriousness

The single most important step in a turnaround is the one most often glossed over, or skipped altogether, by novice corporate rescuers. Given the need for haste, it is human nature to want to get right to the solutions. Don't. You have three immediate objectives. First, quickly determine the viability of the sick company. Second, stop the cash drain, perhaps holding off creditors. Third, identify the root causes of the problem.

The central question is whether the business can be saved, or is even worth saving. In dealing with this dilemma, it must be understood that the longer the company has been earning less than its cost of capital, the lower the odds are of achieving a turnaround, and the more painful the remedies. The alternatives are shown in Exhibit 18–2. The high road, of course, is the preferred one. However, it takes only three creditors who are owed $5,000 in aggregate to force you down the low road—bankruptcy. "However, in reality, it usually takes six or more creditors, because some get disqualified by the courts," Donald Bibeault says. Under Chapter 11 of the Federal Bankruptcy Code, a company forgoes paying its debts for a 120-day "exclusivity period," during which management can file a reorganization plan. It is submitted to the company's seven largest creditors, while final approval is subject to a vote by all the firms' creditors. If rejected, the company can be liquidated.

This brings me to the second question posed above. Can the company make sufficient profit after a fresh start? If the answer is no, filing under Chapter 11 will be a huge waste of time and money, and Chapter 7— straight liquidation—is the optimal move. However, it must be remembered that there are no sure formulas for making this crucial decision.

EXHIBIT 18–2

Turnaround Decisions Structure

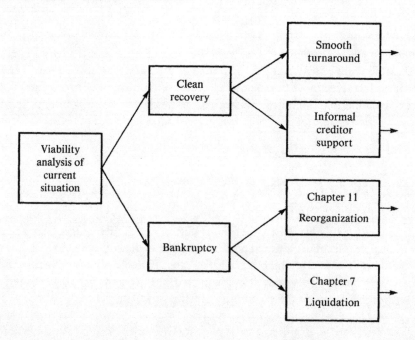

Companies left for dead, under new management, have come roaring back. Take British Leyland's nationalized Jaguar, which faced disaster in 1980, having sold only three thousand cars that year. (The car company's quality at the time was ridiculed by the joke that you had to buy two so you could have enough spare parts to keep one running.) But instead of burying Jaguar, as had been done with MG and Triumph, the British Government stepped in with a tough new CEO, John Egan. His orders: Save the Cat. He did. Quality improvement was his first order of business. Reorganization was his second. By 1987 Jaguar was selling 40,000 cars a year for revenue of $1.3 billion and profit of $193 million.[10]

By the time a turnaround pro is brought in, a company is generally running on fumes. Its cash position needs to be stabilized and replenished—usually immediately. Roy Wright, a turnaround specialist who brought Victor Technologies through bankruptcy and sold the company, says he starts thus: "I ask, 'How do I get as much cash as quickly as possible? What is my plan to use the cash to get more revenue to get more cash?'" He goes on to say: "Cash is probably one of the three most important things you need to make a company go. The other two are cash and cash." Anyone who has been through a turnaround will attest to this.

Where do you find cash? Exhibit 18–3 presents some suggestions. Which ones you follow depends on the severity of the situation. One place to turn is to certain lenders that specialize in troubled companies. "Chapter

EXHIBIT 18–3

Creating Cash

- Sell inventories, particularly excess finished goods, even if distress prices are necessary. Raw materials can also be sold.
- Collect receivables by pressuring customers to pay overdue accounts. Then shorten payment terms, offering discounts if necessary.
- Stretch payables by negotiating more lenient payment plans with suppliers. Make partial payments.
- Accrue part of the salary and bonuses of top executives, in exchange for stock or future bonuses.
- Renegotiate loans with all financial sources, asking for forgiveness on principal or interest.
- Sell all nonessential assets. Sell and lease back essential ones. Sublease excess space.
- Put on hold all capital expenditures.
- Monitor cash flow daily with a detailed report weekly.
- Inform everyone in the company of the severe situation and that there will be an austerity program until times are better.
- Streamline the organization, if necessary, down to only the most essential people needed to save the company in the short term.

---

11 bankruptcy reorganization does not have to be the last chapter in your company's evolution!'' That is how Foothill Group in Los Angeles starts its sales literature. The company makes asset-secured loans to small and medium-size businesses needing specially tailored financing terms.

If at all possible, hold off on downsizing the organization until you've gotten to the core of the situation. Before you can fix a problem, you have know what it is. One master of finding and solving turnaround problems in Q.T. Wiles, chairman of the board of Hambrecht & Quist. What he says when he walks into a company in need of a turnaround is, ''Gentlemen, I'm going to break this down into small enough pieces so that even you guys who couldn't do anything right before can run it.''[11] Strategic insights are what he is after, and, later, accountability for each of the pieces. Wiles's supporters say a company could be dead, buried, and decomposing and he could still save it. ''I'm absolutely convinced that Q.T. can turn around almost anything,'' William Hambrecht, president of Hambrecht & Quist, says. ''He's just got an intuitive smell for problems, and then he knows how to flush them right to the top.''

How do turnaround specialists begin analyzing a situation so they can take quick action? Here is what they do.

1. *Review Current Financials.* This is an extension of the severity analysis described above. They are looking for reasons why the company is performing badly in the first place and what measures could be taken to correct it. Are manufacturing costs too high? What about overhead? Is sales expense per dollar of revenue out of line with industry averages? An excellent place to look for sources of problems is receivables. Are customers paying slowly because they are financially strapped themselves, or because of disputes on quality, delivery, or other reasons?

2. *Collect All Lists.* Ask all managers and supervisors for any and all lists used in operating the company. Then assemble lists of the top ten of everything: customers, products, markets, inventoried raw materials and finished products, costs, assets, et cetera. Ranking these gives you an instant feel for the focus of the company. It may not match what management says.

3. *Interview Everyone in Upper Management.* Ask each person privately questions covering their personal perception of:

  • The cause of the turnaround predicament (envision the past, when the problems started)
  • Why the problems occurred

- What can be done to correct them in the short term
- What can be done in the long term
- What they would do if they were president and had unlimited funding
- A variety of other questions that provoke strategic insights and creative leaps

4. *Interview Middle Management and Front-Line Employees.* Turnaround specialist Morris Lasky told *Success* magazine: "I'd say that 95% of a good bailout campaign comes from the comments of the people who are already there . . . who know what the problems are, but have never been asked." When asked why they don't bring these up with top management, the usual reply I hear is: "The last messenger is no longer with us." Bill McGowan specialized in failing companies before he plotted the overthrow of Ma Bell's monopoly with the startup of MCI Communications. He explains: "What I would do was come in and ask what the problem was with the company, and for the most part they all knew—in fact, I never really ran across anyone who didn't know the answer."[12]

5. *Isolate the Core Problem.* What you find through these interviews is that the problem as perceived from the top is rarely the one seen at the bottom. Reconcile the two, and you are on your way to saving the firm. But you may have to dig deeper. Bill McCormick, forty-seven, the chairman of Fireman's Fund who turned the company around in the mid-1980s, is reported by colleagues to ask incessantly, "Why?"

Trace symptoms back to root causes and then rank them. You'll isolate the core problem. In 1984 the only ribbon color needed to type the bottom line of the Smith-Corona's U.S. typewriter manufacturing plant in Cortland, New York, was red. Losses since 1979 totaled $100 million. G. Lee Thompson, CEO of Smith-Corona in New Canaan, Connecticut, stated in 1986: "We analyzed the core problem. We needed an entirely new product line that could be cost-competitive worldwide." The company focused on electronic typewriters, primarily ones geared for consumers and small businesses. Smith-Corona's market share in this segment since 1980 increased from 5% to 50%.[13]

6. *Strategic Analyses.* With the company's problems broadly defined, it's now time to employ the analyses described in Part Three of this book: profitability, market, competition, et cetera. The profitability analysis, for example, will enable you to estimate cash flow by product line, market segment, and other variables. This and the other work you have done will prepare you for the next step.

Step Two: Alternative Cures

"There were no thousand-dollar items; there were lots of $110-dollar items," reports Stanley Hiller, a corporate paramedic, about his turnaround of York International, an air conditioner manufacturer in Pennsylvania. In 1985 York lost $18 million before taxes. In 1987 it earned $50 million before taxes.[14] The point is, as in any creative problem solving, that many ideas are needed in turnaround management. Here are some common themes.

1. *Vigor and Intensity.* If they are combined with closeness to the customer, à la Tom Peters, all the better. One turnaround manager of a $50 million consumer products company made all his senior officers, himself included, undertake a thirty-day sales blitz. Aside from stimulating sales, they found out that a major customer was dissatisfied with quality and about to take his business elsewhere.

2. *Participation.* This is particularly important. Consider all new ideas that come up in your interviews with employees. According to J. William Grimes, his turnaround of ESPN was largely due to delegation. For example, even though he thought paying $2 million for the America's Cup was too much, he went ahead with the decision of his young head of programming, Steve Bornstein. The result: a $2 million profit and a major victory for the fledgling business. Moves like this transformed ESPN from an ill-fated firm losing $40 million a year to a $1 billion company expected to net $80 million in 1988.[15]

3. *A Fresh Top Management.* I have already mentioned that many boards of directors or creditor committees bring in a new CEO to turn a company around. This can be overdone, as well. Coleco had three CEOs in twenty-four months during its attempted turn in the late 1980s. But usually an entirely new top management team is needed. Lee Iaccoca did this in his first year at Chrysler. He developed internal knowledge by immediately choosing a highly respected Chrysler executive as his second in command. He recruited a number of Ford executives, some of whom had recently retired. Then he went to work identifying young people with leadership potential within Chrysler, as well as old-timers who had been overlooked by the previous management regime.

Replacement CEOs often meet with resistance because they "don't know the business." One turnaround pro dealt with his perceived lack of experience and the inability of the management team to change its ways as follows: A week into the new assignment he had the marketing, operations, and accounting officers switch jobs, then announced, "Okay, since I now have been in my job longer than any of you three, we will . . ."

4. *Focus on the Core.* Once you have identified the products and markets of highest profitability (or near-term potential for it), develop a vision of the ideal company focusing exclusively on these areas. Then, while cutting back on all other areas, spend money on the core. Robert Wilson, who was part of the dramatic turnarounds of Memorex, GAF, and Collins Radio, feels it is important to cut expenses in most areas but to invest in others. "You've got to have a game plan, otherwise you just hack around and destroy what you're trying to preserve." At Memorex, for example, he continued to increase research and development expenditures on selected projects while cutting expenses elsewhere.[16]

5. *Raise Prices.* Sometimes this can be done immediately. Other times raising prices requires a repositioning of the company as described in Chapter 11. The Great Atlantic and Pacific Tea Company, better known as A&P, almost buried itself with its low-price strategy for conventional supermarkets. Its much-heralded turnaround in the mid-1980s was due to an innovative merchandising strategy that provided a format and a price for almost every type of shopper: Futurestores (featuring gourmet foods) for exclusive neighborhoods, Superfresh (conventional) stores for middle-class neighborhoods, and Sav-a-Center (warehouse stores) where appropriate. Sebastiani Vineyards in Sonoma, California, was turned around by Marty Adams, a turnaround pro, by upscaling the wine's positioning while increasing revenue. The high ground can be an effective place to focus.

6. *Radical Restructuring.* Overhauling the entire company is frequently necessary in a turnaround. That is what Irving Azoff did when he became CEO of MCA's Music Entertainment Group in 1983. It went from a $7 million loss to more than $40 million in earnings in 1987. He fired forty-one of the forty-six acts on the music roster, negotiated a deal with Motown Records to distribute its records, and hit on a number of top-selling albums, including "Miami Vice" and "Beverly Hills Cop."[17]

The Pittsburgh Pirates were turned around both financially and on the playing field through a total restructuring. In 1985 the team was twenty-three games out of first place and losing $7 million a year through terrible attendance. In the face of losing its franchise, ten of the city's major corporations put up $2 million apiece and the city raised $220 million through a bond issue. A new sixteen-member board brought in a new general manager, Syd Thrift. He traded away all the big-name, high-paid players, spent $2 million on improved food concessions, and revamped the marketing effort. With the team's $12 million payroll reduced by half, the Pirates are now one of the "lowest-cost producers" in the league.[18] The Baltimore Orioles in 1988 were trying the same model to revive their club.

Step Three: Selecting a Strategy

Halfway measures won't accomplish anything in a turnaround. So when selecting options, keep in mind two words: "change" and "quickly." Rarely do you have a lot of time. Which of your options will put the company into position to make money in the immediate future? Frequently, labor concessions are in order. Iaccoca did it. Gerald Grinstein of Western Airlines in Los Angeles did it. Many other turnaround managers had to do it. Most unions will agree that it is better than closing the plant down.

While pruning expenses, keep in mind that you have to preserve some part of the business for future growth. Scale back selectively. Black & Decker dubbed its strategy "cut and build." In the early 1980s the company was faced with severe offshore competition and was barely above break-even. To reverse the slide, overhead was dramatically cut, and plants were consolidated to make the company profitable at a modest sales level. When profits returned, Black & Decker purchased General Electric's housewares business, giving it a marketing system not geared solely to hardware merchants.

Steps Four and Five: Planning and Implementation

Developing a plan and executing it in a turnaround situation is similar to doing it under normal business conditions, except for the focus on cash flow and immediate results. Accountability is of utmost importance. Q. T. Wiles generally splits up a company's workforce into small groups, each responsible for a product, research project, customer, or manufacturing program. He then authorizes each group to plan its own sales targets and prepare its own budgets. In doing so, he quickly wins loyalty of middle managers by increasing their roles in setting the company's course. He also hands out bonuses for exceeding quarterly objectives.

Providing an overall vision to guide this spreading of responsibility is crucial. Once Fireman's Fund began to turn, Bill McCormick, its chairman, pursued his dream of making the company "the insurance industry's best." For him, nothing less than excellence would do. Lee Iaccoca took a tradition-heavy company that was behind the times and on the brink of bankruptcy, with little cash for R&D and other new projects, and turned it into an innovative, high-quality, automated winner.

Spain has been making a rapid economic turnaround because of the government's will to change from the old autocracy that kept the country a hundred years behind the times. The ghost of Francisco Franco was laid to rest, and the country now hopes to become the "Florida of Europe." It has plans for luring both tourists and businesses with its mild climate, low labor costs, and open opportunities for development, particularly in light of EC 1992.

LIFE AFTER DEATH

Assuming your turnaround plan works, you are now faced with a new challenge: staying turned around. To do this, you need to get back on the growth track and create a winning spirit.

A stunning turnaround was achieved in the early 1980s by Fiat, led by CEO Cesare Romiti. In 1981 the company had an aging product line, low productivity, and poor quality. A popular joke was the letters in "Fiat" stood for "Fix it again, Tony." From 1982 to 1987, management cut 75,000 jobs, invested $15 billion, doubled annual productivity to twenty-nine cars per worker, became Europe's lowest-cost producer, and achieved a 61% share in Italy. Sales doubled from $15 billion to $30 billion, and profits soared from break-even to $1.8 billion. Industry experts wonder, however, if Fiat's management can keep its growth record going. Italy's trade barriers, which now hold Japanese producers to a 2% market share, will be loosened in 1992. Management is coming out with new midsize and full-size automobiles, trying to leverage its 1987 acquisition of Alfa Romeo and to beef up its nonauto businesses.[19] Only time will tell.

My final point on turnarounds is that pulling a company out of trouble and spurring growth requires that a new spirit of winning be established. You have to motivate everyone in the organization to give extra of themselves. Irwin Federman did this to turn around and rebuild Monolithic Memories, Inc. (MMI) when he was named president in 1979. Currently vice chairman of Advanced Micro Devices and chairman of the Semiconductor Industry Association (not bad for an accountant), he describes what happened at MMI as follows:

> In the mid-1970s, MMI de-focused from its base business and failed. In 1978, it was sunny outside [the market was strong], but raining

inside. By spring of 1979, when Í became president, we had 125% turnover. I became suspicious of anyone who applied for a job. No other company could have wanted them. To stop the outflow, we began recruiting our own people before our competitors did.

To salvage barrels of bad bipolar chips, we taught our R&D engineers to write new test software for them. Employees worked extra shifts of three hours, and we worked all hours of the night to test them. Friends of employees helped straighten leads. Because of the tight chip market, customers accepted our less-than-spec products.

In six weeks, MMI turned from a $600,000 loss per month to a profit of $60,000 per month. Once revived, the company went through three industry recessions without losing a single dollar in any month. We were the only semiconductor company not to have a layoff. Not that we had a no-layoff policy. Our only policy was that profit was nonnegotiable.

The key to our turnaround was making people feel important—to have dignity and self-esteem. Extracting ideas from the lower ranks, this underutilized and taciturn group, is the supreme management challenge. I am convinced ordinary people are capable of grand achievement. Draw out this silent treasure. And when you are president, never forget what it felt like to be at a lower level.[20]

Conclusion: How and When to Start

CREATIVE Planning can drive innovation and positive change throughout your organization. A high-impact change tool, it promises a dynamic new style of management, for not only will it help your team conceive an innovative strategy, the commitment created will inspire everyone to execute effectively.

This book has explained not just the overall approach to creating profit but also how to customize the process for various parts of your business and what specific techniques to employ. Can you put off doing it? Hardly. Azure skies are not necessarily ahead. Stronger foreign competition, changing markets, and technology discontinuities are just a few of the reasons the 1990s will be challenging. GE's Jack Welch says it will be a "white-knuckle decade for global business."[1] It will be the same for domestic companies, whether or not they are threatened by imports. Every company needs to take a totally fresh look at the way it does business.

HOW TO BEGIN

The best way to start Creative Planning depends on the size of your organization, the number and diversity of your divisions and product lines, the degree of participation you initially want to achieve, the geographic dispersion of your operations, and other factors. Here are seven ways to begin.

1. *Corporate Plan*. Develop a vision of where your overall company is going. Include in it the strategies for achieving both short- and long-range goals, and the milestones to be used to measure whether you have achieved them. This will provide a framework for decision making at all levels of your firm. Then have each division prepare a Creative Plan of its own.

2. *Division Plan*. Undertake the process first in one of your divisions or departments and use the positive results to sell the concept throughout the rest of the company. As division plans are completed, integrate them into an overall corporate plan.

3. *Marketing/Sales Strategy*. Start by concentrating on the customer-driven aspect of your company. Creatively segment your market and use it to drive the strategy of the rest of your company. Market research can discover unfulfilled needs, new product and service ideas, and ways to attack new classes of customers.

4. *Technology Assessment*. Your R&D effort can be more effective if you clearly determine your current technology position and identify your future priorities. Finding ways to speed up a new product development process is another area on which to concentrate.

5. *Quality/Productivity Program*. Both areas require wide participation and teamwork in order to achieve sustainable improvements. What is frequently discovered is a need for change in operations philosophy, systems, and structure.

6. *Profitability Improvements*. Focusing on reducing costs, increasing cash flow, and improving return on equity (or net assets) can be an excellent way to start Creative Planning. Both operational and strategic aspects have to be addressed.

7. *Creative Team Building*. Effective teamwork can increase cooperation, resolve conflict, improve communication, establish trust, and foster commitment. Once teamwork is enhanced, all other forms of Creative Planning are easier to implement.

It is not so much *how* you start, but *that* you start. Here are some suggested times to begin.

WHEN TO DO IT

Most companies realize that the time to take a fresh look at their strategy is now. For some executives, however, it seems never to be the right time.

One response is: "We are making so much money we don't need it. It is all we can do just to keep up with our present level of business." The opposite is: "Our business is doing so poorly, we don't have the luxury of thinking about tomorrow."

The first type of management should realize the best time to build a plan for the future is when the outlook is brightest. The second type needs a plan immediately, or there may not be any tomorrow. Aside from these extremes, here are situations, or times, when it is appropriate to undertake Creative Planning.

1. *Don't Have a Plan.* One was never prepared for your company, or the one that was prepared focused exclusively on the numbers. Or it is outdated. Whatever the reason, you cannot afford to run your business without one.

2. *Growth Opportunities Are High.* Your goal is to make sure you fully capitalize on them, but at the lowest possible risk. A Creative Plan provides you with both the strategy and the tactics for exploiting opportunities.

3. *Company or Department Has a Major Issue.* Your major competitor just implemented a new strategy. The key technology of your industry is changing. Your markets have matured. The innovative process outlined in this book is ideal for addressing these and other challenges to your organization.

4. *Seek an Acquisition or Joint Venture.* Making the best deal requires determining the characteristics of your ideal partner, search skills in finding the partner, shrewdness in negotiating the best agreement, and leadership.

5. *Anticipate Major Investment.* Your company is committing to a major change in strategy or capital investment in the near future. Given the magnitude and irreversibility of the decision involved, a plan that integrates all viewpoints is essential.

6. *New Venture or Department.* Whether it is a group of entrepreneurs or a major corporation, a plan is needed before a new business unit is launched. It's the same when a new department is created. Strategy and execution together determine success.

7. *Promoted to a New Level of Management.* If you are a CEO, division manager, planning director or department manager, Creative Planning can quickly give you a grasp of the situation, guide your decision making, and position you as a dynamic leader.

8. *Decline in Profitability or Cash Flow.* The time to have prepared an innovative plan was before you got into trouble, but better now

than never. An innovative strategy focusing on rapidly improving profitability and restoring cash flow can put your company back in the black.

9. *At Annual Corporate Conference.* Your management team will be meeting for a few days. Using some of that time to address corporatewide issues and opportunities creatively will boost your organization's future performance.

10. *At Marketing or Technology Conference.* Your national sales meeting, marketing conference, or technology retreat can be enlivened by employing group creativity and consensus building techniques. Excellent ideas will emerge.

11. *Entering the Off Season.* Seasonal businesses can use the less hectic months (from management's viewpoint) to reform their strategic and departmental plans. Your organization will be better focused during the upcoming season.

U.S. COMPETITIVENESS

Now what about for this country? In October 1988 John East, vice president of the logic division of Advanced Micro Devices, put it this way:

> I'm terrified. We used to be better at everything—shoes, cars, clothes— but today it's weaponry, agriculture and high-tech. And if you lose high-tech, you lose the military. If we lose high-tech, we're an also-ran nation. We're an England.[2]

Bunker Ramo, the "R" in TRW, predicts in his book *The Business of Science: Winning and Losing in the High-Tech Age,* "By the year 2000 four out of five technological breakthroughs are likely to originate outside the U.S." Our great country must reverse its current slide in world competitiveness before the turnaround measures become unpalatable. Or impossible.

How Far Have We Slipped?

Four of the top five most valuable companies in the world are Japanese. Nippon Telegraph & Telephone's market value as of May 31, 1988, was $295 billion, more than four times that of IBM, America's most valuable company. Ten years ago U.S. banks dominated world finance. In 1988 all ten of the world's largest banks were Japanese.

While IBM demonstrated in 1988 a major leap in semiconductor production technology—X-rays—the Japanese are rapidly pulling ahead in this crucial technology, which will be used to manufacture chips in the mid-1990s.

U.S. researchers in total get more patents than the rest of the world combined. But the U.S. Department of Commerce reports that Japan's Canon topped the list of individual companies at the U.S. Patent & Trademark Office in 1987 with 847. Hitachi was second with 845, Toshiba third with 823, and G.E. forth with 779.

If a war broke out, our adversary would need only to knock out a small plant in Germany 30 miles west of the Czechoslovakian border. Then our missile production would be stalled for months, because the facility makes all the high-purity silicon the U.S. buys for semiconductors in our missile guidance systems.[3] In fact, there is no more silicon in Silicon Valley. The last U.S. producer of silicon wafers, Monsanto Electronic Materials Co., was sold in February 1989 to Huels AG of West Germany. Japanese firms account for 70% and European firms 26% of the world's supply.

These and other situations account for the United States' $12 billion trade gap in August 1988 and $95 billion federal deficit. Unless the trend is reversed, eventually our economy will weaken and our population's standard of living will spiral downward. It's sad. Very. But, the Nobel Prize economist Robert J. Samuelson points out, "At most, only 20 percent of the U.S. trade deficit reflects 'unfair' foreign practices." Even if the percentage were higher, blaming our competitors for our problems is not going to solve them. As was emphasized in Chapter 12, one must first understand the opposition.

Japan's Strategy

I have tremendous respect for Japan and its accomplishments. It has 170 million people, occupies less land than California, and imports 98% of its oil and 97% of its iron ore. How has this nation threatened the United States for leadership in only three decades after complete wartime devastation? It plays our game—capitalism—but by its rules.

What are its rules? The martial arts offer a clue. Eleven years ago I studied karate. Instructors demanded unwavering discipline and impeccable execution. On the other hand, karate assumes that in a fight there are no rules. When threatened with death, the groin is a lower-priority target than most people think. Karate teaches: eyes first, throat second, knees third, and then the groin. I am thankful that I have never had to use it.

Japan feels it is in a life-or-death economic battle. Given the Samurai philosophy that insists on being dominant, here are just some of its strategies:

1. *Long-Term Vision.* "Export or die," a phrase familiar to every Japanese schoolchild, symbolizes the national attitude.[4] Given this priority, Japan selects industries in which to compete and then does everything possible to win. The Ministry of International Trade and Industry (MITI) guides industrial direction and policy. But more important, the country as a whole has a clear picture of its destination and a consensus as to what has to be done.

2. *Collect Ideas.* Japanese companies are expert at finding nascent technologies in other countries and commercializing them first. In particular, they harvest U.S. know-how by sending engineers and managers to research our companies, purchase embryonic high-tech firms or enter joint ventures with them, fund our top American universities, and hire our scientists. For instance, in November 1988 a twenty-five-member team came to the United States to study our service industries (an area in which we still lead). Konomu Matsui, a professor at Tokyo's Rikkyo University, says, "There is still much to learn from the United States."[5]

3. *Manufacturing Offense.* In the 1960s Japanese companies embraced Deming's and Juran's quality approaches. In the 1970s it was JIT and productivity through people. In the 1980s it has been lightning-fast product development and productivity through automation. In the 1990s, it will be continued innovation in manufacturing and services operations. Japan has consistently been a decade ahead of the United States.

4. *Subtle Defense.* Japan shuts out competitors by failing to publicize sales opportunities; suggesting domestic companies buy locally; maintaining its difficult distribution system of "papa-mama" shops, as the Japanese call them, which account for half of retail sales; and other techniques. When pressed, Japan will bend a bit for show. For example, in 1987 a number of Cray Computers were purchased when the heat was on about Japan's barriers to entry.

5. *Low-Cost, Reliable Finance.* Japan's prime rate equivalent in May 1988 was 4% (as against 9% in the United States). In addition, its major banks lend up to 80% of equity and don't insist on quarterly profit increases. This gives Japanese companies an advantage when investing either at home or abroad. And when times are tough, manufacturers make more profits from investments than product sales, which they call "zai-tech" (financial engineering).

6. *Long Term, Win with Creativity.* Canon USA President Fujio Mitarai

says, "cost-cutting can only be a temporary solution to the *endaka* problem. The real answer lies with innovation." Quality was once the primary focus in Japan. Now it's creativity. Anyone who thinks the Japanese can only imitate is dangerously underestimating the country's current strategy. "Science cities" are being constructed as part of their strategy to do basic research and become the technology leader in the 1990s.

These strategies resulted in a 10% growth in Japan's GNP in 1988 and a spending spree by cash-rich Japanese individuals and companies. In addition to multibillion-dollar investments in U.S. real estate, they are eying our major film studios and have purchased two of the three most expensive works of art in the world: Van Gogh's *Sunflowers* for $39 million and Picasso's *Acrobat and Young Harlequin* for $38 million. The spoils of war.

The United States will need some radical strategies to slow down Japan's momentum. But don't count on the Japanese to alert us. They have a proverb: Don't ever wake the sleeping lion.

Imaginative Solutions Needed

A useful definition of a country's competitiveness is the ratio of quality to cost of the goods that it produces—with the winning hand being the best quality for the cheapest cost. The other factor is volume sold domestically and exported. The central question is then: How can the United States as a whole increase its competitiveness? All five constituents—federal and state government, industry, labor, education, and the people—have to work together toward one common objective.

My approach to conceiving and implementing a strategy for U.S. competitiveness would be to form multi-disciplinary task forces of high-level people from the five groups and lead them through the Creative Planning process. Step One is a thorough strategic analysis of our country's profitability, markets, competition, technology, operations, and organization. In Step Two, I would invite radical ideas under two assumptions: (1) in the long term, this is a life-or-death game, and (2) employ business martial arts, or Business-Fu, if you will. Step Three would be the most critical: taking the wild ideas and coming up with strategies that would both work and be acceptable to the philosophy of capitalism. Step Four would be to work out an overall plan and detailed action programs, and Step Five would be to implement. There are no quick fixes to the United States' competitiveness situation, but I am convinced a plan for winning can be developed and executed.

Government Sets the Climate

The Council on Competitiveness, lead by John Young, CEO of Hewlett-Packard, has already told our bureaucrats what they need to do. The Council's report, *Picking Up the Pace: The Commercial Challenge to American Innovation,* implores the U.S. government to "create an environment more conducive to the rapid commercialization of technology by American companies and workers." Exhibit C–1 presents a summary of their comprehensive recommendations. Here are some of my own creative leaps:

1. *Stimulate Savings.* Capital is needed for industrial growth. Reinstate tax-free interest income, but with a higher threshold, say $10,000 per year. Reinstitute capital gains treatment with a sliding scale based on the number of years the investment was made.
2. *Export and Win.* Set a national goal of increasing exports 50% a year over the next ten years. Streamline all regulations that constrain them and use powerful fiscal stimulants. Make the profits on all incremental export business tax-free to the manufacturing companies and the financial institutions lending the funds to the exporter.
3. *Defense.* Help cut the federal deficit by decreasing our national defense budget by $50 billion in 1990 and another $50 billion in 1991 and 1992. Tell NATO countries and, especially, Japan that they have to make up part of the difference in proportion to their country's GNP—or they are a low priority in time of war.
4. *Receivables Collection.* Make it law that all companies pay invoices in thirty days (except in cases of dispute), or a 2% per month charge is automatically added on. This would eliminate the huge productivity waste of hundreds of thousands of people in industry collecting accounts receivable. It would also remove one of the major reasons companies, particularly small ones, get caught in a cash squeeze when trying to grow.

Industry Must Deliver the Goods

The focus of business should be innovation and production—in other words, technology and manufacturing. Beyond using Creative Planning

Exhibit C–1

Summary of Recommendations of
Council on Competitiveness

Macroeconomic
A. Fiscal policy
   1. Federal deficit: Credible multiyear reduction program
   2. Tax policy: Promote savings and long-term investment
B. U.S. trade policy
   1. Open foreign high-technology markets
   2. Protect our intellectual property

Technology Policy
A. Appoint Assistant to the President for Science and Technology (S&T) to:
   1. Coordinate S&T across agencies and set priorities
   2. Ensure that regulations support industry S&T development
   3. Develop President's four-year strategy on S&T
   4. Monitor implementation and coordinate with industry
B. Congress's role
   1. Consider technology issues in all policy setting
   2. Set S&T budget priorities across all agencies
   3. Provide two-year funding of S&T programs
C. Other government strategies
   1. Permanent R&D tax credit
   2. Double budget of National Science Foundation in five years
   3. Speed approval of new products and standards
   4. Consider competitiveness in all policy making
D. Education
   1. Invest in science and engineering education
   2. Faculty development grants and forgivable loans
   3. Federal funding to modernize university S&T facilities

National Research
A. Mission of federal laboratories
   1. Reevaluate mission and get consensus on scope and strategy
   2. Streamline and consolidate labs
   3. Stress technology transfer to industry
   4. Exchange personnel with industry
B. Manufacturing technology
   1. Cooperate R&D among industry, government, and universities
   2. Determine best structure for industry usage
C. State technology programs
   1. Coordinate at federal level
   2. Clearinghouse for information on state programs
D. Department of Defense: Use procurement policies to strengthen U.S. industrial base

throughout the company, industry should consider how to make these leaps feasible:

1. *Play Japan's Game.* "The realistic challenge in the future," says Bunker Ramo, "won't be how to keep U.S. technology from being exploited by foreign rivals, but rather how to acquire theirs." Find ways to make joint ventures a one-way street in *our* direction for a change.
2. *Technology/Manufacturing Focus.* A top priority in companies should be that all managers understand technology and production. Have everyone in the company, from CEO down, spend three months in the plant identifying and solving operational problems or supervising production. Have them spend three months more in R&D and product design. While we are at it, why not another three months in the Far Eastern or European office?
3. *Quality.* Each company must continue pushing to improve with the goal of surpassing the quality of Far Eastern competitors (which is getting even better) in three years. Germany is a good example of a country with high wages but with a total commitment to quality.

A Motivated Public

I speculate that the average American knows about the competitiveness issue but really doesn't understand it. Lee Iacocca says we have to get people alarmed, and I wholeheartedly agree. Just as corporations have to get everyone aligned, the United States has to do the same with its people. What must be communicated clearly and repeatedly is the significance of competitiveness, our country's strategy for it, the consequences of less than perfect execution by everyone, and what each and every person can do to help, including children.

Restructure Education

The free market approach to education has been used in Minneapolis, Minnesota, since 1971 and has proved successful. In this approach, known as "choice," parents decide which public school their children attend, and the schools compete. San Francisco is considering legislation of this nature, and it is being investigated at a national level. Something has to be done to improve education.

A six-country survey released in January 1989 by the Educational Testing Service showed that thirteen-year-old American schoolchildren scored the worst in mathematics and below average in science. Only 50% of the American children thought that "much of what you learn in science classes is useful in everyday life," but 82% of the Korean children did.[6] South Korea is becoming a fierce international competitor.

Clearly, our children need to be sold the vision of a technology-driven world, and how they personally will benefit from being knowledgeable. Furthermore, science must be made more intriguing. How about teaching it through the eyes of the great discoverers and inventors, and telling kids they can do the same?

At the collegiate level, all business majors should have mandatory courses in engineering, manufacturing, teamwork, and competitiveness. Engineering schools have to cover theory, but they must also teach practicality. Mandatory courses for all engineering majors should include quality, design for manufacturing, manufacturing engineering, and creativity and invention.

Creativity training should be a separate course for all high school and college students. A survey of 1,188 colleges and universities in 1987 showed that only 6% of them had a formal course on the subject. Yet it is creativity in the development and rapid use of technology that will determine this country's future.

Obviously, these leaps have to be massaged into feasible strategies before they can be made policy. But they all must be seriously considered.

We Can Do It Again

Japan fell in World War II not so much because of the skill of generals as because of the skill of scientists. It was this country's ability not only to develop a new technology first—in this case the atom bomb—but to be the first to deliver it to the market.

The popular World War II saying was: "The difficult we do immediately. The impossible takes a little longer." There is no shortage of competitive spirit in the United States today. It just needs to be focused on the task and provided with the climate to succeed.

Remember, you *can* outperform your competitors. To do so, you need to innovate and implement, innovate and implement, and innovate and implement again. This requires insight into your industries and markets, imaginative ideas, astute decision making, actionable strategies, and an inspired organization—the five steps of Creative Planning.

Appendix: The Nature of Genius

THE following words are engraved in stone in the lobby of Carnegie–Mellon University's Graduate School of Industrial Administration: "Industrial opportunity means the opportunity to create."

Yet many managers view strategy development as purely an analytical process. They believe that analyzing a situation leads to answers. The successful executives I've interviewed tell me otherwise. They say imagination and creativity lie at the heart of the process. Analysis sets the stage for provocative thinking and later is used to verify results. But the conception of breakthrough strategies is grounded in creativity.

A second finding of my extensive research into creativity is inspiring:

> Scientific geniuses—the lone rangers of discovery—and innovative executives think alike when they are creating.

Presumably, if we can delve into the minds of geniuses and see how they work, then maybe we can pattern our thought processes after theirs. Any understanding we gain, though, will help us incorporate more creativity into our strategic thinking.

I began my research into the field of creativity in the mid-1970s when

I realized that innovative thinking should play a central role in both strategy development and implementation. Since then, I have:

1. Reviewed the creative techniques and processes used in the fields of scientific research, new product development, advertising, creative writing, the fine arts, and other fields
2. Researched what psychologists have found out about creativity, from Freud and Jung to modern-day practitioners
3. Interviewed the heads of planning of twenty-five major corporations on how they go about injecting creativity into their planning
4. Observed and recorded as a consultant how top and middle management conceive successful strategies, and how they motivate organizations to execute
5. Interviewed more than eighty top executives on how they have conceived ideas and what they did to get them implemented
6. Studied the biographies of great thinkers—Leonardo da Vinci, Plato, Einstein, Newton, Edison, Freud, and others—looking for common traits and thought processes

This Appendix presents a composite of my conclusions on the pseudoscience of creativity. I call it that because it is far more art than science. Let's now turn to a model of a genius's mind and look for a while at the path it follows in conceiving breakthroughs.

MEET A GENIUS

Creative geniuses go through three distinct steps in developing ideas:

1. Analyze the situation to gain understanding
2. Create or generate ideas
3. Judge the ideas to select the best

Recall that analytical, creative, and judicial thinking are the first three steps of the Creative Planning process. One thing that separates creative geniuses from the rest is that they undertake these three steps *sequentially* rather than *simultaneously*. Sequential thinking, or the isolation of thought, allows the prolific individual to be sharply analytical one minute, boundlessly creative and speculative the next, *and* decisively judgmental a moment later. As shown in Exhibit A–1, it is as if they have three mental channels, each of which can be controlled and used separately. Their creative productivity, as a result, is far greater than that of the average

Three Heads Are Better than One

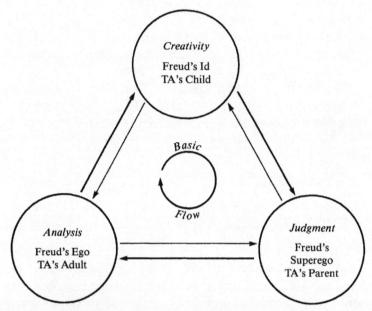

Creative geniuses can control which mental "channel" they use, making them highly
productive thinkers. Most people attempt to use all three channels at the same time, which
prevents them from developing dramatic insights. Worse yet, people may use the wrong
mode of thinking in a given situation; for example, being creative when harsh judgment is
called for. This three-step process coincides with Freud's model of the human psyche as well
as that of Transactional Analysis (TA).

person, who attempts to think in all three modes at once. Their result is
mediocrity of all three.

This isolation of thought is important throughout the entire creative
process, but it is crucial during the second step, when new ideas first
come to mind. The most important principle, then, in this phase—the
golden rule of creativity—is "deferral of judgment." No negative
thinking or censoring of ideas is permissible. To do otherwise would be
like trying to drive a car with its brakes on. These polar opposites—
creativity and judgment—would work against each other, with the result
that neither would be done well. Note that this is one area where
conventional planning frequently falls down—when creating and
judging are done together rather than sequentially. The three states of
mind have to work together in a synergistic way, not against one
another.

MANAGING THE FAMILY
IN YOUR MIND

According to Transactional Analysis theory, everyone's personality has three parts: *adult*, *child*, and *parent*. I find that these are excellent labels for the three steps shown in Exhibit A–1.

The adult in us analyzes. It wants to solve problems in practical ways, through collecting and understanding facts. It has a balanced point of view, not too positive, not too negative. Freud named this part of our psyche the *ego*.

The child in us creates. It is the wellspring of our creativity. It loves to try new things. break the rules, rebel, be mischievous, fantasize about the ideal world, and get what it wants. Freud called this part of our personality the *id*, the instinctive animal in us. He believed a newborn baby to essentially be all id.

The parent in us judges. It is our moral and ethical conscience. It is also great at rejecting new ideas, or at least finding fault with them. Freud designated this our *superego*. It forbids, prohibits, and drives out creative thinking.

Do you remember when you were a small child and fantasized? What you might call "childhood foolishness" today is actually highly functional. It is the wellspring of your creativity. "The creative person is a perpetual child," said John Huston. A master film director who let "the child roam in him," he acknowledged that he did as a man what excited him as a boy.[1] Highly creative people often display childish behavior. Wolfgang Amade Mozart (he only used "Amadeus" when he was being flippant) was both a faultless genius and a perpetual child. We are not born leaders, but we are born creative.

The problem is that the creative child is programmed out of us during the growing-up process. Psychologists who have tested creativity in various age groups confirm that on average 90% of five-year-olds rate highly creative, 10% of ten-year-olds, 5% of eighteen-year-olds, and only 2% of forty-year-olds.[2] We start to have our creativity squelched when we are old enough to be repeatedly told by our parents and others not to do things. Creative rigor mortis really sets in when we enter school and learn there is "one right answer" to problems. Conformity and conservatism are educated into us.

What is ironic is that our intelligence (defined as the ability to deal with abstract concepts and learn from experience) goes up with age. (See Exhibit A–2.) However, it is the synergistic combination of creativity and intelligence that leads to breakthroughs.

EXHIBIT A–2

Creativity and Intelligence Versus Age

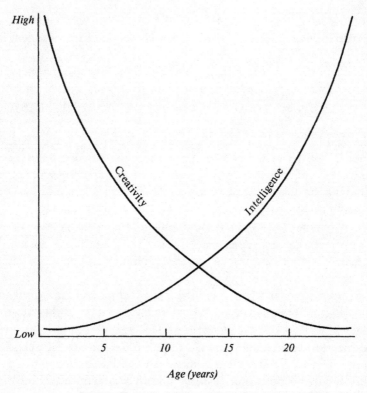

Age (years)

So let your youthful sense of wonder run rampant. Set your child free and watch the ideas flow. As the psychologist Abraham H. Maslow put it:

> The really creative person is not afraid of his unconscious. This is the person who can live with his unconscious . . . his childishness, his fantasy, his imagination, his wish fulfillment, his poetic quality, his crazy quality. He is the person who can regress in the service of the ego . . . voluntary regression.[3]

A genius combines the creativity of the child with the intellect of the adult and applies the wisdom of the parent.

THREE WAYS TO BREAKTHROUGHS

Delving deeper into the creative process, I find that geniuses use three distinct thought mechanisms in coming up with breakthrough concepts: (1) insights, (2) leaps, and (3) connections.

Perhaps insights are more closely related to analytical thought than to creativity *per se*. But since they lead directly to creative solutions, I classify insights as creative mechanisms. The overriding principle of attaining insights is to break the problem or situation down into its homogeneous components. Do this in as many ways as possible, from many angles. Fresh approaches to the problem are what you are after. One method is to define all negativism in the situation—things needing improvement, issues, challenges, customer needs, and so on. Another method is mentally to distill all available information about a problem down to one or several all-encompassing concepts or patterns. A third is to develop a deeper understanding of how and why the various elements of a problem interact. Viewing the situation from a totally new vantage point (your customer's, for example, or your competitor's) is a fourth method. Insights help us to grasp the inner nature of a situation and fuel the imagination.

The creative leap is the most esoteric approach of creative thinkers, involving the formation of totally new concepts rather than connecting existing things. The "mountaintop experiences" of the great minds fall into this category. Plato called them "hypotheses." Einstein described them as "thought experiments." Many technological breakthroughs are conceived in this manner. Among scientists, a leap consists of formulation of a theory in an extreme situation to see if it is still valid. This is the approach Einstein used to develop $E = mc^2$, which relates energy, mass, and the speed of light. All mass is congealed energy, and all energy liberated matter. Specific techniques for taking leaps were described in Chapter 3.

Making connections is the most common definition of creativity—the bringing together of previously unrelated items to form a new whole, one that is more useful and valuable than the sum of the parts. It is based on the supposition that rarely is anything invented that is truly new. Connections are made when the brain (primarily the right, intuitive hemisphere) is allowed to think freely in a childlike manner. This kind of thinking requires training (or retraining) the mind to engage in the activity Freud called free association, while watching for intriguing combinations—the "turning on of the light bulb" experience.

The bottom line of the above three thought mechanisms is that creative genius is thinking in unconventional ways.

CREATIVE CHARACTERISTICS

What common denominators did I find in both the world's great thinkers and highly innovative executives? The top nine are explained below. One has to be careful about generalizing, though. For instance, many creative people are eccentric. That doesn't mean all eccentric people are creative.

Creativity over Intelligence

Einstein claimed, "Imagination is more important than knowledge." Edison said, "I never remember anything that I can look up in a book." Most researchers agree that the crucial element of innovative genius is not intelligence quotient (IQ), but creativity. IQ, of course, is important. But only up to a point. Scoring much over 120 on the Stanford-Binet test (with a mean of 100) is not essential. IQ is a measure of general knowledge and logical, deductive abilities. It does not assess the ability to break the set—to see significance in the irrelevant—or to take leaps of imagination to "radical practicals," ideas that are both unconventional and feasible. No level of mental ability of the kind measured by IQ tests is in itself sufficient to produce a genuine new idea. On the other hand, a low IQ doesn't mean you are creative.

Einstein's great achievements could never have been predicted from his mediocre grades in school. Edison was sent home from school by a teacher because he was a slow learner—so his mother taught him. Dr. Robert Jarvik, the inventor of the artificial heart, had lousy grades in college and had to start medical school in Italy. It is the synergistic combination of intelligence, creativity, and judgment that differentiates the great innovators from the barren intellectuals.

Problem Finding

Gifted, creative people do not take the world as it is. They believe anything that has been done can be done better. That attitude, plus their insatiable curiosity, equals someone who is working on problems the rest of us don't know exist. Albert Szent-Gyorgyi, a Hungarian biochemist, defined it as follows: "Innovation consists of seeing what everyone has seen and thinking what no one else has thought." A genius aims at something no one else can see and hits it.

While Dr. Edwin H. Land was taking photos in 1943, his three-year-old daughter asked why she couldn't see them right away. Perhaps that elementary challenge kindled a flame, for several years later, thanks to her dad, she could. In the United States, Dr. Land's 533 patents, including the Polaroid process, are second only to Edison's 1,093.

Bruce Mills was changing his grandchild's diapers and had a creative flash. Or maybe he just got sensitive right then to a market need. But anyway, he was determined. He invented a new billion-dollar product segment we know as Pampers.

Why does blood contain iron? How do catalysts make chemical reactions go faster? Henry Taube turns simple-sounding questions like those over and over in his mind. The result is eighteen major advances in the study of chemical reactions, particularly inorganic ones, and Taube's Nobel award by the Swedish Academy in 1987. Problem finding is opportunity finding.

Think in Pictures

Geniuses speak of vivid images, mental pictures, and fantasies when describing how many of their breakthrough thoughts appear to them. The most important element of Darwin's development of the theory of evolution turned out to be an image of an irregularly branching tree. It helped him pull together his thoughts on the principle of natural selection. He revised the tree image many times, and it became the only diagram in his seminal book, *The Origin of Species*.

When Einstein was trying to understand why the law of gravitation did not fit his special theory of relativity, he imagined a person falling from a rooftop. He realized that if this person dropped something in midflight, it would remain, relative to him, in a state of rest. This led directly to his discovery of the principle of general relativity that revolutionized physics. He certainly didn't come up with his theories by crunching numbers. He did that later, only to verify what he had imagined.

This visualization or imaging, by the way, is similar to the way innovative top executives develop strategy. They mentally picture one or more alternative futures, see the necessary relationships, synthesize the overall situation, and envision a way to capitalize on it. The result is a clear vision of the company.

Mental Fluidity

Great thinkers have agile minds. They use all possible modes of thought in attacking problems, freely switching between them as needed. They will try to identify insights or solutions logically, spatially, even paradoxically. If they run into a block on one portion of a problem, they table it for future thinking and work on another part. They will zoom in to solve a small portion of a large, complex problem, or they will take a wide-angle view in an attempt to see and redefine new patterns. They will oscillate between creative, childlike daydreaming and critical, parental thinking. They use everything in their tool chests—tools, by the way, that are available to all of us.

Entertain Contradictions

Geniuses feel comfortable solving ambiguous problems, especially those steeped in contradictions. This is an important characteristic. In fact, they seek out opposites, realizing that creating a new context where these make sense can lead to breakthroughs. This is why they do not discard theories that seem in conflict. In 1895 the German physicist Wilhelm Conrad Röntgen noticed an unusual green glow on the screen of a cathode ray tube. Other scientists had seen it and ignored it, because it didn't fit in with what they knew about cathode ray tubes. Röntgen investigated it and discovered the X-ray. Einstein was convinced that the universe could be explained by logical, mathematical formulas. Yet he relied on flights of fantasy to discover the truths.

Wide Interests

Creative geniuses are noted for being Renaissance people who work or play in a variety of unrelated areas. This is stimulating to them; they make connections between disparate fields to achieve breakthroughs. This is not the case with experts and specialists, who have closed minds. They are susceptible to tunnel vision and resist change.

Samuel F. B. Morse, inventor of the telegraph and the code that bears his name, made achievements in commerce, politics, art and, of course, science. When he came to New York University as a member of its faculty, he was the first and only person in the country to hold the title of Professor of Fine Arts. His 1832 painting *Gallery of the Louvre* sold for $3.25 million in 1982.

George Bernard Shaw, the playwright who ranks among the wittiest men of all time, offered opinions on all the major issues of his day from artificial insemination to homosexuality. Thomas Jefferson was a master architect, scientist, educator, and public servant, excelling in disparate fields. Einstein did much the same. These were men for all seasons.

Diverse skills are essential in business as well. Leading an organization through multiple growth phases requires an extraordinary range of talents and motivations.

Seize Opportunities

Geniuses are alert to serendipity. In the words of Louis Pasteur, "Chance favors the prepared mind." Fleming's discovery of penicillin, Becquerel's identification of radioactivity, and Nobel's discovery of nitrocellulose were all exploitations of accidents. Sometimes the opportunities are obscure, and distant connections need to be made. The cardiologist Garrett Lee invented the technique of melting fatty deposits that clog arteries with a laser in a catheter after watching laser sword fights in the movie *Star Wars*.

Michael Korda, author of *Power*, says: "Achievers tend to be more observant than nonachievers. You don't get ahead unless you learn to notice things." Tom Wilson, in one of his cartoons, has Ziggy remarking, "Every time opportunity knocked, I was out back taking out the garbage."

Intellectual Playfulness

A sense of humor is another trait of great thinkers of the past. The process of contriving humorous remarks certainly is a form of creativity. Irreverence also comes in handy when breaking with tradition. Sir Alexander Fleming, the Scottish bacteriologist who discovered penicillin, used to like to paint pictures with germs in petri dishes. He knew how to play. "I play with microbes," he once said. "It is very pleasant to break the rules."

R. Buckminster Fuller, known as the inventor of the geodesic dome, was awarded the Presidential Medal of Freedom, the highest official honor the country can grant a civilian. He enjoyed watching the reporters' shock when he told them he had been expelled twice from Harvard, once for squandering his tuition money on a party for the cast of the Ziegfeld Follies. Preferring to be known as "Bucky," he later returned to Harvard as a professor. Imagine calling Leonardo da Vinci, with whom Fuller has been compared, "Lenny."[4]

Patient Persistence

John Foster, the nineteenth-century American diplomat and author, called genius "the power of lighting one's own fire." The most prominent characteristic of geniuses is their high level of motivation to solve problems, evident in the energy and length of time they spend doing so. The "Eureka!" usually comes after a complex and lengthy process. Howard Head, inventor of the metal sandwich ski, said, "If I'd known it would take forty-two tries to get it right, I would never have started." Michelangelo said it differently: "If people knew how hard I worked to get my mastery, it wouldn't seem so wonderful after all." When someone referred to Edison's "Godlike genius," he proclaimed, "Any other bright-minded fellow can accomplish just as much if he will stick like hell and remember that nothing that's any good works by itself. You've got to make the damn thing work."

Here is what one reporter said about two of the most creative people in the movie business:

> I think I've discovered the professional secret of George Lucas and Steven Spielberg: They are the hardest working dreamers around. These guys aren't lazy. They have a limitless appetite for taking pains, for being perfectionists even about the little things that take place in the corners of their screens. And so when we enter one of their worlds, it is a full world we're inhabiting, not just a movie notion.[5]

Highly creative people have many common denominators that underlie their talent for invention and innovation. I have described only an important few. Additional characteristics will emerge in the discussions that follow.

GETTING TO EUREKA!

One major aspect of creative thinking deserves special attention: incubation. It can be made less mysterious and more intentional. Here is how.

Passive Incubation: Be Receptive

Have you ever tried to remember someone's name, only to have it come to you after you stopped trying to think of it? Often referred to as "sleeping on the problem," incubation consists of mentally getting away from a problem or challenge and letting ideas come to you. A response that one innovative president made after hearing an intriguing yet ostensibly unfeasible idea sums up this concept: "Let's put it in a dark closet for a while and see what develops."

Intensely focus on a problem for a while, and then put it out of your mind. Do, however, set a personal deadline (don't tell anyone what it is) for coming up with a solution. Ideas will appear in your mind when you are relaxed and thinking of nothing in particular. However, ideas appear only after the focusing stage. Incubation without previous concentration is goofing off.

Creative people find ideas "popping into their minds" when they are walking, relaxing alone, falling asleep, waking, taking a shower, and doing repetitive tasks. It's surprising where and when ideas strike. In 1968 Eugene Richeson, M. Kenneth Oshman, Walter Lowenstern, and Robert Maxfield came up with the concept of Rolm Corporation at their monthly poker game. The first letters of their last names spell "Rolm."

Einstein used to get ideas while shaving or walking (rain or shine) to and from his laboratory. Mozart wrote in a letter that it was most natural for him to compose when he was in a cheerful mood—traveling in a carriage or strolling after a hearty meal. "Whence and how [my ideas] come, I know not. Nor can I force them." His process of idea development (which I call "concept building"—the subject of Chapter 5) he described as follows:

> All this fires my soul, and provided I am not disturbed, my subject enlarges itself, becomes methodized and defined, and the whole, though it be long, stands almost complete and finished in my mind, so that I can survey it, like a fine picture or a beautiful statue, at a glance. Nor do I hear in my imagination the parts successively, but I hear them, as it were, all at once. What a delight this is I cannot tell!

Perhaps you have noticed that all of the above situations described by great thinkers are outside the office. But relax; you can incubate in the office too. Be sure, however, to do it with your door closed. Ralph Waldo Emerson once observed, "If a man sits down to think, he is immediately asked if he has a headache." The same occurs in corporations.

Write down ideas the instant you get them. They will pop out of your head as quickly as they popped in. If you were looking for just one or two ideas, remembering would be easy. But since you are looking for as many pieces to the strategic puzzle as you can find, capturing them all is necessary.

Active Incubation: Relax and Focus

You can also be proactive in inducing a state of consciousness that is conducive to creativity. How do you enter an altered state of inspired thought? You calm yourself way down, then daydream about the problem.

Relaxing can be accomplished by using the Yoga breath method. Get comfortable in your chair. Take a slow, deep breath, filling first your stomach (you are pushing down your diaphragm, giving you twice the air intake capacity), then your chest. After a count to five, slowly exhale, first from your upper chest, then from the stomach. To enhance the effect, close your eyes and visualize the air flowing in as you inhale. See it move. As you exhale, visualize all the tension flowing out of your body, starting from the top of your head, down through your neck, and out your fingertips and toes. See the tension as a colored liquid flowing right out of you. Ten to fifteen minutes of Yoga breathing, and you will be highly relaxed. You are ready to fantasize ideal solutions to your strategic situation. Now, in the words of William James, "Get your mind whirling and see what happens." No mental editing, either. If you're lucky, you may experience an idea avalanche.

Sound like meditation? It is related to it. Mitch Kapor, inventor of Lotus 1-2-3 and former chairman of Lotus Development Corporation, was a meditation instructor in his earlier years.

Peak performance in sports occurs when one has achieved relaxed concentration and is thinking in pictures. Professional athletes call it "the zone." I extensively researched this in the mid-1970s and interviewed top performers in developing a line of cassette tapes on tennis, golf, and skiing for *Psychology Today* magazine. Jack Nicklaus and many other top golf pros use a ritual before each shot of relaxing through deep breathing and visualizing the perfect swing. Nicklaus says: "I never hit a shot, not even in practice, without having a very sharp, in-focus picture in my head." Billy Kidd, the only skier to win both the world amateur and the world professional championships in one year, described to me how he relaxed in the chairlift before each race and visualized the perfect run, gate by gate, turn by turn. O. J. Simpson described his use of mental imagery this way:

> I used to run plays in my mind all the time. Visualization, someone called it. I'd run the play over and over and over against certain defenses, and I would know an outside linebacker should be in a certain place. I didn't have to see him, or look there. I knew his responsibility and I knew by this time where he should be. So if I run a play (during a game), sometimes a guy says, "how did you fake that guy? You never even looked to see him, and you faked him." Well, I knew he should have been there.[6]

If you are resistant because this seems uncomfortably new or strange in business, be assured that it is accepted. Michael L. Ray, professor of marketing and communication at the Stanford Graduate School of Business, teaches a unique course entitled "Creativity in Business." He exposes his students to meditation, the "I Ching," and other Eastern techniques to awaken their creativity. The course has also included talks by such successful entrepreneurs as Nolan Bushnell and Steven Jobs. Through question-and-answer sessions, the class explores how the "big ideas" occurred to these thinkers and doers. Incidentally, Ray's book, *Creativity in Business*, is excellent reading (Doubleday, 1986).

There are other methods. The Japanese billionaire Dr. Yoshiro Naka-Mats has 1,267 patents, the world record. (Edison had 1,093.) One was for the floppy disk, which established his wealth. Dr. NakaMats says his best ideas come in one of three ways. He swims to the bottom of his pool and stays there until he almost drowns. "I stay under maybe four or five minutes until I come close to death when images of one's past life flash through the mind," he says. "Instead of past, I've trained myself to use this period of extraordinary brain activity to create new things."[7] Another is sitting in his Cerebrex brain chair, which he invented, and having electrical current shot through the back of his neck to his feet; this, he says, increases blood circulation to the brain. His third choice is listening to Beethoven's Fifth Symphony. I prefer his third method.

Music-Induced Creativity

Psychologists have found that the steady beat of baroque music, specifically the largo (slow) sections of concertos, induces a relaxed, high-performance state of mind. The pathfinder in this area is Dr. Georgi Lozanov, a Bulgarian psychiatrist and educator who has researched and documented this phenomenon over the past thirty years. His concepts are now used in more than a dozen countries.

The baroque period, 1600–1750, was the first of four classical music eras. Its notable composers include Bach, Vivaldi, Telemann, Corelli, Purcell, Scalatti, and Handel. Not all baroque music will shift your mental gears, however. Largo movements in 4/4 time (or sixty or fewer beats per minute) are required. Choose these appropriate movements from your favorite classical pieces or, if you have no favorites, otherwise famous ones. Largo is a tempo 40–60 beats per minute; Larghetto, 60–66; and Adagio, which seems pleasantly slow, is nonetheless out of the range at 66–76. Andante (76–108) and Allegro (120–168) are far too fast.

Your heartbeat and metabolism—your state of being, really—tend to synchronize themselves with the rhythm of the music. For example, when listening to largo movements, your pulse will slow down from its normal 80 to about 60. Your brain waves will also tune into the tempo, albeit at a much higher frequency. You are being helped into the relaxed state of alpha. I sometimes play special tapes of baroque largo sections during creativity sessions with clients. Their behavior changes. Scientifically, this has been proved to improve group rapport, enhance concentration, and stimulate creative thinking.

UNDERSTANDING YOUR OWN CREATIVITY

A provocative exercise I use in my seminars on imaginative thinking involves analyzing past creative moments. This Freudian self-analysis directed specifically at your innovative talent can be revealing. Undertake it as follows:

1. Make a list of some business ideas you've had that were successfully implemented. They need not be major ones.
2. Think back. What motivated you to solve each problem? What thoughts gave you a handle on it? Where were you when the first glimmer of solution came to you? Did you have to refine the idea? What did it take to put the idea into action? Did the final strategy resemble your initial idea?
3. Now compare your modes of thinking with those of geniuses described earlier. Is there anything you could do differently to increase your creativity?

The key to corporate success is providing an environment which fosters imaginative thinking and motivates people to act.

Notes

CHAPTER 1   THE CREATIVE PLANNING PROCESS

1. Carol Kennedy, "Planning Global Strategies for 3M," *Long Range Planning,* February 1988, pp. 9–17.
2. Interview with Kent Dorwin, senior vice president of planning, Charles Schwab & Co., August 15, 1988.
3. Donald E. Noble, "Rubbermaid's Strategy to Achieve Above Average Profitability and Growth," speech to the Cleveland Chapter of Association for Corporate Growth, 1986.

CHAPTER 2   DEVELOPING STRATEGIC INSIGHTS

1. Nicholas Colchester, "The Man Who Took the Hiss Out of Entertainment," *Financial Times,* September 11, 1979.
2. Interview with William Jasper, president of Dolby Laboratories, on February 25, 1987.
3. R. Gordon McGovern, "The Key to a Growing Company—Customer, Customer, Customer," *Journal for Corporate Growth,* Vol. 1, no. 1, 1985.
4. Interview with Douglas Phillips, senior director of corporate planning, Merck & Company, in November 1987.

5. John Wright, president of Domaine Chandon, in a speech to the San Francisco chapter of the Association for Corporate Growth, December 10, 1986.

6. David E. Sanger, "Compaq Fools the Experts." *San Francisco Chronicle,* September 2, 1985, p. 52.

7. *Wall Street Journal,* June 13, 1986, p. 1.

8. Charles W. Moritz, "Strategies and Principles That Guide Dun & Bradstreet," *Journal for Corporate Growth,* November 2, 1987, pp. 13–23.

9. Interview with Art Gensler, CEO, Gensler and Associates, December 1986.

CHAPTER 3   TAKING CREATIVE LEAPS

1. Harold Geneen with Alvin Moscow, *Managing* (Avon Books: New York, 1984).

2. Carol Kennedy, "Planning Global Strategies for 3M," *Long Range Planning,* February 1988, pp. 9–17.

3. Mary Ganz, "Move Afloat to Halt Tokyo's Sprawl," *San Francisco Examiner,* July 17, 1988, p. 1.

4. Otis Port, "Why Army Engineers Are Stuck on a New Cement," *Business Week,* October 31, 1988, p. 153.

5. Robert E. Norton, "Citibank Wows the Consumer," *Fortune,* June 8, 1987, pp. 48–54.

6. Interview with Linda Cyrog, vice president of strategic marketing, American President Lines, Oakland, California, November 16, 1988.

7. Interview with William Jasper, president of Dolby Laboratories, San Francisco, February 1987.

CHAPTER 4   MAKING STRATEGIC CONNECTIONS

1. Richard Phalon, "Strawberry, Chocolate, Tutti-Frutti," *Forbes,* March 21, 1988, p. 190.

2. "Now Airlines are Diversifying by Sticking to What They Know Best," *Business Week,* May 7, 1984, pp. 70–72.

3. "The Tough Cookie at RJR Nabisco," *Fortune,* July 18, 1988, pp. 32–46.

4. "Circus Circus 8" videotape, Broad Street Productions, New York, August 1987.

5. Interview with Glenn Schaeffer, CFO, Circus Circus, Las Vegas, June 1988, and the company's 1988 Annual Report, p. 4.

6. Fred Hiatt, "Pay Now, Buy Later a Hit in Japan," *San Francisco Chronicle,* December 26, 1988, p. D–1.

CHAPTER 5   BUILDING STRATEGIC CONCEPTS

1. Walter Kiechel, "Getting Creative," *Fortune,* July 25, 1983, p. 109.

2. From a speech by Regis McKenna in 1983. A detailed account of Jack Kilby's integrated circuit invention appears in Richard Foster, *Innovation: The Attacker's Advantage* (New York: Summit Books, 1986), pp. 81–85.

3. From an interview with Tom Abbott, manager of public relations, Xerox, March 1989.

4. Epictetus, "Discourses," c. 50–120.

5. "Give Shape to Imagination" was the heading of a Lockheed corporate advertisement in *Fortune* on April 1, 1985.

6. Kevin McKean and Tom Dworetzky, "Fuzzy Means to Logical Ends," *Discover*, February 1985, pp. 70–73.

7. Peter F. Drucker, *The Age of Discontinuity* (New York: Harper & Row, 1969), pp. 56–57.

CHAPTER 6   STRATEGIC DECISION MAKING

1. Theodore Levitt, *The Marketing Imagination* (New York: Free Press, 1983), p. 164.

2. Michael Emerson, "Why Coca-Cola and Wine Didn't Mix," *Business Week*, October 10, 1983, p. 30.

3. Patricia Sellers, "How King Kellogg Beat the Blahs," *Fortune*, August 29, 1988, pp. 54–64.

4. From an interview with Larry Davis, president, DG Mouldings, Marion, Virginia, November 1984.

5. Carol Kennedy, "Planning Global Strategies at 3M," *Long Range Planning*, February 1988, pp. 9–17.

6. "The Miracle Company: Excellence in the Lab and Executive Suite Makes Merck a Powerhouse," *Business Week*, October 19, 1987, pp. 84–90.

CHAPTER 7   FORMULATING STRATEGY

1. James K. Brown, "Corporate Soul-Searching, the Power of Mission Statements," *Across the Board*, March 1984, pp. 44–52.

2. "Forbes Annual Survey of the Most Powerful People in Corporate America," *Forbes*, May 30, 1988, p. 122.

3. Kathy Rebello and John Hillkirk, "Sabbaticals at Core of Apple Perks," *USA Today*, June 10, 1988, p. B–1.

4. Louise Ackerman, "Reebok: Tennis' Billion-Dollar Superstar," *Tennis*, December 1987, pp. 46–53.

5. Rick Molz, "How Leaders Use Goals," *Long Range Planning*, October 1987, pp. 91–101.

6. Kathleen K. Wiegner, "And the Last Shall Be First," *Forbes*, November 16, 1987, pp. 100–102.

7. From an interview with Kent Dorwin, senior vice president of planning, Charles Schwab & Co., July 29, 1988.

8. Frederick W. Gluck, "Vision and Leadership in Corporate Strategy," *McKinsey Quarterly,* Winter 1981, pp. 13–27.

9. "Corporate Strategies: Bill Marriott's Grand Design For Growth," *Business Week,* October 1, 1984, p. 62.

10. Janet Guyon, "Combative Chief: GE Chairman Welch, Though Much Praised, Starts to Draw Critics," *Wall Street Journal,* August 4, 1988, p. 1.

CHAPTER 8   ENTHUSIASTIC IMPLEMENTATION

1. Donald F. Craib, Jr., "Communicating for Growth: A New Strategic Challenge," *Journal for Corporate Growth,* Vol. 2, no. 1 (1986): pp. 57–69.

2. From interviews with Larry Davis, president of DG Mouldings, and Art Ramey, vice president of sales and marketing, November 1984.

3. From an interview with J. Douglas Phillips, senior director of corporate planning of Merck & Co., November 1988.

4. Thomas Rohan, "Do Something Outrageous!" *Industry Week,* January 7, 1985, pp. 86–87.

5. Charles L. Hughes, "On Being Systematically Outrageous," *Supervisory Management,* September 1985, pp. 2–5.

6. "Who Made the Most—and Why," *Business Week,* May 2, 1988, p. 50; "The $60 million Chairman," *Business Week,* May 16, 1988, p. 42.

7. John Sculley, "A Look into the Future," speech to the Contra Costa County Council, California, June 12, 1987.

8. "The New Breed of Strategic Planner," *Business Week,* September 17, 1984, p. 68.

9. "Reagan Takes Responsibility: Iran Deal—'It Was a Mistake,' " *San Francisco Chronicle,* March 5, 1987, p. 1.

10. Maynard M. Gordon, *The Iacocca Management Technique* (New York: Ballantine Books, 1985), pp. 13–16.

11. David A. Silver, *Entrepreneurial Megabucks* (New York: John Wiley & Sons, 1985), p. 405.

12. Leonard Lieberman, CEO of Supermarkets General, speech at the 1984 meeting of the Food Marketing Institute.

13. Bill Saporito, "The Tough Cookie at RJR Nabisco," *Fortune,* July 18, 1988, p. 32.

14. Christopher Power, "At Johnson & Johnson, a Mistake Can Be a Badge of Honor," *Business Week,* September, 26, 1988, p. 126.

15. Joshua Hyatt, "Too Hot to Handle," *Inc.,* March 1987, pp. 52–58.

16. Tom Peters, "Constantly Improving Your Business" (syndicated column), *San Francisco Chronicle,* October 7, 1988, p. B–4.

CHAPTER 9   LEADING CREATIVE TEAMS

1. Ronald Bailey, "Not Power but Empower," *Forbes,* May 30, 1988, pp. 120–123.

2. Robert Lefton and V. R. Buzotta, "Teams and Teamwork: A Study of Executive-Level Teams," *National Productivity Review,* Winter 1987–88.

3. Editorial staff, "Tom Peters' Formula for Supervisory Excellence," *Supervisory Management,* February 1985, pp. 2–6.

4. Carol Hymowitz, "Five Main Reasons Why Managers Fail," *Wall Street Journal,* May 2, 1988, p. 25.

5. Bailey, "Not Power, but Empower," p. 123.

6. Rayna Skolnik, "Meetings Carry the Message," *Sales and Marketing Management,* November 14, 1983, pp. 66–77.

7. Connie Leslie with Shawn D. Lewis, "Collection-Plate Blues," *Newsweek,* October 17, 1988, p. 78.

8. Interview with Henri Lipmanowicz, vice president of economic and strategic planning, Merck Sharp & Dohme International, Rahway, N.J., January 1986.

9. Stuart Gannes, "America's Fastest Growing Companies," *Fortune,* May 23, 1988, p. 28.

10. Jonathan B. Levine, "Sun Microsystems Turns On the Afterburners," *Business Week,* July 18, 1988, pp. 114–18.

11. Alan M. Webber, "Red Auerbach on Management," *Harvard Business Review,* March–April 1987, pp. 84–93.

12. Jolie Solomon and Carol Hymowitz, "Team Strategy: P&G Makes Changes in the Way It Develops and Sells Its Products," *Wall Street Journal,* August 11, 1987, p. 1.

CHAPTER 10   PROFITABILITY IMPROVEMENT

1. Brian O'Reilly, "Steve Jobs: What's Next?," *Fortune,* November 7, 1988.

2. "Face to Face: Federal Express's Fred Smith," *Inc.,* October 1986, p. 34.

3. Craig Webb, "World Bank Cuts Staff, Regroups," *San Francisco Chronicle,* May 5, 1987, p. C–1.

4. Michael Ceiply, "Universal Problem: MCA Is in Front Line of Hollywood's Fight to Rein in TV Costs," *Wall Street Journal,* March 3, 1987, p. 1.

5. Interview with Steve Wood, director of planning, Moore Industries, Sepulveda, California, December 1988.

6. Sanford Goodkin, "We Must Take a Lesson from Japan for Management Success," *California Business,* August 1985, p. 109.

7. From an interview with James Manning, chief financial officer, Medco Containment Services, Inc., Fair Lawn, New Jersey, September 27, 1988.

8. Arthur M. Louis, "America's New Economy: How to Manage in It," *Fortune,* June 23, 1986, pp. 21–25.

9. John H. Sheridan, "Attacking Overhead," *Industry Week*, July 18, 1988, pp. 49–55.

10. John Byrne, "The Rebel Shaking Up Exxon," *Business Week*, July 18, 1988, pp. 104–111.

CHAPTER 11   MARKET POSITIONING

1. Theodore Levitt, *The Marketing Imagination* (New York: Free Press, 1983), p. 19.

2. From an interview with Paul Erickson, a San Francisco consultant, February 1988.

3. From an interview with Fred Cutler, director of strategic marketing, Compaq Computer, Houston, July 1987.

4. Michael E. Porter, *Competitive Advantage* (New York: Free Press, 1985), pp. 238 and 247.

5. Sylvia Nasar, "America's Competitive Revival," *Fortune*, January 4, 1988, pp. 44–52.

6. From an interview with Art Gensler, CEO, Gensler and Associates, February 1987.

7. From an interview with Art Ramey, vice president of marketing, DG Mouldings, November 1987.

8. Ibid.

9. "Local Lunch Meat Makes Good," *People Weekly*, July 20, 1987, p. 53.

10. William Davidow, "In High-Tech Markets, 'Slightly Better' Is Dangerous," *Business Marketing*, June 1986, p. 58.

11. F. G. "Buck" Rodgers, *The IBM Way* (New York: Harper & Row, 1986), p. 47.

CHAPTER 12   CREATING THE COMPETITIVE DIFFERENCE

1. David Lieberman, "The Wall Street Journal Makes News of Its Own," *Business Week*, February 8, 1988, pp. 31–32.

2. "Unions: It's Union vs. Union in the Scramble for Members," *Business Week*, September 3, 1984, p. 27.

3. Raymond Serafin, "Making Domino's Deliver," *Advertising Age*, November 28, 1988, p. 10.

4. "Federal Express Spreads Its Wings" (Interview with Frederick Smith), *Journal of Business Strategy*, July–August 1988, pp. 15–20.

5. Deirdre Fanning, "The Ultimate Paper Chase," *Forbes*, May 2, 1988, p. 108.

6. From an interview with Sigi Ziering, CEO, Diagnostics Products Corporation, Los Angeles, August 26, 1988.

7. Peter T. Johnson, "Why I Race Against Phantom Competitors," *Harvard Business Review*, September–October 1988, pp. 106–12.

CHAPTER 13   TECHNOLOGY MAPPING

1. "Developments to Watch: The Corrugated Box Goes High Tech," *Business Week*, April 13, 1987, p. 99.
2. Richard Foster, *Innovation: The Attacker's Advantage* (New York: Summit Books, 1986), p. 33.
3. "Research & Development: Key Issues for Management," *Conference Board*, 1983, no. 843.
4. Don Clark, "IBM Strikes Again in the Fast Chip Race," *San Francisco Chronicle*, March 17, 1988, p. C–3.
5. Richard Saltus, "Outdated Optical Microscope, New Video Technology Join Forces to Shed Light on the Tiny," *San Francisco Examiner*, November 19, 1988, p. D–1.
6. Associated Press, "Return of the Leeches," *San Francisco Chronicle*, January 5, 1989, p. B–5.
7. Eric von Hippel, *Sources of Innovation* (London and New York: Oxford University Press, 1988).
8. Stuart Gannes, "America's Fastest-Growing Companies," *Fortune*, May 23, 1988, p. 36.
9. "Technology—Philips' High-Tech Strategy: If You Can't Beat 'Em, Join 'Em," *Business Week*, May 28, 1984.
10. Stanley J. Modic, "Strategic Alliances," *Industry Week*, October 3, 1988, p. 47.

CHAPTER 14   REINVENTING OPERATIONS

1. Michael Berger, "U.S. Producers Told to Shape Up," *San Francisco Chronicle*, January 25, 1988, p. C–3.
2. Susan Chira, "Japan Toughens Up," *San Francisco Chronicle*, February 20, 1988. p. B–1.
3. Alyssa A. Lappen, "Worldwide Connections," *Forbes*, June 27, 1988, p. 78.
4. Peter Petre, "GE's Gamble on American-Made TVs," *Fortune*, July 6, 1987, pp. 50–54.
5. From an interview with James Manning, chief financial officer, Medco Containment Services, September 27, 1988.
6. From an interview with Len Moore, CEO, Moore Industries International, January 20, 1989.
7. Brian Dumaine, "How Managers Can Succeed Through Speed," *Fortune*, February 13, 1989, pp. 54–59.

8. Merck & Co.'s 1986 Annual Report, pp. 18–21, and discussions with the company's manufacturing management.

9. John A. Young, "The Quality Focus at Hewlett-Packard," *Journal of Business Strategy*, Winter 1985, pp. 6–9.

10. J. M. Juran, *Juran on Planning for Quality* (New York: Free Press, 1988), p. 11.

11. Patricia Sellars, "How King Kellogg Beat the Blahs," *Fortune*, August 29, 1988, p. 54.

12. Alex Taylor III, "Lee Iacocca's Production Whiz," *Fortune*, June 22, 1987, pp. 36–44.

13. Emily Smith, "The Fully Automated Factory Rewards an Early Dreamer," *Business Week*, March 17, 1986, p. 91.

CHAPTER 15   LEVERAGING THE ORGANIZATION

1. Stella M. Nkomo, "Prescription Versus Practice: The State of Human Resource Planning in Large U.S. Organizations," Southern Management Association proceedings, 1984.

2. Charles Gitzendanner, Kenneth Misa, and Timothy Stein, "Management's Involvement in the Strategic Utilization of the Human Resource," *Management Review*, October 1983, pp. 13–17.

3. Thomas McCarroll, "Can This Elephant Dance?" *Time*, February 8, 1988, p. 52.

4. Kate Ballen et al., "Big Blue Wants to Loosen Its Collar," *Fortune*, February 29, 1988, p. 8.

5. Bill Powell and Elisa Williams, "Tips for the Hands-Off CEO," *Newsweek*, March 16, 1987, p. 52.

6. John K. Clemens, "A Lesson from 431 B.C.," *Fortune*, October 13, 1986, p. 161.

7. "Every Employee an Entrepreneur" (interview with Alan Kennedy), *Inc.*, April 1984, p. 103.

8. Robert Ingersoll, "The Banker Behind the Shakeup at Daimler-Benz," *Business Week*, July 27, 1987, p. 36.

9. Stephen G. Tompkins, "Sculley's Apple Takes a Bite Out of IBM," *San Francisco Examiner*, May 22, 1988, p. D–3.

10. From an interview with Cheryl Wicks, Apple Computer's management strategy expert, July 26, 1988.

11. John S. McClenahen, "Training Americans for Work," *Industry Week*, September 19, 1988, pp. 53–60.

12. Michael Brody, "Helping Workers to Work Smarter," *Fortune*, June 8, 1987, pp. 86–88.

CHAPTER 16 CREATIVE CORPORATE PLANNING

1. Edward Iwata, "The Restructuring of the U.S. Beef Business," *San Francisco Chronicle,* May 18, 1987, p. 25.

2. Russell Mitchell, with Judith H. Dobrzynski, "Jack Welch: How Good a Manager?" *Business Week,* December 14, 1987, pp. 92–103.

3. Walter Guzzardi, "Big Can Still Be Beautiful." *Fortune,* April 25, 1988, pp. 50–64.

4. Steve Weiner, "Happy Ending," *Forbes,* August 10, 1987, p. 73.

5. William S. Woodside and James A. Long, "The Journey from American Can to Primerica," *Journal for Corporate Growth,* Vol. 4, No. 1 (1988): pp 5–18.

6. Gerald Tsai, Jr., "Restructuring Corporate Assets: What American Can Did," *Journal for Corporate Growth,* vol. 3, no. 1 (1987).

7. Arthur M. Louis, "Clausen's Efforts Could Be Jeopardized," *San Francisco Chronicle,* May 22, 1987.

8. Carol J. Loomis, "Buyout Kings," *Fortune,* July 4, 1988, pp. 52–60.

9. Laurie Itow, "Is There Life Beyond Jeans?" *San Francisco Examiner,* April 10, 1988, pp. D–1.

10. Christine Tierney, "Recession Could Hurt Banks Involved in Leveraged Buyouts," *San Francisco Examiner,* July 6, 1988, p. D–3.

11. "Retiring Westinghouse Chief Executive Talks of Issues Facing Firms and Managers," *Wall Street Journal,* December 30, 1987, p. 15.

12. From an interview with John S. Wheaton, executive vice president of administration, McKesson Corporation, San Francisco, August 1988.

13. Bruce H. Atwater, Jr., "Restructuring Is a Process, Not an Event," speech delivered to the Minnesota chapter of Association for Corporate Growth, December 1987. Information updated by Kristen Wenker, General Mills' Investor Relations Department, on January 16, 1989.

CHAPTER 17 ACQUISITION BARGAINS, DIVESTITURE COUPS

1. From an interview with Alex Ladias, research director of W. T. Grimm, Chicago, February 15, 1989.

2. Richard J. Loughlin, president and CEO of Century 21, in a speech to the San Francisco chapter of Association for Corporate Growth, May 19, 1988.

3. Irwin Federman, "The Growth of Monolithic Memories Leading to a Merger with Advanced Micro Devices," speech to the Santa Clara, California, chapter of Association for Corporate Growth, May 12, 1988.

4. Tim Smart, "Homebuilding: How Ryan Nailed Down the No. 1 Spot," *Business Week,* September 12, 1988.

5. Larry Walker, "Wine and Spirits: Sparkling Wine Maker Looking for Room to Grow," *San Francisco Chronicle,* September 6, 1988, p. C–3.

6. Don Clark, "How National Plans to Make Fairchild Profitable," *San Francisco Examiner,* December 14, 1987, p. C–3.

7. Brett D. Fromson, "Companies to Watch," *Fortune,* May 25, 1987, p. 62.

8. Alex B. Block, "One Man's Trash Is Another's Treasure," *Forbes,* June 30, 1986, p. 70.

9. Roger W. Stone, "The Challenge of Acquisitions: Buy Low and Maximize Returns," speech to the Chicago chapter of Association for Corporate Growth, September 1987.

10. Philip Barbara, "Nippon Mining to Buy Gould Electronics," *San Francisco Examiner,* August 31, 1988, p. C–3.

11. Tully M. Friedman, speech to the San Francisco chapter of Association for Corporate Growth, April 21, 1988.

12. From an interview with James Mahoney, editor of *The National Review of Acquisitions,* Tiburon, California, November 1988.

13. From an interview with Edward McGrath, president of CAMA, Inc., San Francisco, May 1987.

CHAPTER 18   FROM TURNAROUND TO TAKEOFF

1. "The Baby Bells' Weak Sister Is Growing into a Bruiser," *Business Week,* September 8, 1986, p. 69.

2. Donald B. Bibeault, *Corporate Turnaround: How Managers Turn Losers into Winners* (New York: McGraw Hill, 1982), p. 25.

3. Mark Ivey, "Sprint's New Chief Has a Lot of Wires to Untangle," *Business Week,* July 27, 1987, p. 29.

4. Howard Rudnitsky, "Teddy Ruxpin Stumbles," *Forbes,* August 24, 1987, p. 35.

5. Pamela Klein, "What Went Wrong at Coleco?" *San Jose Mercury News,* July 19, 1988, p. C–1.

6. Karen Wolman, "Can an Outsider Fill Aldo Gucci's Loafers?" *Business Week,* November 30, 1987, p. 52.

7. Arthur M. Louis, "Detectives Who Track Trouble at Thrifts," *San Francisco Chronicle,* June 22, 1987, p. 21.

8. Marc Beauchamp, "Learning from Disaster," *Forbes,* October 19, 1987, p. 96.

9. Paul Freiberger, "Jobs Unveils Next as Industry Cheers," *San Francisco Examiner,* October 13, 1988. p. A–1, 12.

10. Don Stanley, "Jaguar: An Independent Breed of Cat," *Contra Costa Times,* July 10, 1987, p. 3.

11. "Face-to-Face Interview: Company Doctor—Q. T. Wiles," *Inc.,* February 1988, pp. 27–38.

12. "Face-to-Face Interview: MCI Founder Bill McGowan," *Inc.*, August 1986, p. 29.

13. Diane Zielinski, "Key Moves Return Smith-Corona to Black," *San Francisco Examiners*, July 4, 1986, p. C–1.

14. Vlae Kershner and Kathleen Pender, "Corporate Paramedic Ready for Next Case?" *San Francisco Chronicle*, March 7, 1988, p. C–1.

15. Andrew Feinberg, "He Dares to Delegate," *Success*, June 1988, p. 34.

16. Robert Wilson, speech at the seminar "Corporate Turnaround," sponsored by the San Francisco chapter of Association for Corporate Growth, March 26, 1987.

17. Michael A. Lerner, "The Hit Man of the Record Biz," *Newsweek*, February 8, 1988, p. 48.

18. Michael Schroeder, "How Business Went to Bat for the Pirates," *Business Week*, July 18, 1988, p. 98.

19. William C. Symonds, "Its Turnaround Was Brilliant—But Can Fiat Stay the Course?" *Business Week*, August 15, 1988, p. 66.

20. Irwin Federman, "The Growth of Monolithic Memories Leading to a Merger with Advanced Micro Devices," speech to the Santa Clara Valley Chapter of Association for Corporate Growth, May 12, 1988.

CONCLUSION: HOW AND WHEN TO START

1. Andrew Kupfer, "Managing Now for the 1990s," *Fortune*, September 26, 1988, pp. 44–47.

2. Paul Freiberger, "How U.S. Got 'Dumped' from Its Throne," *San Francisco Examiner*, October 2, 1988, p. D–1.

3. Tim Carrington, "Vital Parts: Military's Dependence on Foreign Suppliers Causes Rising Concern," *Wall Street Journal*, March 24, 1988, p. 1.

4. Michael Berger, "How Japan Makes Exporting Work," *San Francisco Chronicle*, March 14, 1988, p. C–1.

5. Washington Post News Service, "Japanese Study U.S. Services," *San Francisco Chronicle*, November 10, 1988, p. C–1.

6. Los Angeles Times News Service, "U.S. Scores Dead Last in Math among 6 Nations' 13-Year-Olds," *San Francisco Chronicle*, February 1, 1989, p. 1.

APPENDIX: THE NATURE OF GENIUS

1. "John Huston," *Creativity with Bill Moyers*, an installment of a PBS television series made possible by a grant from Chevron, 1984.

2. Harold R. McAlindon, "Toward a More Creative You: Unlocking Human Potential," *Supervisory Management*, October 1979, pp. 2–8.

3. Eugene Raudsepp, "Are You a Creative Executive?" *Management Review*, February 1978, pp. 10–15 + .

4. Jim Wood, "Bucky Fuller Left a Legacy of Good Ideas Worthy of Leonardo," *San Francisco Chronicle,* July 3, 1983, p. 1.

5. Roger Ebert, "The Real Key to the Success of Lucas and Spielberg," *San Francisco Examiner,* May 14, 1984, p. B–11.

6. "O.J. Simpson," segment of *Sportraits* show on ESPN, November 13, 1988.

7. Al Morch, "The No. 1 Inventor," *San Francisco Examiner,* April 25, 1988, p. B–1; letter from Dr. NakaMats and articles he sent to author on November 25, 1988.

Index